A Post-Analytical Approach to Philosophy and Theory of Law

Polish Contemporary Philosophy and Philosophical Humanities

Edited by Jan Hartman

Volume 14

PETER LANG

Andrzej Bator / Zbigniew Pulka (eds.)

A Post-Analytical Approach to Philosophy and Theory of Law

Translated by Jan Burzyński and Mikołaj Golubiewski

PETER LANG

Bibliographic Information published by the Deutsche Nationalbibliothek
The Deutsche Nationalbibliothek lists this publication in the Deutsche Nationalbibliografie; detailed bibliographic data is available in the internet at http://dnb.d-nb.de.

Library of Congress Cataloging-in-Publication Data
A CIP catalog record for this book has been applied for at the Library of Congress.

This publication was financially supported by the Faculty of Law, Administration and Economics of the University of Wrocław.

Cover Design: © Olaf Gloeckler, Atelier Platen, Friedberg
Translation by Jan Burzyński and Mikołaj Golubiewski
Printed by CPI books GmbH, Leck

ISSN 2191-1878
ISBN 978-3-631-74626-4 (Print)
E-ISBN 978-3-631-76656-9 (E-PDF)
E-ISBN 978-3-631-76657-6 (EPUB)
E-ISBN 978-3-631-76658-3 (MOBI)
DOI 10.3726/b14869

Peter Lang – Berlin · Bern · Bruxelles · New York · Oxford · Warszawa · Wien

This publication has been peer reviewed.

www.peterlang.com

Contents

Andrzej Bator and Zbigniew Pulka

Introduction

In the Western tradition, the primary function of philosophical cognition was to optimize the perception of an object by proving it to be a carrier of a specific order. Within the philosophical realm, the analytical current was the most far-reaching attempt to tame the chaos of ideological frenzy of the 20th century, or at least to distance oneself from this chaos. Neo-positivism reduced philosophy to the logical analysis of academic language. Within the philosophy of law, an attempt to seek order in legal and political phenomena was the analytical philosophy of law, which reduces the academic image of law to the logical and linguistic dimensions. There is a definite correlation between neo-positivism and the analytical philosophy of law, at least when considering Polish theory and philosophy of law. The post-analytical approach is a critical response to the idea of order introduced into the language of science by the analytical tradition. It does not *in extenso* undermine the principles and claims of analytical philosophy, but instead seeks to relativize it, bringing the logocentric image of language reality, as founded by analytical philosophy, to one of the available scientific discourses. Post-analytical philosophy does not, therefore, negate the existing practices of language sciences, but rather thrives on their critique. It urges to broaden the field and perspectives of academic perception. As any research current of the "post" type, the post-analytical approach also cannot exist without ideas founded on its own tradition.

The post-analytical vein of the philosophy of law separates itself from the tradition of philosophical cognition in its purely sense-making and optimizing activity. Its main goal is not to tame or introduce order into the chaos of legal and political sphere, but rather to deconstruct the philosophical and legal analytical narration by showing that it is a collection of simplifications, which in consequence partly mystify the legal and political reality. The chief goal of the post-analytical philosophy of law is to challenge the universal and objective character of the notions of the analytical philosophy. These will be related both to the picture of legal phenomena and process of cognition of law.

One of the fundamental myths undermined by the post-analytical philosophy of law is the myth of the legal system. It may be found in the ontological variant, which assumes that a systemness is a necessary property of law and therefore law exists as an ordered collection of norms, perceived as utterances. An epistemological version will entail an assumption of systemic character of law, which is deemed necessary in the process of cognizing law. In postanalytical thinking, logocentric picture of the system of law as an ordered whole is replaced with the vision of law as an agonistic social practice that manifests itself in asystemic or desystemized legal regulations. The undermining of the assumption of systemic character of law goes hand in hand with the questioning of its systemic binding force which entails that the binding effect of one norm is the result of the existence of another, related, binding norm. As a consequence, there also falls the myth of the limits of law defined by the notion of systemic binding force. In the post-analytical picture of law as a dynamic praxis, borders between legal and non-legal phenomena become blurred. Specifically, the political character of law and its ideological sense are exposed. Law as a social praxis, entangled into the game of conflicting political interests, ceases to be perceived as rational entity, that is, one that fulfils the criteria of instrumental or communicational rationality. According to the post-analytical thinking, the myth of a rational lawmaker as the creator of law is therefore undermined. It is also hard to maintain taking into account the ongoing globalization of legal and political reality, where informal and supranational normative rules become dominant, as exemplifies, for example, the corporation law. In the conditions of a dominating normative order being established outside of any democratic control, the category of individual rights attains a mythological sense.

In turn, in the epistemological dimension, the post-analytical reflection undermines the myth of the analytical method as legal cognition free of evaluation. Demystification of the analytical method refers to both the reconstructionist and descriptivist variants of the study of language. A critical approach to traditional legal analyses reveals that legal phenomena are axiologically entangled also in the language dimension. When the theory of legal interpretation is considered as a method of legal cognition, the breaking of the myth of the analytical method takes the form of rejecting the concept of statutory interpretation as an act of cognition. Such an act would, when employing a set of commonly accepted interpretational directives, arrive at the same result: an objectively existing meaning of a legal text. The post-analytical reflection leans towards hermeneutic concepts of interpretation which relativize the results of interpretation by taking into account the context of a given interpretative community. In the epistemological dimension, this equals hermeneutic universalism or "paninterpretationalism," in which the opposition of the subject and object of cognition, deeply exposed by the analytical philosophy, vanishes. The post-analytical vision of law entails that philosophical reflection results in the emergence of space, in which a number of idiosyncratic images of legal phenomena exist, relativized to the perspective of the person cognizing law. In consequence, the post-analytical philosophy of law also undermines the postulate of creating a single image of legal phenomena, that would be equipped with value of scientific character and universality.

Philosophers in the post-analytical vein have never formed an integrated academic school. They were bound by the common way of thinking, even if it was delivered independently by each of them, constructed on the conviction about the autonomy of humanistic and social sciences. This may be called an anti-naturalistic attitude. However, the extent of critical involvement of individual philosophers in the existing ways of practicing science varied. It ranged from a cautious critique of the previously dominating analytical traditions to a more radical questioning of the fundamental assumptions of these traditions – which is evident in the postmodern approach or the area of Critical Legal Studies in case of law education. The range of variety also is evident in the texts from this book. The reader will find texts related to the fundamental theses of analytical philosophy itself, its criticism, evaluations of the leading theses of the post-analytical philosophy with attempts of application to the theory and philosophy of law, as well as fragments on selected issues of jurisprudence. Moreover, criticism of the individual authors towards the analytical tradition and, consequently, their writing style varies, at times reaching even towards the postmodernist manner of argumentation.

The authors of all the texts from this book are professors or PhD candidates at the Department of Theory and Philosophy of Law at the University of Wrocław and represent a spectrum of academic generations.

We would like to express our gratitude to Wydawnictwo Uniwersytetu Wrocławskiego for their agreement to reproduce some of the texts contained within this book.[1]

Andrzej Bator, Zbigniew Pulka
Wrocław, December 1, 2017

1 The agreement covers fragments of text published in *Czy koniec teorii prawa* (P. Jabłoński, ed.) in the series "Prawo," No. CCCXII, Wydawnictwo Uniwersytetu Wrocławskiego, Wrocław 2011; *Postanalityczna filozofia prawa* (M. Jabłoński and M. Paździora, eds.), "Przegląd Prawa i Administracji" No. CII, Wydawnictwo Uniwersytetu Wrocławskiego, Wrocław 2015; and *Systemowość prawa* (Z. Pulka, ed.), "Przegląd Prawa i Administracji" No. CIV, Wydawnictwo Uniwersytetu Wrocławskiego, Wrocław 2016.

Andrzej Bator

Post-Analytical Theory and Philosophy of Law. New Problems, New Research Perspectives?

1 Introduction

In the beginning, I would like to offer a few remarks about the title of this chapter, as well as about the goal of the deliberations articulated in the subtitle. The post-analytical idea itself is a notion that provokes doubt,[1] especially if used in the context of the philosophy of law. It is a relatively new notion and not yet grounded in general jurisprudence. The doubt arrives already with an attempt to place law research in the post-analytical perspective either on the side of theory of law and philosophy of law. Traditionally, the problem of the analytical character of law was located unambiguously in the area of the theory of law, even when its roots may be traced back to "analytical philosophy." It turned out, therefore, that not all "philosophy" needs to be speculative and this certainly is not true of analytical philosophy. The term "analytical philosophy" seemed to have been reserved to the general reflections on language. When applied to law or jurisprudence as a detailed discipline it was usually perceived a "theory." It was accordant with the rule of "analytical philosophy" as a general discipline that cooperates with various specialized sciences, while employing and establishing its own universal rules of research methodology. In jurisprudence, there seemed to be no place for a "particular" philosophy, so the name of the discipline contained a clearly dominant "analytical theory of law."[2] However, the post-analytical approach breaks the established rule of separating "philosophy" from "theory" in the study of language. It is naturally distrustful towards divisions and distinctions of notions. However, in the situation led by post-analytical caution, it was decided that the title of this work ought not to omit the word "philosophy."

---

1 The term first appeared in a book edited by J. Rajchman and C. West, *Post-Analitic Philosophy*, Columbia University Press, New York 1985. However, Bernard Williams was of major influence on its conceptualization. So claims A. Głąb in *Rozum w świetle praktyki. Poglądy filozoficzne Marthy C. Nussbaum*, Wydawnictwo Łośgraf, Warsaw 2010, p. 10.

2 An influential exception in Poland was the work of J. Woleński, *Z zagadnień analitycznej filozofii prawa*, Kraków 1980.

The question mark at the end of the title of this chapter reveals yet another doubt, about what we wish to call a "post-analytical" theory and philosophy of law and whether it bears the ability to articulate new notions in jurisprudence. In my opinion, it does. This text will try to prove that the application of the post-analytical notion to a category of general jurisprudence makes sense and may be applied to name cognitively serious problems. Such situations may otherwise disable the possibility of adequate consideration of the traditional analytical philosophy. Problems generated by the language as offered by the post-analytical approach are, however, not new to the contemporary theory and philosophy of law. Cognitive value of this scientific approach is reduced, in my opinion, not so much by the fact that something new can be "discovered" using this approach, but rather because it allows to articulate and order the opinions and positions largely already present in different scientific concepts and research, even if they are separated. The common front of disputing the logocentric tradition of analytical philosophy – also frequently authenticated by the "analytical" biographies of leading "post-analytical philosophers" – seems to bind this loose milieu. Undoubtedly, already the common name for a defined group of opinions and attitudes strengthens and legitimizes specific research and non-research practice, allowing to identify it as something that is recognized and accepted by the milieu. As each "post," however critical of its source current, may not live without the current it seeks to criticize. Each "post" broadens the perspective of the reader and sensitizes them to the phenomena that were unavailable in its traditional form, but it does not seek to undermine the achievements of its original current, with some exceptions. It rather strives to relativize the achievements, showing their overt claims and the tendency to monopolize the existing scholar consciousness.

Content analysis of the notion of post-analytism may be approached in two ways: (a) by calling forth the ideas of these authors – usually opposed to the prevailing methods of practicing analytics – who openly formulated not only the need to alter the approach to the study of language but also claimed that it deserves its own notional categorization, called "post-analytical approach"; (b) by appealing to the opinions of philosophers of similar scientific attitudes and programs, who decline to use the term and are, instead, included in the post-analytical current by their commentators.[3] Practicing a given scientific

3 G. Duke, E. Walsh, J. Chase, I. J. Reynolds, "Postanalytic" Philosophy: Overcoming Divide," *Postanalitic and Metacontinantal: Overcomming Philosophical Divide* (J. Reynolds, J. Chase, J. Williams, and E. Mares, ed.). "Continuum IPG" 2010 indicates the following representatives of the current: Wittgenstein, Davidson, Rorty, Mc Dowell,

approach need not always be combined with a label which others may apply to the approach, with the example of R. Rorty, commonly classified as a post-analyst although rejecting the name. While characterizing the notion under scrutiny, I will use both these approaches, since their combination provides a wider image of what the current's composition.

One more remark to limit the scope of the following considerations: I will refer only to those attributes that differentiate the post-analytical approach, which are the most accentuated and the strongest influence on the image of the problems of legal sciences. The attributes are extensive and not always unanimous among the philosophers. It needs to be clarified that my examples mainly originate from Polish jurisprudence. The selection is far from accidental. The Polish scientific output, shaped in the last few decades, comprises achievements based on analytical philosophy, with a special role of the so-called Lviv-Warsaw school.[4] This is yet another reason that when characterizing the attributes of the post-analytical approach, one should contrast them with the "standard" understanding of analytical research. Naturally, the last phrase, if disconnected from the Polish context, appears risky. If we scrutinize the differences between logical positivism, as practiced by the Vienna Circle and the Oxford School of the Common Language, it will not be easy to show assumptions in the study of language that are common to these approaches. For this work, these differences do not seem valid, though. The object of questioning for the post-analytical philosophers mainly stemmed from the traditions shaped by the program of the Vienna Circle, as well as its developments in continental Europe and America. Linguistics practiced as part of the common language school was a somewhat positive inspiration to the representatives of the post-analytical current.

Putnam, while at the same time adding that the current is most commonly associated with the achievements of R. Rorty (ibid, p. 7.) P. Strawson is also indicated as one of the authors of the revolution in analytical philosophy that marked "a transition from analytical to post-analytical philosophy." Cf. A. Beckermann, "Wprowadzenie," P. Prechtl, *Leksykon pojęć filozofii analitycznej*, translated by J. Bremer, Kraków, Wydawnictwo WAM 2009, p. 14.

4 Cf. J. Wolenski, *Logic and Philosophy in Lvov-Warsaw School*, Dordrecht Boston 1989. R. Rorty, "Filozofia analityczna a filozofia transformacyjna," *Analiza i Egzystencja* 2007, Vol. 5, p. 8: "In 1945–1960, analytical philosophy dominated the majority of important American institutes of philosophy. Such emigrants and logical empiricists like Carnap and Hempel replaced Dewey and Whitehead in their roles as heroes of the younger generation. This replacement led to striking holisitic changes."

Below, the reader will find some of the leading notional and problematic distinctions between what, for the sake of these considerations, will be called analytical and post-analytical approaches in the widely considered studies of language. We will only be interested in these differences that seem valid for the studies of theory and philosophy of law.

2 Professionalization of Traditional Analytical Studies

Professionalization based on scientific specialization is the first trait which post-analytical current representatives approached, with major reservations. Their own attitude was based on an ecumenical inclination towards synthesis. Such synthesis is based on problematic similarity, intuitively shown via, for example, analogy and metaphor rather than synthesis in the strict sense.

The way of practicing analytical research, initially, was supposed to be close to the way specialized sciences deliver their research, in precise language devoid of easy generalizations, and mainly with the use of logical tools.[5] Specialization was not combined with the properties of the object, with an extra-linguistic area of research – because analytical sciences were supposed to have no such area. The language of science in analytical research became a tool accessible for subject-unspecific areas of knowledge. Specialization was therefore evident in the language used by science. To be a scientist was equal with the ability to name the observed phenomenon in accessible language, accepted by the group in question, even if the described phenomenon was already well known. The language served to specify more or less intuitively formulated and justified beliefs. Therefore, professionalism is language accessible to a narrow group of researchers, mainly logicians that pattern their work on mathematics, capable of explicating knowledge and views present in defined specialist professional practice. This type of program also influenced academic science, including, naturally, the area of law. Teaching law in the so-called analytical jurisprudence meant teaching specific sets of definitions which would then allow for linguistic ordering, quantifying, and explaining of the knowledge available to a lawyer, such as information provided by lawmakers or court rulings, in distinct language categories. These categories were founded by science and practically verified by legal doctrine and practice.

Post-analytical response to professionalization is synthesis based on different areas of human cognition and practice. This is more a case of an individual's

5 Cf. T. Szubka, *Filozofia analityczna. Koncepcje, metody, ograniczenia*, Wrocław 2009, p. 26.

view of the world and their ethical and political sensitivity rather than of clarity and precision of the presented claims. The individual's attitudes may be shaped in varied ways, not only through the activity of socially involved science. In this, science not only ceases to be neutral in its view of the world but also opens to the language offered by other forms of social discourse. Post-analytical synthesis is based on describing problems holistically, treating them as belonging to different, inseparable areas of human knowledge and practice: science, culture, ethics, social philosophy, law, and legal sciences. Despite different origins of each of these types of narration, they are considered "a single set of problems, one area of reflection where light is shed from different angles in various aspects."[6] This leads to inevitable superficiality and intuitive character of the formulated theories. This is, however, a cost that – according to the post-analytic philosophers – is worth taking. Academic theorems are meant to address the reader's imagination – where the reader need not always be a professional – rather than be combined to make linguistically clear and objectively verifiable beliefs. R. Rorty considered the divisions of American university institutes of philosophy into – according to himself – "analytical technicians" and "non-analytical [post-analytical] murkies" as harmful and incomprehensible.[7] These circles were so intolerant of one another, or even mutually hostile, that the division became a necessity. It was symptomatic that the "analytical technicians" were primarily to exhibit the attitude of exclusion from the rest of the environment, whose activity in the eyes of the analysts failed to fulfill the standards of being academic. The effort to break such divisions became one of the challenges of the post-analytical current.

The expectation of professionalization of law and legal sciences seems deeply rooted in the continental, and especially Polish, reflections on law. This is mostly due to legal dogmatics, built on the conviction that instituted law is the point of reference for legal science and practice. Branch differentiation of the legal system, ceaseless searching for the criteria of separating the individual areas of legal regulations – subject, object, method of regulation, or concepts of legal interest – are still the basis for the legitimization of academic existence of individual, deeply technicized legal dogmatics. The sciences, also called specific jurisprudence, were built on a strong assumption that the point of origin for the research is always some form of selecting the analyzed objects: texts produced by the legislator.[8] In our domestic legal doctrine, the conviction is still

6 A. Głąb, "Postanalityczność – nowa kategoria?," *Znak*, May 2007, Vol. 624.

7 R. Rorty, op. cit., p. 6.

8 Cf. Z. Ziembiński, *Szkice z metodologii szczegółowych nauk prawnych*, Warsaw 1983, p. 14.

prevalent that only an expert in, for example, civil law is capable of competently talking about legal incapacitation, while only an expert in penal law is capable of explaining causality of desistence. In such an order of research, the role of analytical theory of law continued to be constructing axiologically neutral definitions whose scope reached beyond the borders of specific legal sciences or ex-post systematicizing of theses of these sciences. The vision of the theory of law as a serving science corresponds to similar expectation in the relation of legal dogmatics and legal practice, where the role of legal dogmatics is to formulate a practically useful set of definitions and offer ready-made interpretations of legal texts. Legal science thus becomes, at its different levels of theory of law, or specific sciences, a specific "concept technology" to support the practice of law. Each of the levels has at its disposal a generally separate, autonomous language of analysis. The languages of specific sciences become "thematized," the language of the theory of law becomes formalized. The structure of the legal system, language shape of the norm, or the construction of a normative act become – when considering such divided tasks – problems belonging to the theory of law. There is no place for the philosophy of law as differentiated from analytical philosophy.

Post-analytical response to the issues of general legal sciences will be a depreciation of such defined role of theory of law and its replacement with the philosophy of law. Overall erudition will be preferred to specialist legal knowledge of the language. For a lawyer, in this setup, a philosopher of law becomes a guide to other, non-legal practices, a mediator between legal sciences and its external environment. On the other hand, the crisis of traditionally considered analytics in legal dogmatics can be seen in difficulties in defining borders between individual legal sciences and building respective legal disciplines. The crisis may be regarded as an exaggerated commitment of these sciences to perceive the internal workings of the legal system in categories resembling logical ones. It manifests itself in an increasing count of the so-called complex branches of law – areas of regulation impossible to be clearly defined in the system of law based on one dominant criterion of division. Even recently, legal doctrine considered economic law as one of the most prominent complex branches of law. Currently, the list keeps expanding, with admiralty law, IT law, consumer law, tourism law, and so on. Subjective specialization in the area of legal dogmatics appears increasingly often as a limitation in the study of law. In this case, again, general erudite knowledge of law, open to other branches and disciplines of law, appears to be more highly valued than professionalism and specialization.

3 Scientific Character of Analytical Philosophy

Analytical philosophy was born as part of the opposition to classical philosophy which the analysts themselves called "speculative philosophy."[9] The term "analytical philosophy" was rarely used by the analysts, because "philosophy" was to be replaced by the positive "science," based on an existing pattern, such as mathematics or physics. Analytical and empirical theorems were, therefore, the only ones of cognitive value. Other theorems, since they were neither logically justified nor empirically verifiable sentences, were considered devoid of any sense, and therefore moved into the area of metaphysics. Things that could not be reduced to tautology, contradiction (analytical theorems), and verified with facts or empirical theorems are pseudo-problems, eliminated outside the realm of science. Therefore, science was defined very restrictively.

Post-analytical philosophers consider the "scientific character" built on predefined criteria as a form of stigmatization. According to them, there are no reasons for a priori self-limitation with the use of one or another definition of science. According to post-analytical philosophers, problems located on the border of recognized scientific disciplines are much more interesting. As evidenced by later debates on some of the basic assumptions of analytical philosophy, such as concepts of truth or meaning, concentrating on the mere standards for the scientific character of theorems caused philosophy to become overly involved with "itself." R. Rorty named such involvement in issues founded by the current itself as the capability to solve riddles that are valid and meaningful only to the authors of these riddles. The post-analytical current, following the rule of pragmatics, attaches no meaning to such meta-theorizing. In authentic social debates that scientific circles are engaged into, such ways of practicing theory bear no argumentative value. Analytical philosophy ought to abandon the aspirations to be a science that orders the individual bricks of available knowledge according to rules of construction imposed by logic. Instead of building the "edifice" of science, it ought to become philosophy which is – as Rorty said, quoting Hegel – "time seized in a thought."[10] The skill of capturing the problems of "one's own time" in thoughts is, according to the representatives of the current, more of the domain of literature, poetry or film rather than many of the university sciences based on institutionalized grounds. For instance, Shakespeare or Kafka may have a lot more to say on authority or law than many philosophers, political scientists,

9 Cf. J. Wisdom, *Problems of Mind and Matter*, Cambridge University Press, Cambridge 1934, pp. 1–3.

10 R. Rorty, op. cit., p. 7.

or lawyers who take the scientific patents as their points of reference. Artistic view on the reality is from its nature more sensitive to the surrounding social problems and has much stronger persuasion at its disposal, so science should not be indifferent to its existence. Extensive humanistic erudition becomes a scientific value. There are no reasons, therefore, for post-analytical science to separate itself from such a meaningful source of problematic inspiration and argumentation.

Polish law-making, mainly thanks to analytical models of science, also underwent a period of questioning its own scientific identity. Apart from the achievements of the Lviv-Warsaw school, an additional motive for the construction of worldview-neutral, or scientific, theory of law was the need for the science to distance itself from the then dominating Marxist philosophy. J. Wróblewski's handbook *Zagadnienia teorii wykładni prawa ludowego* (Questions of the Theory of People's Law Interpretation, 1959) and *Zagadnienia teorii prawa* (Questions of Theory of Law, 1969) which he co-authored with K. Opałek were long-standing prescribed proper standards of analytical practice of general jurisprudence. As the authors of the latter book remark, "the interest of jurisprudence of its own scientific status is what distinguishes legal disciplines from the other areas of reflection."[11] Already on the grounds of pragmatically oriented scientific methodology, scholars concentrated on the fact that questions about the scientific character of the undertaken deliberations may be said to reflect the immaturity of a given scientific discipline.[12] Science which has outgrown its adolescent period of questioning its own status ought rather to address the issues grounded on specific practice. This was, however, a lacking element in the Polish theory of law which was normally practiced analytically. It is worth mentioning that a similar evaluation of the achievements of domestic general analytical jurisprudence has been formulated in the past by the representatives of specific jurisprudence.[13]

---

11 K. Opałek, J. Wróblewski, *Prawo. Metodologia. Filozofia. Teoria prawa*, Warsaw 1991, p. 34. Reference list to the chapter "Naukowość prawoznawstwa" contained in this work gathers many sources.

12 Cf. E. Geblewicz, "O naukach zaawansowanych i niezaawansowanych," *Problemy epistemologii pragmatycznej. Materiały z posiedzeń konserwatorium naukoznawstwa PAN*, Wrocław 1972; see also: S. Glendinning, *The Idea of Continental Philosophy: A Philosophical Chronicle*, Edinburgh University Press 2006, p. 5ff.

13 See the opinions in the discussion about K. Opałek and J. Wróblewski's handbook, *Zagadnienia teorii prawa* (PWN, Warsaw 1969): A. Stelmachowski's, "Niebezpieczeństwo formalnego ujmowania systemu państwa i prawa," *Państwo i Prawo* 1970, Vol. 5; K. Grzybowski's, "Nauka prawa cywilnego a teoria prawa," *Państwo i Prawo* 1971, Vol. 1;

In the opinion of the representatives of the post-analytical current, humanistic sciences could not attain such maturity, based on methodological naturalism, and therefore should not even aspire to it, lest seeking to harm themselves. There are a number of signals proving that continental legal science has, in recent decades, undergone changes that can be said to "seize time in a thought." Let us limit ourselves to two examples. One is the spreading of theorems reaching back to the achievements of economic analysis of law in the argumentation of theory of law; in Poland, the onset of the popularity of this trend dates back to the 1980s. Theoretical and dogmatic-legal dilemmas of branch separation of economic law within the legal system started to give way to questions on the economic usefulness of legal regulations – whether and to what degree the rationality of the economic entities coincides or collides with the rationality of the lawmaker. The second example is expansion of hermeneutics into the territory of legal interpretation that occurred in a similar timeframe. The said current had profound impact on the need to show the connections between the practice of legal cognition and the experience of philologists or theologians in the process of interpreting texts, so postulated by the post-analytical philosophers (see, e.g., S. Fish).

Therefore, instead of striving to meet the criteria of being scientific, borrowed from some "pattern sciences," post-analytical jurisprudence will seek heuristic and practical inspiration in those disciplines that either directly undertake problems from the realm of law or work with issues that are somewhat similar. In short, it is all about jurisprudence to stop putting itself in the center but, instead, start working on issues relevant to social life, inspired by those disciplines that have something meaningful to say to lawyers in their area of research.

4 The Descriptive-Explanatory Function of Analytical Science Theorems

The function of science with such a description was accompanied by the classical concept of truth, that of correspondence. The notion was accepted by logical empiricism, as evidenced by, for example, the debate on the "base sentences" and "protocol sentences." The concept was afterwards developed by various methodological projects of scientific explanation, the most representative were the nomologic-deductive and probabilistic models, the latter usually called the Hempel-Popper model. The acceptance of such a concept of truth allowed to

and A. Ohanowicz, "Uwagi o współpracy między dyscyplinami szczegółowymi a teorią prawa," *Państwo i Prawo* 1971, Vol. 1.

put the analytical approach into the current described as representationism. On the other hand, to accept that formulating any generalizations, including the so-called scientific laws, in both models, ought to be subject to exclusively cognitive function of science resulted in the elimination of classical reflective involvement of the researcher in his field. Independence and objectivism of the formulated theses became leading values of conduct in science and the basis for scientific qualifications of achievements.

In the culture of analytical philosophy, quoting Rorty, there is a "deeply rooted ideal of searching for truths that are not time-bound and are not subject to revision."[14] Objective knowledge derived from science is sometimes opposed to unverifiable "opinions" (history, socially involved literature and art) which may be found on the side of the post-analytical current. Objective knowledge – truth – is replaced here with imagination which serves more to "create new examples rather than serve the function of expressing opinions." For this reason, when referring to the post-analytical concept of philosophy, we mainly have in mind "such a philosophy which widens many of our anxieties."[15] Therefore, instead of polishing the means of linguistic expression, subject to thoughts that are usually trivial or unimportant in the life of an individual, constantly pondering on the same problems-riddles, love of the analysts for permanent solving of different paradoxes, it is better to make the readers aware of the phenomena that are related directly to them and which they often accept without reflection as something obvious.[16] This new approach may be called the "imaginative" sense of philosophy: humanistic philosophy that builds narrations for the individuals or groups to identify themselves in their social contexts when making life-crucial choices. It is worth stating that such claims are raised not only towards traditional humanistic approaches. Similar expectations are raised towards empirical sciences like physics, which have been until recently considered, on the grounds of analytical philosophy, to be the role models for "scientific" humanistic studies.[17]

---

14 R. Rorty, op. cit., p. 19.

15 A. Głąb, "Postanalityczność – nowa kategoria?," op. cit.

16 R. Rorty, following Kierkegaard, calls for a differentiation of "what is existential and important from what is objective and relatively of minor impact," and what in his opinion gives reason to "ignore the question about consensus and certainty" – op. cit. p. 16.

17 L. Smolin, *Kłopoty z fizyką*, Warsaw 2008, p. 305: "Instead of believing in contemporary knowledge, the members [of an imagined community] invest their expectations and hopes in future generations, handing down ethical rules and mental tools, both

Attempts at applying a model of science that would be similar to the empirical-nomological one may also be found in the Polish theory of law from a few decades ago. Of special importance for the current was J. Kmita's concept of humanistic interpretation, and in legal science the application of the concept in legal text interpretation proposed by L. Nowak. It included the counterpart of "general law" as the assumption about rationality or internal perfection of the lawmaker. It is striking that the author of the concept, L. Nowak, concluded in his final remarks that jurisprudence, or dogmatics of law, cannot fit into such a model of science. The rationality of the lawmaker assumed in jurisprudence does not allow for empirical verification. At the same time, the aim of jurisprudence is not to provide a cognitive goal, which would form the basis for the creation of the empirical-explaining model. The theorems of jurisprudence, as the author concludes, are not descriptions of law but projects of its improvement.[18] This conclusion involuntarily fits into the post-analytical train of thought, despite original intentions at the basis of "general law." It appears that this scientific practice, most characteristic of lawyers – we are mainly referencing dogmatics of law here – does not fit into patterns typical of the descriptive-explaining model of science. The activity of science of law is inevitably practical, oriented at optimizing lawmaker's legal decisions, and critically involved in the "researched" area.

The post-analytical philosophy of law luckily does not need to tackle such dilemmas. It questions the principle of the abovementioned model(s) of scientific practice as inadequate to legal research, including the interpretation of law. It is an openly critical philosophy, involving the engagement on the side of the researcher, abandoning the distance so characteristic of the nomological-empirical models of explanation. What is more, for the post-analytical philosophers, the legal assumptions present in the process of exegesis of legal texts, including the assumption of the rationality of the lawmaker, their "knowledge" and "preferences" become a graceful area for demystifying the hidden "legal knowledge"; that is, power by knowledge. In their radicalized version, such doubts may be found in numerous research examples from the so-called Critical Legal Studies Movement.

individual and collective, which are to enable these future generations to cope with conditions reaching far beyond our current imagination."

18 L. Nowak, *Interpretacja prawnicza. Studium z metodologii prawoznawstwa*, Warsaw 1973, pp. 173–175.

5 The Primacy of Scientific Methodology Over Subject-Specific Research

I have already mentioned that analytical theories do not have an assigned external object, a defined research area in an extra-linguistic understanding. The construction of such theories bases on the description and analysis of language, which elements – definitions, theorems – in further analysis serve to express beliefs on an external subject area. The ground for theoretical considerations in analytical research is provided by the adopted scientific methodology, the character of the problem, and the internal structure of the considerations;[19] not the area related to the analytical considerations. Subject order serves a secondary role, as a possible proof of adequacy (satisfiability) of the adopted research assumptions, such as the definitions adopted as basis for the considerations. These assumptions validate the conviction that "the [analytical] theory creates its subject, not the other way around."[20] In this sense, analytical philosophy fails to provide new truths and broaden our knowledge about any subject and, instead, assists in clarifying and specifying the expression of such knowledge which is already known and intuitively expressed in common language, or the existent language of science. An analytical philosopher, therefore, merely "serves old truths in new depictions."[21] In this sense, the problem of analytical philosophy is not what is being researched, since one can practice analytical philosophy on practically any issue, but how it is being done; how precise assumptions and definitions emerge from it. This results in the visible domination of methodological theorems.[22] Research problems tend to be created by science itself and, therefore, are of mainly meta-theoretical character. This results in the separation of analytical research both from the social environment and other disciplines which undertake extra-linguistic issues or concentrate on language in its practical sense.

Post-analytical attitude associates itself with the rejection of the primary character of scientific methodology over subject-specific research. It is not theory that creates its research area and forces the academic environment to work on issues emerging from the patterns of the adopted scientific methodology; exactly the opposite, theory serves to address ready-made issues resulting from real life.

---

19 J. Woleński, "Dyscyplina a teoria naukowa," *Zeszyty Naukoznawstwa* 1981, Vols. 1–2, p. 7.

20 J. Woleński, "Spór o status metodologiczny nauki o polityce," *Metodologiczne i teoretyczne problemy nauk politycznych*, Warsaw 1975, p. 40.

21 A. Pap, *Elements of Analytic Philosophy*, Macmillan, New York 1949, p. 478.

22 E. Nagel, "Impressions and Appraisals of Analytic Philosophy in Europe," *The Journal of Philosophy* 1936/33, No 1, p. 6.

Post-analytical science is to solve the external problems, not to create its own. Imprecision in expressing own thoughts, as the natural cost of such an attitude, is not treated as the weakness of science anymore, but rather as the proof of adequacy of the language towards reality, or maybe even its identity as humanistic "reality." It is an open invitation to practice more casual, "adjective-less" philosophy which rejects slave-like conformity to the limitations of existing philosophical trends.[23] These limitations are mainly categorical distinctions founded on the philosophies of Descartes and Kant, based on the confrontation of the subject of cognition with the object, forms with contents, objectivity with subjectivity, analytic character with empirical, and so on. Critique or even rejection of the oppositions of this kind is the main characteristic of post-analytical philosophy.[24]

The vast majority of works of Polish theory of law, especially from the 1970s, went as far as to include the word "methodology" in their titles.[25] Therefore, among the theoreticians of law, there seemed to be a dominant conviction that without consciously adopting a method there is no science, and meta-theories form the core of science. Even a traditional lecture on cognitive ethics was on occasion replaced with a debate between the supporters of cognitivism and anti-cognitivism, debating on the construction of a moral norm or pointing the differences between absolute and situational ethics. Hence, we knew better how to comprehend ethics or the construction of a moral norm but not necessarily what was the source of ethical behavior. Language concepts of the norm – the structure of the norm – or language concepts of the system of law (system models) became the key components of legal education, and the fairness of justifying the verdicts based on norms or efficiency diminished.

"Methodologies" and "meta-theories" start to fade in the language of Polish works on the theory of law published in the 1990s. Instead of, say, searching for construction differences between the derivative and clarifying concept of the

---

23 Cf. H. Putnam, "A Half Century Philosophy. Viewed From Within," *Daedalus* 1997, Vol. 1 (126), p 202ff.

24 J. Duke, E. Walsh, J. Chase, J. Reynolds, "Post-Analitic Philosophy: Overcoming the Divide?," *Postanalytic and Metacontinental: Crossing Philosophical Divided*, p. 11ff.

25 E.g. *Metody badania prawa. Materiały z sympozjum. Warszawa 28-29 IV 1971 r.* (A. Łopatka, ed.); *Zagadnienia metodologiczne prawoznawstwa. Materiały z sesji naukowej, Łódź 27-28 marca 1980 r.* (J. Wróblewski, ed.); Z. Ziembiński, *Metodologiczne podstawy prawoznawstwa*, Warsaw 1974; Z. Ziembiński, *Szkice z metodologii szczegółowych nauk prawnych*, Warsaw 1983; Opałek and J. Wróblewski: *Prawo – metodologia, filozofia, teoria prawa* (Warsaw 1991). There are many more such examples.

interpretation of law,[26] contemporary authors ask which concept provides better tools to solve specific challenges resulting from the EU interpretation of law. Even as far back as in the 1980s, there appeared discussions on varied versions of semantics at the core of interpretation of law. In the recent few years, however, the interpreters of law are more interested in the issues of the usefulness of the existing theories of interpretation of law; for example, for the research of the phenomenon of multi-language nature of EU legal texts. Yet, another issue of interest to them is the role of the EU law in the process of interpreting the local laws of EU member states. On the other hand, discussions on the differences between the linguistic form of the norm and the moral norm are starting to give way to socially valid questions within the scope of professional legal ethics or contemporary challenges from the area of the ethics of law. A scientifically significant issue no longer meets the criteria imposed by the correct research methodology, is consistent with the existent order of knowledge, or maybe conceptualized in the language of basic theory, but rather has social impact. What R. Rorty called the analysts' skill in "making up riddles and solving them" is currently replaced to an increasing degree with dilemmas that are interesting for wider circles than the mere elites of a given research group.[27] To paraphrase J. Woleński, one may say that thanks to the post-analytical revolution, the "theory of law regained its subject."

6 Systematicity of Knowledge

Systematicity of knowledge or its verification is one of the positions adopted by the post-analytical philosophers which seemed to raise the strongest critique. On the one hand, this position involved humanistic studies in a risky identification with the naturalistic current where – similar to natural sciences – gaining knowledge was supposed to have an element of "discovery" which would cumulatively broaden our vision of reality. These were the "bricks" or the "gaps" in knowledge, metaphors so characteristic of the empirical scientists and the element of "discovery" came with the so-called coherent concept of truth, preferred

26 Cf. K. Płeszka, T. Gizbert-Studnicki, "Dwa ujęcia wykładni prawa. Próba konfrontacji," *Zeszytu Naukowe Uniwersytetu Jagiellońskiego. Prace z Nauk Politycznych*, 1984, Vol. 20, pp. 17–27.

27 A very current example of such a shift in research orientation may be the deep involvement of Polish theoreticians and philosophers of law in the debate of the Constitutional Court of Poland, at the time of the related crisis. What is interesting, this co-occurred with a very distanced approach to the dogmatics of constitutional law.

by the majority of analytical philosophers. For instance, for R. Carnap, the truth of a sentence is verifiable by setting the sentence against the predetermined order of sentences. On the other hand, another risky effect of naturalism was the pronouncement of the rule of unity of science, which included the postulate of adopting a homogenous "intersubjectively verifiable" language that would be common to all sciences. In the area of linguistics, it led to the primate of theorems from the area of syntax, and consequently a strong binding of language theorems with the achievements of formal logic. Such character can be primarily ascribed to the continental branch of logical positivism.[28] Analytical philosophy practiced with a "scientific" angle ceases to limit itself to the syntactic dimension and begins to permeate into the area of semantics, therefore encompassing the logical analysis of notions, such as R. Carnap's procedure of explication. This expansion does not only refer to basic notions in a given science, serving to clarify its analytical research instruments but also started to refer to notions embedded in the social functioning of individuals, such as notions from ethics or aesthetics. The idea of the formalization of the language of science at the semantic level is connected with the preference for reconstructivism as a research approach towards language.[29] The rule of universalism of the language of science is, thus, complemented through the rule of linguistic simplicity.

Post-analytical resistance stems from antipathy towards primarily the latter vision of science, equaling a uniform order of scientific efforts integrated with the rule of universal linguistic structure and filled with properly worded set of definitions. The first understanding of systematicity – an internally coherent collection of scientific theorems – does not bring any threats to humanistic studies and seems an inadequate vision for this area of science, because the aspirations of humanistic science to state the "truth" were not treated seriously. However, the second understanding of systematicity – which means coherence of thinking and expressing oneself with the use of language – already brings such threat,

28 T. Szubka, *Filozofia analityczna*, op. cit. pp. 17, 20–21, remarks that this related to only one of the two dominant currents of analytical philosophy; that is, the tradition originating from the Vienna Circle. Citing the opinion of Black and G. Bergmann, Szubka remarks that Cambridge philosophers such as G. E. Moore and L. Wittgenstein "do it in a more casuistic way; i.e., they are satisfied with the application [of analytical methods] to specific cases, while the continental logical positivists have a tendency to bind the results in a systematic whole." This forms ground for dividing analytical philosophers into "casuists" and "systematists" (ibid., p. 17).

29 J. Kotarbińska, "Spór o granice stosowalności metod logicznych," *Studia Filozoficzne* 1964, Vol. 4, p. 25ff.

according to a number of post-analytical philosophers. Reality has a number of possible dimensions that may be expressed in a number of ways. Additionally, a number of its aspects, especially the humanistic understanding of "reality," are considered permanently ambiguous and blurry. Therefore, describing them fully with a single scheme is from the cognitive point of view a complicated task and one that would usually be evaluated as a deforming or simplifying characteristics of the described objects. Hence, we ought to be aware – add the post-analytical philosophers – that also the linguistic order imposed by a system based on formal logic is just one of many. The idea of "a uniform determined notional vocabulary where the structure of reality can be described once and for all ... is all but unfeasible."[30] Even identical words may take part in "various games" and may be organized by various "grammars," as defined by Wittgenstein; these are not only the rules of syntax but also of the impossibility to reject some sentences. Moreover, not all "games" have the goal of recognizing the reality or the truth.

From the post-analytical perspective, studies of individual cases, their collection, description, and explanation through referencing appropriate contexts of language use, or their potential grouping, will be more scientifically significant than systematicity understood as a single dominating form of organizing thought through language. The former attitude allows to adequately describe and comprehend reality "as is," while the latter limits and simplifies the existent image of human practice, always distorting it to a degree, thus having some traits that postmodernists will call a hidden "oppressiveness" of systems, be it language or culture. Post-analytical resistance to the idea of understanding science as a uniform whole organized by language is constructed in the name of defending a multi-centric, multicultural humanistic studies; for example, Rorty's ethnocentrism. What the representatives of this current had in mind was not an elimination of formal logic from the scientific discourse, but rather for formal logic to abandon its privileged position within science.

The feature of research systematicity seems to be a malfunction that is especially visible in those legal analyses which cooperate with the culture of instituted law. The order of the system of law corresponds to the internal order of research, with subject division into individual disciplines, diligently keeping to their research domains; I have already mentioned this when characterizing the professionalization of legal research. In the following section, I will reference only the second interpretation of science's systematicity; that is, science as an

30 H. Putnam, "The Uniqueness of Pragmatism," *Think. Philosophy for Everyone* 2004, Vol. 8, p. 101.

endeavor aiming at the construction of a uniform image of the researched reality. This issue is one of the fundamental questions discussed on the grounds of the analytical theory of law in the few recent decades. The matter divided the academic environment, on one side forming a group of supporters of standardizing the network of notions, including the notion of "norm"; for example, J. Austin with the concept that reduced law to "an order" or H. Kelsen's imperativism that brought legal order to the level of competence norms and their sanctioning. The other side hosted ideas accentuating the need to differentiate the ways of expressing normative character of law by the use of notions. Probably the most widely recognized concept following this line of thought is the concept of the system of law as internally differentiated rules – primary and secondary ones – proposed by H. L. A. Hart. Similarly, to Hart's methodology based on constructing the notion of law through reconstructive analysis of the linguistic usage context, the latter is definitely closer to the postulates proposed by post-analytical philosophers than the ideas of J. Austin or H. Kelsen. The post-analytical current will also undoubtedly benefit from the differentiation of legal standards into norms-principles and norms-rules (R. Dworkin, R. Alexy). The wealth of legal standards present in legal practice ought to be accompanied by appropriate differentiation of notions in the area of the language of legal sciences. Such an approach need not lead – as proven, for example, by Hart – to doubt in the systemic character of law; although it does indeed complicate its image as a whole by differentiating it internally.

It should also be mentioned that these divergent tendencies in the notional mirroring of law by nature reappear in academic teaching. A symptomatic example will be the program evolution of the teaching of logic observed in the recent decades at law faculties. Currently, this area of education increasingly more orients itself towards the professional needs of lawyers. Since quite recently, common and uniform "logic" taught at Polish faculties of law is losing ground in favor of "thematic logics" such as the logic of law, which is making vast references to the achievements of the argumentation theory.[31] Didactic popularity of legal variations of rhetoric or legal adaptations of discourse theory further evidences the tendency. It may be seen as a valid confirmation of the idea of supporting legal argumentation on informal logic formulated by Ch. Perelman

31 My lecturer in logics, employed by the Faculty of Philosophy, convinced us a number of years ago, while we were still students of law, that there is no such thing as "legal logic," similarly as there is no "housewife logic" and similar. Logic was supposed to be single for everyone because rules of correct thinking are the same for everyone.

and L. Olbrechts-Tytec as early as in 1958 in their *Traité de l'argumentation: la nouvelle rhétorique*.

7 The External Integration of Sciences

Yet another feature of analytical, paradigm-based philosophy is the search of a pattern idea, an order that individual disciplines which are to be "scientific" ought to base on in their research efforts. This order would take the form of either a "scientific research program" that imposes a given course of research and the type of problems undertaken, in its stronger variety, or at least a predefined language and a set of notions that could serve as heuristic inspiration for research in the applied area. Physics and formal logic, with underlying mathematics, were usually considered such patterns. The former was an archetype of an empirical science, therefore encompassing the type of a research area for the analytical philosophy that originally created its achievements; the latter provided neutral, precise, and universal research tools. Reasoning with the use of laws of logic was indifferent to whether it will be related to facts described by the language of physics, biology, or chemistry. It was only important for these sciences to have the traits of the so-called empirical facts. Since analytical philosophy had no subject of its own, it could adopt practically anything to serve as its subject and, therefore, aspire to be a "common good" of all the sciences. The study of language put into universal rules of formal logic thus started becoming the center of integration for the methodological sciences of lower development. These were naturally those sciences that analytical philosophy initially made no mention of; that is, non-empirical sciences, including the wide spectrum of humanistic subjects. The effect of such a variant of external integration of sciences was the weakening of internal integration of sciences that were standardized in this manner.

Can the external integration of sciences be, therefore, delivered with no cost for the internal image of science? It seems that the post-analytical philosophers, when confronted with this question, could give both a positive and negative answer. When it is related to the holistic vision of science, including the humanistic studies, the question will bring a decidedly negative answer, since research is strictly separated from the order of nature (truth as correspondence, the drive to objectivity of decisions) and culture (shared character, relativism of beliefs). The tendency for the former dimension of science to dominate over the latter is constantly criticized by many of the representatives of the current. If the question of external integration was limited to humanistic studies alone – seen as reflection within a specified cultural surrounding – it will bring a decidedly positive answer. R. Rorty describes the distinction of the two orders as the sense of life of the individual perceived differently in each case. The former is delivered through an individual as "a person situated in direct relation to reality," while the latter relies on developing the tale of the person and their "contribution to the life of the community."[32] The former aspires to "touching the sense of the matter" without relying on the opinions of the community, while the latter assumes the community is not only essential as the platform of communication, but also that the definite goal of science is the preservation, creation, or perfection of the community itself.[33] Community perspective is inspired by the belief of the pragmatists, negating the classical subject-object opposition and interpreting cognition as a "form of activity" – to quote, for example, J. Dewey, whose opinions are frequently referenced by R. Rorty. Hence, the humanities ought to "look totally different from natural sciences," and the goal of their research process is to "lead towards a properly balanced combination of sincere agreement and disagreement respecting the rules of tolerance."[34] The objectivity of truth is replaced with solidarity of the community whose composition is limited by ethnos, common to those who "share someone else's beliefs at least to a degree guaranteeing fruitful conversation."[35]

Looking from this perspective, it seems a malconstructed dilemma between the demand for the post-analytical philosophers to support external or internal integration and the agreement for some cooperation of these two points of view. This owes to the fact that it is based on categorization, so close to the heart of scientific positivism and analytical philosophy, which post-analytical philosophers would adopt reluctantly. It would seem that there could be no other integration than "internal," but post-analytical opening of institutional science into new areas or discourses that can share common ethnos – film, literature, or theater – allows us to leave the boundaries of traditional specializations and disciplinary divisions. The post-analytical philosophers reflecting on the areas that were considered "external" to science is becoming a valid argument in favor of the post-analytical current de facto leading to external integration of sciences to a larger degree that was declared by the traditional analytical philosophy. Each of these currents definitely set different goals for itself, as well as varied areas of

32 R. Rorty, *Objectivity, Relativism and Truth. Philosophical Papers Volume I*, Cambridge University Press 1991, *passim*.

33 Ibid., p. 69.

34 Ibid., pp. 62, 64.

35 Ibid., p. 49.

inspiration. Naturalistic patterns were replaced with opening towards broadly understood multidimensional humanities.[36]

The idea of external integration of jurisprudence based on some "model science" has been a topic of debate also for Polish theoreticians and methodologists of law for many years. It would seem the virtue of logical empiricism, and in Poland partially Marxism, that naturalism was considered a good model of scientific approach, while anti-naturalism was perceived as a form of abandoning the fight for scientific character of jurisprudence. Attempts to apply a humanistic interpretation to jurisprudence, referencing the so-called surface and deep structure of science or legal adaptations of the idealistic model of empirical sciences, along with the accompanying formal-logic tools (L. Nowak, W. Patryas), was to introduce jurisprudence into the reach of science in its positivistic definition, on the one hand, while protecting the discipline from axiological context created by the time when such projects originated on the other.

It seems that, on the grounds of philosophy of law, an example similar to R. Rorty's cultural ethnocentrism may be the so-called integral concept of law coined by R. Dworkin, and to some degree all those concepts which form part of the current of legal hermeneutics. Defining the tasks of judges and law specialists as the search for optimal understanding of law in the context of cultural norms and values entails the existence of a political alliance[37] – a community that through negotiation integrates the areas of politics and morality through mechanisms of court interpretations.[38] It causes the collapse of a number of dichotomic patterns that analytical theory of law made so popular. It is also true of the distinctions between internal and external integration of science which, according to the post-analytical discourse, are impossible to be selected from their community environment.

Similar ideas and assumptions were also the basis of the Polish philosophical-legal concept called juriscentrism; for example, abandoning of the cognition subject-object distinction, together with ones of norm-description and cognition-action.[39] The notion of a community has a more exclusive character, limited to the

---

36 R. Rorty, "Philosophy in America Today," *Consequences of Pragmatism (Essays: 1972–1980)*, University of Minnesota Press Minneapolis 1994, p. 211: "Analytical philosophy became … the same kind of discipline which we may find in other 'humanistic' institutes."

37 R. Dworkin, *Law's Empire*, Harvard University Press Cambridge, Massachusetts 1986, pp. 410ff.

38 Cf. M. Zirk-Sadowski, [introduction to the Polish edition of] R. Dworkin, *Law's Empire*, op. cit., p. XXIII.

39 A. Kozak, *Myślenie analityczne w nauce prawa i praktyce prawniczej*, Wrocław 2010.

professional group of lawyers. The last concept is common to the post-analytical current also in its pragmatic dimension because the achievements of analytical theory of law are seen through the theory's social function. Analytical theory of law ceases to be seen through its expected scientific character, but rather in the perspective of its social usefulness; that is, as a component of legal argumentative discourse. To a lawyer, it ought to provide strong support in their professional activity, conditions that would not be negotiable with the social environment, and a framework for legal dispute. It is primarily analytical-legal knowledge that ought to make a lawyer immune to attempts from other practices, primarily political ones. Strong internal integration is therefore delivered at a visible cost of external integration. On the one hand, the proposition on the level of the adopted research criteria shows visible similarity to post-analytical approaches while, on the other hand, it largely enriches the traditional achievements of the analytical theory of law. It places it in a new perspective, however, as well as ascribes it with different tasks.

8 Ahistoricism

Ignoring the historical perspective and subsequent "aculturalism" is yet another feature of research attitude that may be considered characteristic of analytical philosophy. Knowledge of the past is either completely absent because it is considered redundant from the perspective of an analyst's toolbox[40] or – if it appears at all – it serves only to show the mistaken philosophical ideas and speculations, individual case fallacies, or mistakenly formulated notions with the resultant misunderstandings and simulated problems. According to E. Nagel, also counted among analytical philosophers but refusing to share the belief of the uselessness of historical knowledge, history of philosophy is shown here only from its "negative" side.[41] In the opinion of the analysts, history serves not to teach us something but rather to un-teach, showing the mistakes of earlier generations. Such attitude is the consequence of a popular interpretation of the role of history in analytical philosophy: "problems that have been the center of attention of philosophers for centuries are very similar, as is the fundamental set of possible

40 E.g., W. Quine, according to R. Rorty, "approached studying history of philosophy with contempt." Quine did not read works on the history of philosophy and also asked his students not to. In this approach, Quine mirrored R. Carnap, *Filozofia analityczna a filozofia transformacyjna*, p. 10.

41 E. Nagel, *Impressions and Appraisals of Analytic Philosophy in Europe*, op. cit., p. 7.

solutions."[42] The difference lies in that currently, thanks to the achievements of contemporary analytical philosophy, we are capable of addressing these issues much better, mainly by showing their origins. Why, then, are we to reach into history, which offers still unshaped research tools, when we have much better counterparts nowadays? Practicing philosophy in a "scientific" manner is close to a technological vision of progress: new technology pushes its predecessor out of circulation, and the predecessor eventually finds its potential place in a museum, in the history of doctrines. As a rule, history plays no part in the shaping of cultural community. Among analysts, there is a trend towards common belief of their separateness or even elite character of their circles. It is not, however, common history that founds such beliefs, but rather the shared vision of science, similar type of questions, and the language used to articulate them.

Post-analytical competition brings back the conviction, characteristic of traditional philosophy and the inability to reject one's own history. For some representatives of the trend, like B. Williams or M. Nussbaum, this will be an open quoting of European culture personified by Greek philosophy and literature that are treated as the canon of humanistic studies and form an asset, without which the understanding and participation in contemporary culture is impossible. Cultural self-awareness, understanding of the place and context of a given issue are the starting point for any theory related to society, economy, or law. In another version, closer to Rorty's considerations, one would rather speak of historicity – in the spirit of Hegel's maxim of philosophy as "time seized in a thought" – but without the universalizing and objectivizing pitfalls stemming from the language of classical philosophy or Christianity. If philosophy is to be the tool for solving problems, then the problems of contemporary times call for new articulation, their own history, and at the same time the rejection of "the ladder that our predecessors used to climb."[43] In the first version, history and culture are synonymous with tradition based on common grounds, also allowing the contemporaries to better understand their doubts; in the latter, it is contemporary time itself, which cannot be comprehended without the understanding of cultural autonomy of human practice or the ethnos that is shared within the community.

References to history are also hard to find in the analytical theories of law. Standard works in the current begin with the formulation of the so-called

42 T. Szubka, "Czy zmierzch filozofii analitycznej," *Diametros, Internetowy Serwis Filozoficzny*, http://www.diametros.iphils.uj.edu.pl, p. 5.

43 Cf. A. Głąb, "Postanalityczność – nowa kategoria?"

research assumptions, in the form of definitions, potentially contrasted with the assumptions made previously by other authors. This practice is replacing the describing of shaping of a given legal institution or the accompanying doctrinal reflection. In legal analytical research, history is mainly the critique of the achievements of the predecessors, but rarely expands beyond the timeframe of when the paradigms of the theory under criticism were formed. What was before is classified as "ancient history" that would qualify as material belonging to lectures on history of law or history of doctrines. For instance, Polish theory of interpretation of law starts for many adepts with the 1959 work by J. Wróblewski, *Zagadnienia teorii wykładni prawa ludowego*. Some interpreters of law may even reach out for pre-war works of E. Waśkowski and S. Frydman but usually with little or no consequence to their own opinions. History is replaced with a drive towards universalism, showing that there is, for example, only one scientifically valuable and cognitively efficient theory of interpretation of law or concept of the linguistic shape of a norm; hence, there are no reasons whatsoever to tolerate any branch independencies. The history of law and jurisprudence as each history – according to the teachings of Windelband – primarily brings idiographic value and, in consequence, favors the grounding of time-space (branch, cultural) particularisms. However, the general analytical theory of law does not agree with this approach.

The other, post-analytical side is a broadly understood hermeneutic attitude with its characteristic metaphors of "spirals," "working in chains," and "historical horizon" which reflect the role of history and tradition. The attitude integrates what is sometimes called a diachronic approach. Objectivized, culturally integrated cognition of law is achieved through the consistency of decisions with the whole of legal tradition, and the decision is to be based "on the most acceptable political validation of a tradition, which embodies itself in available past legal material."[44] Juridical argumentation is not merely the culture of common law. Contemporary continental dogmatic and theory of law literature also makes this method of argumentation almost universal, and it needs not necessarily be associated with some variety of hermeneutics. Currently, even law theoreticians and philosophers who write glosses for judgments rarely make the news. It is little wonder, nowadays, if a theoretician of law starts their work by analyzing the judgments. The history of judgment is currently not only the search of grounds for the undertaken legal decisions, associated with common law and concurrent with the rule of stare decisis, but a much wider phenomenon. It also reaches

44 M. Zirk-Sadowski, op. cit., p. XXII.

into the realm of research in civil law and is a sort of proof for a different legal research methodology, a testimony to what I called "regaining the subject" by the analytical or practically post-analytical theory of law.

9 Sentences and Norms

Differentiating sentences from norms and judgments by description of facts or empirically oriented issues is one of the canons of analytical philosophy and, at the same time, the embodiment of positivistic descendants of this philosophy. This categorical distinction was to serve as the basis to draw the line between what is scientific (cognitive, theoretical) and non-scientific (metaphysical, practical, ideological). The efforts of the representatives of logical positivism driving towards constructing the so-called protocol or base sentences, so important to the Vienna Circle, were attempts at defining the nature of the connection between theory and its empirical basis. These were connections deriving from the conviction of the need for theoretical considerations to remain neutral towards their own research subject. The evaluation of the effort is of little concern, since the authors of the endeavor had doubts of their own. Another aspect seems more valid, namely a specific paradox, at least prima facie, in which the lack of involvement of theoretical claims towards the researched facts suggested by logical empiricists is confronted with the normative program of analytical philosophy. As T. Szubka observes, the term "analytical philosophy" was from the very onset of a normative dimension: it meant philosophy that was practiced in its own way; that is, by obeying the methodological constraints that give the best cognitive results."[45] Hence, there is no program conflict, because this is exactly why the language of science is confronted with such strict requirements. It can prepare tools that will give results in the form of objectivized theorems about the researched area: the described facts. It was research methodology and the resultant postulated language of nature that ought to serve as the normative dimension to the analytical philosophers. This order derived from the assumptions of Descartes' and Kant's philosophies such as separation of cognitive categories according to the researched contents, subject-object opposition in research, external versus internal, scientific, and practical points of view; with representationalism as the rule for constructing such dichotomous divisions.

Post-analytical reaction to its own tradition – in the benign variety that, despite all, sought to remain "within" the broadly understood analytical

45 T. Szubka, *Filozofia analityczna*, op. cit., p. 27; W. Janikowski, "Normatywna definicja filozofii analitycznej," *Analiza i Egzystencja*, 5 (2007).

philosophy – leads to the undermining or at least relativizing of the above oppositions.[46] Currently, language philosophers find it increasingly hard to claim that practicing science can be reduced to discovering the truth, and practicing analytical philosophy is to be reduced to the sharpening of linguistic tools that serve the truth. Philosophical problems turned out to have been created by the language practice of philosophers itself, and each attempt at approaching them with a solution led to the proposal of new ways to describe them. In this situation, social and cultural criticism, including ethical and political areas, becomes the task of the "new" analytical philosophy. The language of post-analytical philosophers is becoming more of a tool of intentional activity rather than that of mirroring of the existing reality. An acceptable role for a philosopher may be that of a therapist; a demystifier of the myth of the truth and objectivity at the foundation of the so-called theoretical cognition (Wittgenstein). In another perspective, this may be the position of a mediator between different variants of untranslatable discourses (Rorty). Thus, instrumentalism replaces representationism (Davidson).

Separating the description from the norm is especially difficult to achieve in jurisprudence, where the norms form the core of the research area, with an attempt at such descriptive science of norms proposed by H. Kelsen. The founding fathers of analytical philosophy, especially when related to the "logical" stage developed until the 1930s, did not make this an issue, because the reference point for analytical theorizing was supposed to be facts, and only the methodology of researching them was to be normative; the language of science, prepared for the purpose of mainly syntactic operations. However, at a later, "linguistic" stage, associated with attempts to apply the achievements of analytical philosophy to humanities, it appeared that the same notions can be found in double roles: as tools of linguistic cognition and subjects of research. It is exactly this type of situation that we commonly face in legal sciences. In consequence, establishing what is the effect of the legislator's actions and those of a law expert may prove impossible in a variety of situations.[47] For exactly these reasons, even influential

46 D. Davidson, *Inquires into Truth and Interpretation*, New York 1984, Oxford University Press, pp. 183–198; J. Duke, E. Walsh, J. Chase, J. Reynolds, *Postanalitic Philosophy. Ovecomming Divide*, op. cit., p. 8. In the radical version, post-analytical philosophy rejects the starting tradition as a mistaken project and replaces it with a new philosophy. See, for example, H. Putnam, *Realism with a Human Face*, Cambridge MA, Harvard University Press 1990, p. 19.

47 Cf. F. Longchamps, "Uwagi o używaniu pojęć w naukach prawnych," *Zeszyty Naukowe UWr. Series A*, Vol. 27, Prawo VII, Wrocław 1960, pp. 14–15; idem, *Z problemów poznania prawa*, Wrocław 1968, p. 14.

theoreticians of law in the analytical current, but especially those sympathizing with the reconstructionist current, frequently stressed that jurisprudence greatly influences the creation of its own subject.[48] Polish legal literature contains a characteristic evolution of the opinions of J. Wróblewski in this regard, in reference to the cognitive theory status of the theorems on the interpretation of law. From initial drive towards objectivizing meanings and battling the theses on the creative character of the interpretation of law – called "nihilistic"[49] – to pragmatism visible in the later period, situating the interpretation of law in the area closer to practical discourse.[50]

The weakening and relativization of the opposition of descriptive and normative character of the theorems of legal science can be found in the works of numerous contemporary supporters of differentiating external (descriptive, observational, communal) and internal (critical-reflective, individual) points of view in how we perceive rules. If we add a thesis of the cognitive predominance of the internal point of view over the external one,[51] we will move still further from the naturalistic roots of analytical philosophy. Looking from this perspective, the so-called refined legal positivism like Hart's is a visible step towards an attitude that will be described as post-analytical. Usually, however, when critical involvement of post-analytical philosophy is referenced, it means a lot more; that is, it includes the impact of the said philosophy on social, political, and ethical life; all the matters crucial for a group or an individual. The distinction between sentences and norms does not have that much of a profound meaning. Knowledge is to serve activity. Using Kierkegaard's words, it is all about the "objective and trivial" to be replaced by the "existential and important" for a group or an individual. The philosophy of law is becoming a politically and ethically sensitive reflection on humans, to some extent following the Greek example. Numerous

---

48 See, for example, Z. Ziembiński, *Szkice z metodologii szczegółowych nauk prawnych*, op. cit., p. 14.

49 J. Wróblewski, "Opisowa i normatywna teoria wykładni prawa," *Państwo i Prawo* 1958, Vol. 7.

50 A. Kozak, *Pojmowanie prawa w teorii wykładni*, Wrocław 1997, pp. 44–48. On the other hand, M. Zieliński, *Wykładnia prawa. Zasady. Reguły. Wskazówki*, Warszawa 2002, p. 76, described J. Wróblewski's already shaped concept of interpretation as a "normative concept," but "based on excessively grown assumptions that sum up to make a descriptive concept."

51 J. Woleński in the introduction to the Polish edition of H. L. A. Hart, *The Concept of Law*, Warszawa 1998, p. XX.

concepts from the area of the Critical Legal Studies movement will be merely more or less radical consequences of adopting such an attitude.

10 Some Conclusions

A post-analytical approach in combination with the traditional analysis of language phenomena propels itself into new problem areas, as well as adopts modified research approaches. Are they new for contemporary theory and philosophy of law, though? Some of them can be seen within the so-called refined legal positivism, some reach beyond the thinking set in the widely understood positivistic legal culture. Legal research of the post-analytical current draws towards itself problems from a variety of currents of contemporary theory and philosophy of law and shows that authentic problems of science reach beyond divisions into disciplines and professed scientific approaches. What seems to integrate the representatives of the current is (neo)pragmatism associated with a critical attitude towards the existing scientific practice, especially such practice in which science, or the humanistic aspect, is dominated by some external, uniform patterns. On the one hand, in jurisprudence it leads to the restoration of traditional philosophy of law problematics, forgotten during the domination of the analytical current, such as the restitution of the ethics of law, legal professions, and research, referencing the Greek ancestry of legal rhetoric. On the other hand, it results in the emergence of relatively new oppositions, which used to be excluded from science, such as law versus literature. There is also certainly no changing of research paradigm involved, let alone revolutionizing it in the meaning ascribed to the notion by T. Kuhn. It would be safer to assume that we are facing a slow but consistent disassembly of the positivistic paradigm of practicing research, or rather the rejection of the very idea of forming scientific theorems on the concept of paradigms.

It is also worth noting that post-analytical diagnoses of reality fundamentally change the expectations towards legal education, because the role and responsibility of a lawyer are perceived differently. Open involvement of science in social practice reveals new ways to question the responsibility of jurisprudence and the effects of the actions of scholars, including the model of legal education. On the grounds of analytical theories, activity of science had been unpersonified; all due to the ideal of unpersonified objectivism and truth as fundamental values of science. In consequence of the post-analytical critique, education and professional analysis of a lawyer received subjectivity. Legal science and education are not merely subject knowledge, but a form of an imaginative sensitive attitude. Hence, education ought to be more versatile and open to external environments.

Undoubtedly, studies in law as a "preparatory course" for future legal professions do not serve the purpose, since one would rather see in their place studies open to different branches of humanistic and social sciences. The role of the subjects in general law and history of law therefore grows at the cost of traditional dogmatics of law. Classical vision of a university as a community based on knowledge and values is also thus revived, but nowadays it is dominated by universities serving as pools of "human resources," educated for labor market demands.

The emergence of a spectrum of attitudes identifiable with post-analytical current may also raise anxiety. I will mention only two. First is the danger of making science more political, which may result in extremely dangerous consequences. The political of institutional law culture has always strongly legitimized lawmaking, but more or less successful attempts have been made to make the application of law independent from politics. The achievements of analytical theory of law served well to separate professional practice of lawyers from current politics. The considerations of the representatives of the post-analytical current are not only the professional activity of lawyers but also academic lawyers; hence, they are inseparable from politics. The political seems to return as a socially and scientifically valid dimension of the existence of groups and individuals.

The second anxiety is the decay of institutional authority of science. Post-analytical science has a tendency to disperse itself in other areas of cultural practice – "games" – therefore losing its socially privileged position. In the case of a game, as in law and legal sciences which ultimately serve safety and justice, there is a possible risk of these values also getting dispersed in debates between the lawmaker, judge, and philosopher of law, on one the hand, and a politician, economist, and literature or film expert, on the other. Taking debates on law and justice outside the realms of the philosophy of law – which provide a minimal level of consistency of discourse – "into the streets" may allow us to better identify with law but with a lower social agreement to the results of such debates. The authentic dispute based on conflicting interests calls for a meta-rule or, at least, a common idiom. Otherwise, even a dispute simple from a legal perspective may transform into an unsolvable political, economic, or cultural conflict founded on disproportionate discourses.[52] A rather obvious question will then arise: why do we need law, the theory of law, and lawyers at all? Conversely, we may agree that the rules of discourse available to lawyers and lawmakers are merely forms of their collective professional "life-world" and that there is no hidden social role behind them.

---

52 J. F. Lyotard, *The Differend: Phrases in Dispute*, transl. G. van den Abbeele, Manchester University Press, Manchester 1988, p. xi, calls this a "differend."

Jakub Łakomy

Hermeneutic Universalism: A Post-Analytical Inquiry into the Political of Legal Interpretation

1 Introduction[1]

Recently, there is no shortage of opinions that legal interpretation, especially performed by courts and tribunals, including international ones, belongs to the area of the political. It is said, for instance, that specific judgements of national constitutional tribunals or the Court of Justice of the European Union (CJEU) have a "political character."[2] One may even find opinions that the settlement activity of the said tribunals has an inevitably political character. It is symptomatic that the political diagnosed in court judgments is considered something normal by part of the authors,[3] while others go as far as calling it a pathology, twisting the meaning of the application of law.[4] Still other authors present a

1 The article was prepared as part of a research project for the National Center of Research, ID 2016/21/D/HS5/03912. I would like to express my gratitude for the critical reading of the manuscript and fruitful discussion to Rafał Mańko, PhD., Wojciech Małecki, PhD., and Klaudia Gaczoł, MA.

2 See, e.g., G. Beck, "The Court of Justice, legal reasoning, and the Pringle Case – Law as the continuation of politics by other means," *European Law Review* 2014/2; A. Sulikowski, "Trybunał Konstytucyjny a polityczność. O konsekwencjach upadku pewnego mitu," *Państwo i Prawo* 2016/4; R. Mańko, "Symbolic Violence in Technocratic Law and Attempts at its Overcoming: Politicisation Through Humanisation?," *Studia Erasmiana Vratislaviensia* 2017/11; R. Mańko, "Homo iuvens przed Trybunałem: wyrok Leitner w perspektywie teorii i filozofii prawa," *Prawne aspekty podróży i turystyki – historia i współczesność. Prace poświęcone pamięci Profesora Janusza Sondla*, P. Cybula (ed.), Kraków 2018.

3 E.g., R. Mańko, "Ideology and Legal Interpretation: Some Theoretical Considerations," *Constitutional Values in Contemporary Legal Space*, K. Torgans (ed.), Riga 2016, p. 124.

4 E.g., G. Beck, *The Legal Reasoning of the Court of Justice of the EU*, Oxford 2013; G. Conway, *The Limits of Legal Reasoning and the European Court of Justice*, Cambridge 2014. These authors, despite different assumptions and methodologies, agree with the opinion that decisions of the Court of Justice of the European Union are excessively political and formulate postulates in the current of legal positivism to limit their political character by the introduction and maintenance of strict directives of interpretation of EU legal texts.

much more traditional approach, defending the paradigm of the apolitical of legal interpretation, starting their argumentation with the assumptions of traditional legal positivism.

In this context, the goal of this article is to join the debate of the political of legal interpretation, taking the perspective of philosophy of law with post-analytical philosophy of law in the background. This chapter is, therefore, a tool to reconstruct the beliefs of Stanley Fish in a perspective that would highlight the place of the political in legal interpretation based on hermeneutical universalism. It may be claimed that the adoption of the described perspective will bear major influence on the ongoing scientific debate on the political of legal interpretation, including that of courts and tribunals.

2 Hermeneutic Universalism: Definition Considerations

Hermeneutic universalism is one of the concepts of interpretive philosophy, assumptions of which are shared by the current of post-analytical philosophy, and the subject of consideration of this monograph. From the point of view of this current, the political will inevitably influence the interpretation of texts, including legal ones. Each interpreter, and each interpreting community, will take a position in the structure of social conflicts which constitute *the political*. The main antagonist of such a view of interpretation of law is the positivistic theory of interpretation of texts, whose role is to provide the interpreter with tools that allow for the establishment of objective, universal meaning of texts and, thus, the elimination of the influence of subjective categories of cognition[5] and the influence of the political on the whole process.

According to hermeneutical universalism, each cognition is relativized to the perspective of the cognizing subject; that is, each cognition is interpretation. There is no cognition which is not relativized to any perspective. As the philosopher Thomas Nagel claims, there does not exist "a view from nowhere."[6] As the American pragmatist Richard Shusterman puts it, according to hermeneutical universalism, "we see all through a 'veil' of interpretation, or from a perspective that imposes some sort of interpretation … we do not only see everything through interpretation but … everything is constructed by it. In other words, there is nothing real, or real to ourselves, which would not be interpreted."[7]

5 D. Leszczyński, *Struktura poznawcza i obraz świata. Zagadnienie podmiotowych warunków poznania we współczesnej filozofii*, Wrocław 2010, pp. 11–156.

6 T. Nagel, *Widok znikąd*, Aletheia 1997.

7 R. Shusterman, *Estetyka...*, pp. 115–116.

Shusterman sees the roots of such phenomenon in Nietzsche's perspectivism, and its most complete picture in the contemporary philosophy of interpretation in the works of a neopragmatist, Stanley Fish. In his famous essay, where Fish argues with Ronald Dworkin, the former says that even in a simple, initial act of reasoning, devoid of reflection, "interpretation has done its job."[8]

In his *Pragmatist Aesthetics*, Shusterman reconstructs six valid features of the eponymous current, criticizing it within the constraints of interpretive philosophy.[9] First, while reconstructing the criticized perspective, Shusterman begins with pragmatist "fallibilism," claiming that everything we consider true, properly interpreted, in any given point in time is accidental, temporary, and cognitively situated. Everything undergoes constant changes, improvements, and modifications, is subject to different understandings from new stimuli, data, texts, and contexts.[10] Conclusions are not replaced with truths about the facts, but instead with further interpretations. Hence, interpretation never ceases and no fact, sentence, or understanding may be privileged from the cognitive perspective. A sentence formulated on allegedly objective meanings has the status of a further interpretation.[11]

Second, within hermeneutic universalism, cognitive positioning comes with the inevitable perspectivist character of interpretations. According to Shusterman[12] and others like Michał Paweł Markowski,[13] origins of such thinking can be traced to Friedrich Nietzsche. We always interpret cultural texts from an individual subjective perspective, and consequently, there is a variety of perspectives of other interpretive communities outside of our horizon of cognition. This forces epistemological humility and disables any claims of objectivity.

Third, the fact that we are inevitably cognitively situated in a specific interpretational horizon and that we read cultural texts from a given perspective comes with the assumption that we are equally and inevitably "prejudiced" from the cognitive point of view. We have certain "prejudices," "pre-judgments," and

8 Stanley Fish, "Working on the Chain Gang: Interpretation in Law and in Literary Criticism," *Critical Inquiry* 9 (1982), p. 204.

9 R. Shusterman, *Estetyka...*, pp. 122ff.

10 Ibid., p. 122.

11 Ibid., p. 122: "No possible fact and no true understanding may have an epistemological status higher than that of interpretation, because they can be corrected and replaced with a new interpretation. Interpretation is in turn a paradigm of things that can be corrected and that never end."

12 Ibid., p. 122.

13 M. P. Markowski, *Nietzsche. Filozofia interpretacji*, Kraków 1997, pp. 131ff.

results of prior processes of interpretation. They cause the image of an autonomous subject that follows reason, which processes the testimonies of the senses that result from the interaction of a refined subject with the objective reality of fiction.[14]

Fourth, since cognition is perspectivist and prejudiced, it is also inevitably selective. There is no possibility of a holistic approach to the object of cognition, and interpretational look is merely fragmentary.[15]

The fifth characteristic feature of hermeneutic universalism imposes the reconsideration of the relationship between creating and applying law. The interpreters do not merely mirror the textual or extra-textual reality in a passive manner but actively create reality through interpretation itself.[16]

Sixth, all understanding and cognition are of linguistic character. Cognition equals decoding of arbitrary signals.[17]

The definition of interpretation is understood rather broadly; from this perspective, classical positivist distinction of "text interpretation" seeks to interpret an unambiguous norm from a text that creates legal codes and fact cognition. Such a standpoint towards interpretation and the process of applying law from the perspective of hermeneutic universalism requires this dichotomy to be

14 R. Shusterman, *Estetyka...*, p. 123.

15 Ibid., p. 124.

16 Ibid., pp. 126–127: "Comprehension and perception, as Nietzcheanists, pragmatists, and the followers of Gadamer strongly believe, are actions. They are not passive reflections of things encountered, but active application of an ordered structure. Hearing or seeing something before an attempt at interpreting is made includes the activity of our bodies, specific motoric reactions and tightening of muscles and nerves of the senses."

17 Ibid., p. 127: "All comprehension is of language character, because, similarly to experience, it includes notions that require language. Linguistic understanding is in truth decoding or interpreting signs that are not natural, but rather arbitrary, and transforming them into a sentence requires interpretation. According to Quine-Davidson model, in order to comprehend the meaning of a sentence we need to deliver its translation or interpretation in terms that are already known to us, be it terms of the interpreted language or one that is our "native" and closer to us. Davidson clearly states that "understanding the speech of another person always entails radical interpretation" and openly equals "capability for thinking" with "speaking a language." Gadamer, on the grounds of the Continental tradition, liaises with him, supporting the universal scope of hermeneutics on "character of all human experience of the world, linguistic in itself" and the acceptance of "language itself being a game of interpretation that we all get involved in on a daily basis.""

blurred. This thesis was worded very aptly and concisely by the pragmatist Sanne Taekema:

> facts and norms as interdependent in the legal domain.... Any legal problem arises within a context that already comprises legal norms, which implies that the factual side of the problem is not regarded neutrally; it is regarded against the background of legal normativity. Most jurists recognize that facts are coloured by the norms applied to them, but often this is seen as a separate activity of turning raw facts into legally relevant facts. Such a picture fails to acknowledge that the perception of raw facts is impossible.[18]

From the perspective of hermeneutic universalism, any cognition, including the cognition of facts, is always conducted in a specific context. Therefore, in abstracto, "doctrinal" interpretation in legal comments and dogmatic academic articles is merely an illusion. Legal interpretation needs to blur the dichotomies that have been discussed.

Accepting the truth of such thesis causes the whole process of text interpretation to need a completely new perspective. Blurring the difference between objectivism with a more "scientific" cognition of facts of the case and a more subjective establishing of the meaning of a text raises the need to build a completely different theory of application of law which, similarly to a number of theories inspired by pragmatism and neopragmatism, does not allow for a number of analytical dichotomies.[19]

3 A New Vision of Interpretation: Hermeneutic Universalism and the Interpretation of Law

The consequence of the adoption of the rules of hermeneutical universalism is the redefinition of the word "interpretation" itself and its connection with epistemology. I understand interpretation broadly, epistemologically, following hermeneutic universalists, as denoting cognition relativized to the perspective of the cognizing subject. I would therefore strongly distinguish between a more general, broader view of interpretation, understood as the subjectively relativized cognition, from its narrower expression, understood as reading a text in order to

---

18 S. Taekema, "Beyond Common Sense: Philosophical Pragmatism's Relevance to Law," *Tilburg Working Paper Series on Jurisprudence and Legal History* No. 06–02, March 28, 2006; Version: 1.0, http://ssrn.com/abstract=980204, accessed: 30.11.2017, pp. 4–5. Cf. H. Putnam, *Pragmatism: An Open Question*, Oxford 1995, pp. 57ff.

19 It needs to be admitted, though, that some positivists soften these dichotomies noticeably, especially see T. Gizbert- Studnicki, A. Dyrda, A. Grabowski, *Metodologiczne dychotomie. Krytyka pozytywistycznych teorii prawa*, Warszawa 2016, passim.

capture its meaning. Let us call the latter the "philological" approach. It may be understood as one of the variants of generally understood interpretation in the epistemological sense.

When using the word "interpretation" on its own, I am referring to the epistemological understanding of the notion. I would like to stress this because both the everyday use of this word and referring to interpretation on the grounds of theory of law directs our thoughts towards the philological understanding that is intuitive for the majority of laypersons and researchers. If referring to interpretation in the philological sense, it will be marked directly in the text, by the addition of an adjective or referring to the "interpretation of legal texts" or "interpretation of law." The last phrase, naturally, sets us in the context of the most popular category, both in civil and common law: the theory of law emerging from the positivistic understanding of law as objectivistic scientific claims.

Mixing of the two meanings referenced above may lead to numerous misunderstandings and empty debates. A precise consideration of the legal interpretation is additionally complicated by the fact that philologists and lawyers – when reading texts in order to discover their meanings – sometimes differentiate between interpretation and understanding. Interpretation is a specific reflexive process, in which meaning is not "directly tangible" and does not come to the interpreter instantly, without any reflection. Such authors, within the philological understanding, differentiate between two types of reading: with conscious reflection and without it. In this case, they consider "interpretation" to only be the conscious, reflective process.

One needs to stress the fundamental dispute of the 20th-century Polish theory of law: one revolving around the clarificatory concept of the interpretation of law by Wróblewski and the derivative approach of the Poznań school.[20] Jerzy Wróblewski visibly supported the "psychological" approach, differentiating between the situation of isomorphism, in which cognition occurred in the form of "direct understanding" without the need of initiating the interpretation process, from the situation of interpretation, in which the interpreting subject had doubts as to the meaning of the text and was forced to perform its interpretation.

A few decades later, in the Anglo-Saxon legal positivist discourse, descending from the traditions of analytical philosophy, the above dispute was revived in a similar form. Timothy Endicott, a descendant of such theorists of law as Herbert

20 Especially see T. Gizbert-Studnicki, K. Płeszka, "*Dwa ujęcia wykładni prawa. Próba konfrontacji*," *ZNUJ, Prace z Nauk Politycznych* 1984, Vol. 20.

Hart or Ronald Dworkin, in his November 2013 article[21] disputes with another famous representative of legal positivism, Andrei Marmor.

Marmor claims that legal interpretation occurs only when the interpreting subject is forced to solve an indeterminacy of a legal text.[22] Endicott's perspective is different: if law is indeterminate in some respect, the interpreter is forced to reach for something other than only interpretation, which is then used to determine whether the law is indeterminate at all. Both authors agree to one thing, that interpretation is not omnipresent and it is something different from cognition.

4 Debates About the Proper Interpretation of Legal Texts. Hermeneutic Universalism and the Political

Before I present the argumentation in favor of hermeneutical universalism in the philosophy of legal interpretation as requiring the introduction of the notion of the political into the notional and methodological network, I will ponder on the reasons of unmovable and inconclusive disputes on the proper interpretation of legal texts as explained by the representatives of different currents of the philosophy of law. Varied explanations of the state of things are offered by foundational and antifoundational representatives of the philosophers of law.

Foundationalists, who stand on the grounds of ontological realism but without epistemological realism in reference to the social and humanistic sciences, reject the following thesis. The realistic ontology allows for the emergence of theory of cognitive interpretation which, just like in natural sciences, will allow for the creation of epistemological tools that would conclusively solve the debates on the proper meaning of a given legal text. Such foundationalists may be called "epistemological legal skeptics." They assume that law exists objectively, but that we are unable to completely and objectively get to know it. The "fault" is on our side, on the side of the cognizing subject and their cognitive structure. This structure may be adequate to the complete cognition of physical subjects, in which the naturalistic paradigm of practicing science in the Enlightenment model may be reconciled with our cognitive faculty and dependably solve natural cognitive debates

---

21 T. Endicott, "Interpretation and Indeterminacy," *University of Oxford Legal Research Paper Series*. Paper No 96/2013 November 2013. Article is pending publication in *Jerusalem Review of Legal Studies*.

22 Marmor presented the point of view criticized by Endicott in: A. Marmor, *Interpretation and Legal Theory. Second edition*, Oxford 2005; and Idem, *Philosophy of law*, Princeton 2011, [especially Chapter 6].

that apply to the corresponding theory of truth. Analogically, the tools coming from sociology, including jurisprudence, appears to be inadequate, leading us to aporias that we could overcome only with the application of political, rhetoric, or ethical "prosthetics."

Foundationalists, whose realistic assumptions also stretch towards the epistemology of jurisprudence, claim that although we have cognitive "access" to law, contradictions are inevitable due to specifics of the very object of research, which is different from the object of research within the "physical" reality. Law is imperfect and the tangible effects of its existence are the legal texts formulated in a language that shares all imperfections with the spoken language, which makes the objectively existent contents of legal norms inaccessible, despite the existence of methodologically verifiable tools. There is also the insurmountable tension between the general formulation of norms and the particular character of a studied case. Foundationalists of this camp offer a whole range of methodological prostheses, such as the assumption of a rational lawmaker in the Polish theory of law, serving an optimizing function in the process of applying law.

The constructivist camp within the philosophy of interpretation of law points at various reasons for the undecidable element in the debates on the proper meaning of legal texts in legal practice and jurisprudence. Anti-foundationalists – who support the social creation of reality and knowledge – search for answers to the questions of interpretation of law within cognitive, or interpretational, communities. The common values, cognitive prejudgments, interests, and cognitive tools that members of the community share co-shape scientific reality and truth. Since the debates on the proper meanings of legal texts are so widespread in practically all the legal systems and cultures – from obvious reasons I am omitting here the cases of law in totalitarian systems and fundamentalist systems of religious law – there are two possible reasons for such state of things.

First, the problem may lie in the nature of the interpreting community as such and the relations between different communities that share a common interpreter. In this meaning, the communities would permeate each other to the degree when values, goals, and rules of a one of their members would necessarily have impact on his or her cognitive perspective within another community. This would be true of, for example, a civil lawyer that simultaneously belongs to an interpretative community of fans of crime novels set in Victorian England, who would transplant the cognitive prejudgments of 19th-century Great Britain to the institution of a delict in modern civil law. Their understanding of a text regulating the conditions of compensatory liability would be overwhelmingly different from the perception of the same institution by a different civil lawyer who would work for the same chair of civil law but would be a fully socialized member of a community of avid fans of spaghetti westerns. In such setting, separation and professionalization of cognitive efforts would be impossible. A conceptual, axiological, and methodological wall would never come to be and the switching of perspectives would be incomplete.

Second, the grounds for this fact are to be seen in the nature of a specific interpretative community. In such a vision, each community would be internally strictly pluralized, combined with a variety of permeating and crisscrossing "subcommunities" that would partly differ in their cognitive prejudgments and partly unite under a common denominator. For instance, within the lawyer community, we observe a debate on the proper meaning of a collection of texts related to temporary imprisonment between the interpretative community of criminal lawyers representing the doctrine of material criminal law, positivists, advocates, and the community of criminal lawyers, processualists, prosecutors.[23]

Acknowledging that linguistic arguments are insufficient to judge the debates on the proper understanding of legal texts is a condition for the conceptualization of real sources of extra-linguistic premises in the argumentation discourse on the proper meaning of legal texts. Let us try shedding light on the above by introducing the notion of the political related to hermeneutic universalism as per Stanley Fish's proposal.

Let us start with a quote from Chantal Mouffe, whose work was titled *On the Political*: "[B]y 'the political' I mean the dimension of antagonism which I take to be constitutive of human societies, while by 'politics' I mean the set of practices

23 In this context, see the discussion on the interpretation of EU law by lawyers of national, therefore, separate, interpretation societies, or the emergence of the European legal interpretive community. In literature, see H. Schepel, R. Wesseling, "The Legal Community: Judges, Lawyers, Officials and Clerks in the Writing of Europe," *European Law Journal* 1997/2; A. Kozak, "Niedoceniana wspólnota – prawnicy a integracja europejska," *Z zagadnień teorii i filozofii prawa*, J. Kaczor (ed.), Wrocław 2006; R. Mańko, O. Łachacz, Multilingualism, pp. 87–88; R. Mańko, "Multilingualism, Divergent Authentic Versions of a Legal Rule and Legitimate Expectations of Individuals," *Studies in Logic, Grammar and Rhetoric* 2016/45, pp. 153–154. In reference to the International Court of Justice, see A. Bianchi, D. Peat, M. Windsor, *Interpretation in International Law* (2015), who claim: "For example, an ICJ judge may simultaneously be a member of four interpretive communities: (1) the interpretive community of international judges, (2) the [one] … focused on human rights, and (3) the interpretive community of lawyers in the jurisdiction where the judge received her legal education, was socialized or practised."

and institutions through which an order is created, organizing human coexistence in the context of conflictuality provided by the political."[24]

Whenever I refer to "the political of legal interpretation," I reference Chantal Mouffe's "the political." I am interested in situating the interpreter in the framework of antagonism which permeates the community, and within which the interpreted legal texts function. I do not mean the common understanding of the political entanglement of the interpretation processes as of the connection between the interpreters with current politics in legislative institution or political parties. I exclude the empirical analysis of the entanglement of judges in the sub-world of politics from my interests.[25]

I consciously do not use the currently popular notions of "politics" as "activities aiming at participating in the authorities or exerting its distribution between … the state, individuals, and organizations … with appeal to violence"[26] or as "intentional activity, art or rationalized skill of making decisions in public sphere," which result from Aristotle's considerations related to the common good.[27]

Using the poststructuralist definition of "the political" in the context of epistemology and the methodology of reading texts is valid because the point where the theory-cognitive and political discourses meet is Nietzschean perspectivism and interpretationism, which assume that "there are no certain interpretations." In the Nietzschean world there is no access to objective truth, we witness the clash of varied perspectives whose genuineness is not decided upon by reality itself. By necessity, we are witnesses and participants to an "agon," a clash of different perspectives.

The agon also finds its reflection in the area of the clash of conflicting interests, where the debates of perspectives are motivated from a political view. My research intentions on the surprising connection between the post-structuralist epistemology, the philosophy of text interpretation, and political philosophy

24 Ch. Mouffe, *Polityczność*, Warszawa 2008, p. 24.

25 For more about the political in Mouffe's understanding, see an excellent analysis by M. Paździora, M. Stambulski, "Co może dać nauce prawa polityczność? Przyczynek do przyszłych badań," *Archiwum Filozofii Prawa i Filozofii Społecznej* 2014/1, pp. 55ff. I agree with most of the theses and interpretations of agonistic thinking in the theory of politics and theory of law presented in this text.

26 A. Bator, "Polityczne interpretacje analitycznej teorii prawa" *Integracja zewnętrzna i wewnętrzna nauk prawnych cz. 1*, M. Zirk-Sadowski, B. Wojciechowski, T. Bekrycht (eds.), Łódź 2014, p. 14. This is, naturally, a Weberian definition.

27 Ibid.

seem to have been confirmed by Chantal Mouffe in her latest book, *Agonistics. Thinking the World Politically*,[28] in which she links the notion of the political with "antagonism" and "hegemony."

5 Stanley Fish's Hermeneutic Universalism and Interpretive Communities

One of the most coherent concepts of hermeneutical universalism on the grounds of the philosophy of law was formulated by the American neopragmatist, Stanley Fish. In the essay "Working on the Chain Gang. Interpretation in Law and Literary Criticism," Fish wrote:

> Just as there are those in the legal community who have insisted on construing statutes and decisions "strictly" (that is, by attending only to the words themselves), so there are those in the literary community who have insisted that interpretation is, or should be, constrained by what is "in the text"; and just as the opposing doctrine of legal realism holds that judges' "readings" are always rationalizations of their political or personal desires, so do proponents of critical subjectivity hold that what a reader sees is merely a reflection of his predispositions and biases. The field is divided, in short, between those who believe that interpretation is grounded in objectivity and those who believe that interpreters are, for all intents and purposes, free.[29]

Fish places himself outside the dichotomy that he pictures. I will try to explain it in the below considerations. The key concept of his philosophy is that of "interpretive communities." Explaining it will serve a twofold role in my argumentation. First, understanding the concept is a prerequisite to the analysis of Fish's concept of interpretation; second, it will be subsequently used to describe the political of processes and results of interpretation of law.

It is not easy to define "interpretive communities." The concept evolved in Fish's writings over a few decades. At the beginning of his essay "How to Recognize a Poem When You See One," Stanley Fish formulates a thesis on the meaning of texts that will allow us to comprehend the concept better: "[M]eanings are the property of neither set and permanent texts nor independent readers, but rather that of interpretive communities which are responsible both for the shape of the reader's actions and resulting texts."[30]

---

28 Ch. Mouffe, *Agonistics. Thinking the World Politically*, London 2013.

29 S. Fish, *Interpretacja, retoryka, polityka. Eseje wybrane*, Kraków 2008, pp. 227–228. The translation of the last sentence was modified in order to maintain coherence with the original.

30 Ibid., p. 81.

More detailed considerations can be found in Fish's essay "Change." Fish recalls there the genesis of the introduction of the notion of an interpretive community; the aim to raise an opinion in a valid debate within literary studies. This refers to the sources of interpretive authority that were traditionally found in the text itself or were ascribed to the author.[31]

Stanley Fish puts himself outside of the dichotomy, therefore outside of the dichotomy of "subjectivity" and "objectivity" of interpretation. In the former case, the correctness of interpretation is a subjective matter, determined by the individual reader's point of view, while, in the latter, it is determined by an independent external instance. Another dichotomy that Fish distanced himself from is that of "textualism" and classically understood "intentionalism," in which the external instance deciding upon the correctness of interpretation is either the intention of the author or the text itself.[32] In "Change," Stanley Fish perceives the interpretive community not as a "group of individuals" who share a given viewpoint, but rather as a "viewpoint" in itself, a "way to organize experience" that directs thought and action of a defined group of individuals. The strength of this point of view is so considerable that Fish, when writing about individuals who share it references it as "the property of the community."[33]

Leszek Drong, one of the most dedicated researchers of the Fish's theories in Poland, proposed his own definition of the interpretive community: "It seems better to … use the more reserved notion of a community as a *tool of description* used in order to stress the communal – i.e., socially and ideologically conditioned – character of all cognition."[34]

Let us confront Fish's understanding of interpretive communities with the properties of hermeneutical universalism. As Fish claims, "meanings are the property of neither set and permanent texts nor independent readers." A question arises then as to whose property meanings are, with the answer: "that of interpretive communities which are responsible both for the shape of the reader's actions and resulting texts." The role of interpretive communities is therefore dual. First, they provide the interpreter with cognitive tools, schemes or – referring directly to legal interpretations – directives for the interpretation of legal

---

31 Ibid., p. 251.

32 Fish's attitude towards intentionalism is much more complicated than would seem prima facie. It will be presented in more detail below.

33 Ibid., p. 251.

34 L. Drong, "Od konwencjonalizmu do normatywizmu. Kilka uwag o ewolucji poglądów teoretycznoliterackich Stanleya Fisha," *ER(R)GO. Teoria–Literatura–Kultura*, Vol. 12, 1/2006, Katowice-Częstochowa 2006, p. 27.

texts. Second, by the regulation of a cognitive procedure, interpretive communities influence the shape of the texts which actually arise only in the process of interpreting signs.

Hermeneutic universalism entails cognitive fallibilism. Texts as the results of the activity of an interpretive community are merely temporary "cognitive assumptions," open to further interpretive efforts. On the epistemological level, these interpretations will never end. Naturally, limitations imposed on the process of legal interpretation resulting from the tasks of law and legal process are something completely different, as is the vesting of authority in the interpretations during the process, but as Fish points out in another section, these limitations are of completely different nature, not connected with interpretation in the epistemological sense.[35]

The epistemological temporariness of the results of legal text interpretation is bound by changes that occur within the interpretive community, and these changes result both from the internal dynamics of the community and the dominating point of view within the interpretive community. Broader social antagonisms finding their place in specific court proceedings undertake the form of debates on the "proper" interpretation of legal texts that are to shape the basis for the decision in the proceeding. A conflict, in itself a reflection of the political, is adjusted by institutions from the level of politics; these are courts or organs of public administration. Representatives of these institutions are members of various interpretive communities, similar to the individual sides of court proceedings.

Hermeneutical universalism also entails inevitable perspectivism of interpretation, as well as "cognitive prejudice" of the subject, who will utilize their own "cognitive prejudgments." The vision of an autonomous subject who objectively experiences the reality set on a solid metaphysical foundation is questioned.

No element of reality that we experience, including texts, literary and legal, is objectively accessible. We have not the possibility of experiencing them "as is." In this sense, one may say that we actually create reality rather than experience it. Fish suggests that "interpretational strategies that we set in motion" are the decisive factor.[36] From the classical epistemology or methodology of legal positivism such an attitude will cause accusations of the defense of a hazardous

35 S. Fish, "Stanowisko tekstualne nie istnieje," *ER(R)GO. Teoria–Literatura–Kultura* Vol. 12, 2006, pp. 107–128.

36 S. Fish, *Interpretacja...*, p. 91.

"non-scientific" subjectivism; these are the accusations that Fish rejects in a very orderly and convincing argumentation.

Tools, cognitive pre-judgments, which allow for the process of cognition, and interpretation in the broad epistemological sense are conventionalized and possess a social character. The interpreting self is inevitably socially situated, and "divine view" from a direct perspective is inaccessible to man. Of equal inaccessibility is the purely "human," autonomic, subjective, and private perspective. We are constantly limited by social institutions into which we have been set; institutions that existed before us and that will – in one form or another – exist also after our death. Fish underlines that we are members of these institutions as strongly as the institutions are part of us. We make use of their "interpretive strategies," while having very low impact on their shape. The scope of our freedom is limited to a conscious movement between the institutions and application of the interpretive strategies of various institutions.

Understanding the culturalist, constructivist perspective is the key to abandoning the completely useless notion of "objective" and "subjective" result of the process of interpretation. In other words, the cognizing readers or interpreters never find themselves in the relation of an "adequate" insight into the matter of the issue, into the real meaning of the text. It modifies the traditional opposition of "subject and object of cognition," which seems to be adopted by legal positivism.[37]

Fish states it as follows: "we have readers whose consciousness is constituted by a set of conventionalized notions which, when used, make up a conventionalized and conventionally perceived object."[38] Later, Fish stresses that our personality may not exist without strong roots in the conventionalized categories of thinking. If we adopt such a view, a non-situated personality and completely free consciousness, which aptly cognizes objective reality, will become impossible to grasp conceptually.[39] This, in turn, clarifies Fish's remarks which may be found throughout his books, that a condition for the existence of freedom is the existence of limitations.

Deliberating over what can cause us to frequently observe situations of interpretive consensus which commonly appears in numerous conversations, everyday situations, literature faculties, courtrooms, and among dogmatists that practice the interpretation of legal acts. Thus, we must reject a "common-sense"

37 Cf. M. Zirk-Sadowski, "Pozytywizm prawniczy a filozoficzna opozycja podmiotu i przedmiotu poznania," *Studia z Filozofii Prawa*, tom 1, Kraków 2001.

38 S. Fish, *Interpretacja…*, p. 92.

39 Ibid., p. 95.

hypothesis that it is the agreement of a group of people possessing "the truth about the text" in the understanding of corresponding theory.

6 Instead of a Summary. The Political Character of Interpretation and Interpretive Communities

The thesis that Stanley Fish proposes will serve to explain the political of the processes of legal interpretation:

> The source of our unanimity was rather a specific structure of interests and well-founded goals; a structure whose categories filled our consciousness so much that they became synonymous with it. They immediately vest phenomena with meaning that they need to have, adopting ready-made assumptions on what the intentions of someone's gestures and words are.[40]

Adopting such a view makes us talk about the political of both the process of interpretation and the result of interpretation – the set meaning of the text – even in a situation when interpreters are unanimous and the premises, procedures, and results of the interpretation are not controversial. Unanimity within an interpretive community – in our case the interpretive community of lawyers – which very often is vested with authority and (self-)legitimizes itself with specialist knowledge is in fact used to defend a hegemonic perspective and "the structure of interests" of the professional group. The situation becomes slightly more complicated when lawyers represent conflicting sides of a process and adopt a viewpoint that takes into account the interests of the social group of their clients, or another interpretive community.

The above quote is immensely valid for yet another reason. Just like a lens, it focuses two most crucial elements of Fish's philosophy of interpretation: the "creation" of meanings by interpretive communities with the "inert" power of necessity of the community's members and of "identification" of subconsciously created meanings as "objective" and "proper" intentions of authors. This rather unintuitive claim is self-contradictory only on the surface. It is only possible to reconciling the constructivist and culturalist approach to meaning creation of texts with ontological identification of meaning as the authorial intention when we differentiate the two separate levels of approaching a text's interpretation.

"Creating" meanings by members of interpretive communities happens on the sociological level. The theory of interpretation allows to answer the question of why specific texts in specific contexts are interpreted by the members of

40 Ibid., p. 93.

the community in a specific manner. The acceptance of the intentionalist theory works, on the other hand, on the ontological level: it allows us to answer the question of what the meaning of the text is: "A text whose meaning seems clear and obvious at first glance is a text whose intentional context has already been accepted without reservations, although stability and clarity of such a text can always be questioned, by putting forward arguments for another intentional context and therefore a different obvious meaning."[41]

The above quote calls for a more detailed analysis because it clarifies some doubts that are natural to come to a reader in an analytical-positivist interpretive community of law scholars. Adopting "the intentional context without doubt" is performed within the specified interpretive community. What causes the members of an interpretive community to repetitively and similarly set the intentional context of a text is the cognitive prejudgments which are deeply socialized and create the element of cognitive structure of the interpretive community of lawyers. At the psychological level, interpreters have the impression of a situation of "direct understanding," therefore, no interpretation efforts are necessary. In some extreme formalistic concepts, they are even forbidden on methodological and political grounds. At any rate, the interpretation will have achieved its goals on the epistemological level.

The functioning of interpretive communities allows us to clarify a situation that may seem incomprehensible to a supporter of formalistic concepts of interpretation. Since meaning – objectively, literarily, and ontologically existing on the level of lexical structure – does not exist, how can we justify frequent facts of common agreement about the meanings of specific texts of literature, on the one hand, and on the other, the legitimization of the theory of interpretation and the existence of criteria for assessing arguments that allow to conduct meaningful disputes on the proper meanings of texts?

The reason behind the acceptance of some interpretations as proper and "objective" is the similar cognitive structure of members of a given interpretive community. Theories of interpretation from the neopragmatist culturalist perspective are legitimized through the professionalism of the disciplines,[42] while the evaluation criteria are intradisciplinary, created within the community, and assessed according to the institutional rules.

Both within the literature and legal community there will be frequent situations in which a stabilized meaning, even after a long time, starts to be

41 S. Fish, *Stanowisko…*, p. 108.
42 S. Fish, *Interpretacja...*, pp. 227ff.

questioned. Arguments appear then in defense of the validity of new meanings. As Fish writes, "stability and clarity of such a text can always be questioned, by putting forward arguments for another intentional context and therefore a different obvious meaning." The above fragment is the key to defending the thesis saying that Fish's theory of interpretation should be perceived through post-structuralist concept of the political.

The moment when the alternative result of legal interpretation is subject to discussion on the pages of a legal journal, during a legal conference, in a commentary to an act of law, or in justification of a precedent in court is political per se. The same applies to a courtroom situation in which the attorney ad litem or the counsel for the defense, while following a set process strategy, puts forward an argument that we "should abandon the 'literal' meaning because of the important functional premises" or when "the result of the application of linguistic interpretive directives should be narrowed/expanded."

The debate about the political of legal interpretation conducted on the grounds of the socializing visions of constitutional or European law may now appear meaningless, since all interpretation is inevitably political, including processes of court interpretation and application of law. The above implications to the theory of interpretation of law that result from the philosophy of hermeneutical universalism seem to confirm this statement. In this situation, not only the decisions of constitutional courts and international tribunals, such as the Court of Justice of the European Union, would be political because of normative[43] and methodological[44] conditions. The political would inevitably be included in each process of interpreting and applying law.[45] Adopting such a viewpoint would

43 It is indicated that stylization of the constitutional entries and the points of Union treaties provides an especially wide field for their free interpretation. See, e.g., A. Arnull, *The European Union and Its Court of Justice*, Oxford 2006, p. 612.

44 As an example, the UE Court of Justice's susceptibility to wider argumentation in the "extralegal" or "political" sense that national courts is indicated in, e.g., P. Marcisz, *Koncepcja tworzenia prawa przez Trybunał Sprawiedliwości Unii Europejskiej*, Warszawa 2015, pp. 115ff; R. Mańko, "The Use of Extra-Legal Arguments in the Judicial Interpretation of European Contract Law: A Case Study on Aziz v Catalunyacaixa (CJEU, 14 March 2013, Case C-415/11)," *Law and Forensic Science* 2015/2.

45 That is, even if – for reasons indicated in the above remark – the political remains normally hidden and becomes visible at the moment of interpretative turns, rapid changes to line of decisions, or in "cause lawyers" cases descried by D. Kennedy who, with the use of interpretation tools, fight for the changes of interpretation while openly declaring their political goals.

have significant consequences for the research on the political character of adjudication! The adoption of the political of the process as the starting point would lead to focusing on the more important question of "how" instead of "whether" when analyzing the specific position within the social antagonism assumed by a court interpreter of law.

Michał Stambulski

The Concept of Law in the Analytical and Post-Analytical Theory

1 Two Approaches to Language in Analytical Philosophy

The 20th century was the scene of "linguistic turn" in European philosophy. Independently from one another, researchers in Great Britain, Austria, and Poland noticed the fact that language is an intermediary between the subject and external reality (epistemological issues), co-constitutes reality (ontological issues), may be a cognitive tool (methodological issues), and a tool of influence (ethical and political issues). Idealism was rejected. Instead of creating philosophical systems that embrace the totality of reality, a philosopher was to seek a neutral point of view and focus on a specific fragment of a problem. Classical philosophical problems were reformulated in order to highlight their connections with language. Linguistic analysis became the new promising method of solving these problems. In the analytical philosophy, there was no consensus as to what the method was to look like. Moreover, there was no consensus as to what the "solution" of a philosophical problem should be. Is creating a satisfactory theory that encompasses the broadest possible class of examples an acceptable solution or will it be the reformulation of a question in order to show its invalidity? Nevertheless, similarities of goal, method, and style allow to speak of a single branch within contemporary philosophy. The goal was to overcome idealism and create a scientific philosophy method was broadly understood analysis, modeled on the precision, rigor, and unambiguity of natural sciences. The style was based on the quality of argumentation, where the logical coherence was more important than rhetoric.[1]

Ansgar Beckermann, the author of the introduction to Peter Prechtl's *Lexicon of Analytical Philosophy*,[2] claims that analytical philosophy had three characteristic theses at its beginnings:

1 More on the linguistic turn, see: Richard Rorty, ed., *The Linguistic Turn: Essays in Philosophical Method*, Chicago, The University Of Chicago Press 1992.

2 A. Beckermann, "Wprowadzenie," P. Prechtl, *Leksykon pojęć filozofii analitycznej*, translated by J. Bremer, Kraków, Wydawnictwo WAM 2009.

1. The goal of philosophy is to overcome the philosophy through analysis of language.
2. The only (valid) task of philosophy is to analyze the language, be it common or scientific.
3. The only method at philosophy's disposal is the method of linguistic analysis.[3]

Beckermann also indicates that, since at least 1975, there has been no philosopher who would sign his name under all the three theses. Therefore, he differentiates between traditional analytical philosophy, which accepts the above program, and post-analytical philosophy that dominates contemporary philosophical debates. This change may be described as leaning towards pragmatist approach from the formal-semantic perspective. Post-analytical philosophy has one major thing in common with its predecessor: the style of practicing philosophy seeks precision and clarity of expression even at the cost of being lengthy or boring, based on attempts to solve philosophical problems without relativizing them to a specified time and treating the practice of philosophy as an institutional activity.

Such analytical philosophy is a normative term.[4] It contains the criterion of sensibility, demonstrating what kind of utterances may be accepted in the philosophical discourse. If a collection of sentences does not meet the minimum criteria, it cannot be subject to serious academic reflection. For the same reasons, we may assume that analytical philosophy is another form of classical philosophy that dates back to Kant. It does not point out new arguments in old debates but rather calls for the abandoning of specific problems. It also indicates a defined place of philosophy in the society. In particular, it favors a political and ideological neutrality of philosophy. When the view of the world in the cosmological sense is referenced, it favors common-sense naturalism, intuitively adopting one form of ontological and epistemological realism or another.

Using the notion of "ideal types," we may differentiate two approaches to language in analytical philosophy. The first, formal-semantic, is based on the semantic concept of meaning and the transcendental concept of language. It may be found in the early writings of Ludwig Wittgenstein. This approach adopts artificial language as the model, claiming that natural language is too chaotic, ambiguous, and blurry. Here, analysis stems from the creation of a new language

3 Ibid, p. 18.

4 The normative character of analytical philosophy is independently referenced by Wacław Janikowski and Tadeusz Szubka. Cf. W. Janikowski, "Normatywna definicja filozofii analitycznej," *Analiza i Egzystencja*, 5(2007); T. Szubka, *Filozofia analityczna*, op.cit., p. 27.

and applies it to scientific discourse or makes natural language similar to an artificial one by eliminating ambiguity and blurriness. Language is a set of cognitive rules, and meaning can be reduced to conditions of truthfulness. The second approach, pragmatist[5] approach is based on the contextual concept of meaning and social concept of language. It may be found in the late works of Wittgenstein. Here, the model is natural language, and the representatives of this approach claim that each artificial language is too limited, reductionist, and, therefore, does not reach the majority of human experience. Language is a social practice, and meaning may be found in the conformity of the undertaken actions with the dominant practice. This approach, therefore, is more interested in the world in which speaking occurs rather than language itself. This distinction spreads, to quote Robert Brandom, "between saying and doing."

2 Analytical Jurisprudence

The analytical method started developing in European jurisprudence since the onset of the 20th century. It was a result of a crisis within the model of jurisprudence, in which a code was to introduce exhaustive and casuistic norms to social reality.[6] Together with the development of capitalist economy, a need arose to make legal norms somewhat more flexible, to adjust them to the dynamic exchange of goods and the flow of capital. Generalizations started to replace to detailed descriptions. At the same time, individual legal systems started to be compared, noticing their similarities in the sources, the systematic character of law, and the structure of the legal norm. These tendencies found their place in the theory of John Austin, who defined general jurisprudence in his *Lectures on Jurisprudence*. At its core, it held rules, definitions, and divisions that were common to varied, more mature, systems of positive law. In the legal sciences of the second half of the 20th century, we may notice a drive towards rationalization of the process of creating and applying law. As has already been mentioned, the 20th-century developments in language philosophy, in connection with the linguistic turn, caused an increase in the interest of language, especially natural

5 Joanna Odrowąż-Sypniewska, quoting Janina Kotarbińska, refers to a "descriptionist" approach. However, the name would suggest a "descriptive" character, which maintains the subject/object dichotomy. The notion "pragmatic" does not include such a division. Cf. J. Odrowąż-Sypniewska, "Wprowadzenie," *Przewodnik po filozofii języka*, J. Odrowąż-Sypniewska (red.), Wydawnictwo WAM 2016, pp. 72.

6 K. Opałek, *Problemy metodologiczne nauki prawa*, Warszawa Wydawnictwo Naukowe 1962, p. 63.

language and directive utterances. There met analytical philosophy and theory of law. Analytical theory of law almost dominated the European field of theoretical legal considerations of the second half of the 20th century. The fragmentary character and worldview neutrality of analytical philosophy were a good match for the technical character of jurisprudence.

The most prominent 20th-century advocate of analytical approach in jurisprudence was undoubtedly Herbert L. A. Hart. It was he who introduced logical analysis to jurisprudence, associated with the formal-semantic approach to be supplemented with the analysis of the common language, itself part of the pragmatist approach. Hart supports the vision of analytical philosophy that does not limit itself to tautology and the research of ways to verify empiric sentences. Interpersonal communication is much richer than this. An analytical philosopher ought to show their interest in each method of communicating, one of them being law. In other words, analytical philosophy knows no subject borders.

In the 1953 article "Definition and Theory in Jurisprudence,"[7] debating the usefulness of analytical philosophy in jurisprudence, Hart used the Enlightenment metaphor of "light" and "darkness." We may know something about law, we may even know how to use it, but this does not mean we comprehend law, argued Hart. Knowledge in an area may be distorted by shadows that "not only vary in intensity but are cast by different obstacles to light."[8] According to Hart, what casts the shadow on the theory of law is the wrong way of defining, which causes the theory of law to separate from practice. Definition sheds light merely on a part of law, at the same time concealing the rest. Theory, when confronted with the need to define fundamental legal notions, references philosophical arguments external to law, while practice needs no reference to general philosophy. Seeking to reconnect theory and practice, Hart concludes that the definition ought to contain more than the mere report of how a given notion is understood in legal practice like "law," "authorization," or "contract." Such knowledge, however, is still distant from comprehension. The problem arises because each of the fundamental definitions is related to so many things that it is difficult to define a core that would be common to them all. Moreover, these notions have no simple semantic counterparts in a real world, since they are intellectual constructs. Seeing these difficulties, Hart does not supply another definition of "law" or "authorization" so they would be included in the available

---

7 H. L. A. Hart, "Definition and Theory in Jurisprudence," *Essays in Jurisprudence and Philosophy*, Clarendon Press Oxford, 1983.

8 H. L. A. Hart, "Definicja i teoria w prawoznawstwie," *Eseje z filozofii prawa*, translated by Jan Woleński, Warszawa, Dom Wydawniczy ABC 2001, p. 21.

portfolio of definitions, which form the basis for the division of "schools of law." Instead, Hart ponders on the very act of defining. Quoting the rule of Jeremy Bentham, Hart concludes that legal notions are to be researched in the context of complete sentences in which they appear. The analysis of these sentences allows for the conclusion that they are based on a concealed assumption in the area of law. Singular legal utterances are like individual moves in a game of chess. The possibility criteria for each move appear in the ruleset of the game. At the same time, each move is a consequence of the earlier moves, as well as the ruleset, together creating the so-called context. The language of law is not a descriptive one. The meaning of its ideas depends on the context which causes traditional methods of defining by supplying the type and specific difference are of limited application to legal sciences. The traditional definition does not problematize the type and species. A legal problem arises when a question is asked not about the location of a given notion in relation to other but about the functioning of the notion in reality. According to Hart, legal notions should be defined by analyzing the conditions of truth and the way sentences containing these notions are used. By doing this, Hart attempts to position himself between the semantic-formal and the pragmatist approach. A collection of sentences containing a given notion creates the context. However, analyzing these notions as sentence elements limits the context to mere linguistic dimension. We do not ask about who is involved in communication with the use of legal notions or about what social relations exist between the two subjects. With this statement, Hart "cuts off" the sociological level of communication. A question appears here, however, about what should be the target of this way of defining? In particular, following the popular differentiation by American realists, should defining relate to "law in books" or "law in action?"

In the 1961 *Concept of Law*,[9] Hart states that objects of definitions mostly should be sought in their common use. The everyday use makes the core and convention for the use of a notion, surrounded by some borderline cases, in which users may express their doubts as to whether a specific case can be included in the defined notion. Hart states that if we want to define "law" with cases, the borderline cases are the laws of primitive tribes and international law. Furthermore, this is not a problem limited to law but related to all general matters. Jokingly, Hart adds that "[a] man with a shining smooth pate is clearly bald; another with a luxuriant mop clearly is not; but the question whether a third man, with a

9 H. L. A. Hart, *Concept of Law*, Oxford Clarendon Press 1994.

fringe of hair here and there, is bald might be indefinitely disputed, if it were thought worthwhile or any practical issue turned on it."[10]

Aside from the quantitative borderline cases, we may also point out to qualitative borderline cases, characterized by a missing or added qualitative component. "Is it still 'chess,' if the game is played without a queen?"[11] These problems cause a possible shift of attention into the historical ways of defining a notion in order to extract their common features. Such analysis led Hart to conclude that, when defining law, current notions highlighted the connection between law and the feelings of duty, morality, and rule. This leads to the commonly known and influential vision of law as a set of primary and secondary rules. With the development of society, the level of complication of legal system grows. Apart from simple rules dictating behaviors (primary rules), secondary rules appear related to how the primary rules may be changed, who and how is to oversee and specify primary rules, and which rules are considered binding.

One of the issues outside of Hart's consideration was the problem of legal interpretation. This was the result of Hart adopting the optics of "descriptive sociology," within which the system of law is not so much constructed in the process of interpretation but rather imposes the interpretation rules. If we want to supplement Hart's analytical theory with the problem of interpretation, we may use Jerzy Wróblewski's considerations.[12]

Wróblewski differentiated regulation as a separate fragment of a legal text from its meaning, which is an abstract formula of behavior.[13] Moreover, the formula is made concrete in legal decisions. Because of the imperfection of language, its blurriness and incompleteness, we may be facing a situation, in which the subject that applies or comments on a rule may have some doubts as to the construction of an abstract or specific norm. The need of interpretation arises on such occasions. For Wróblewski, the need for interpretation depends on the situational comprehension. All the potential interpretation doubts are

10 Ibid., p. 4.

11 Ibid.

12 Wróblewski did start the construction of his theory before Hart's *Concept of Law*, but the similarity of the methodological background of both authors and later influence of Hart on Polish theory and Wróblewski in particular seems to justify the comparison. Cf. S. Wojtczak, "Wpływ piśmiennictwa anglojęzycznego z zakresu prawoznawstwa na zmianę paradygmatu polskiej teorii prawa," *Czy koniec teorii prawa?*, P. Jabłoński (ed.), Wrocław, Wydawnictwo Uniwersytetu Wrocławskiego 2011, pp. 81–91.

13 Jerzy Wróblewski, "Semantic Basis of the Theory of Legal Interpretation," *Logique & Analyse* (6), Vol. 21.

impossible to predict, since they arise in specific situations. In most cases, organs applying law make the rule and norm synonymous, acting quite automatically. We then reference the clarity of a rule. If this activity is met with some resistance, there arises a need for interpretation. A rule becomes blurry. This is especially true of the so-called hard cases. For the representatives of the doctrine of law, situation of interpretation is created purposefully, as a didactic aid or an object for study. In a situation, the interpreter calls forth linguistic, systemic, and functional directives.[14] They reference lexical meanings, positioning, relative to other rules, and function of those fragments that raise doubts. Language directives are visibly preferred here. How do we know, however, how to interpret law? Applying Hart's terminology, we may say it results from the accepted rule of recogonition, separating what is law and what it is not. In other words, the very system of law dictates its own rules of interpretation. They result primarily from the properties of the language used to formulate the rules of law. In the course of legal education, subjects of law gain competence to perform interpretation as knowledge of the system. A system of law is, therefore, a meta-language for the specific interpretive decisions that equips the interpreting subjects with appropriate competences.

Hart and Wróblewski analyzed social situations, in which lawyers apply analytical tools. Hart put more interest in the analysis of the architecture of the system of law, while Wróblewski on the interaction of the system and its sustaining elements. The goal of the theory of law is to recreate the system and describe its "deep structure." Everyday legal practice is unwillingly shaped by this structure and therefore looks upon itself in theory, just like in a mirror.

3 Foundationalism and Antifoundationalism

The analytical theory of law is based on something we may call the standard theory of meaning. We may also present it through the metaphor of conduit. American researchers, M. Johnson and G. Lakoff, quoting Michael Reedy, indicate the "conduit metaphor" as the basis for comprehending language in everyday interactions. This metaphor may be reduced to three claims: "IDEAS (or MEANINGS) ARE OBJECTS. / LINGUISTIC EXPRESSIONS ARE CONTAINERS. / COMMUNICATION IS SENDING."[15]

---

14 Jerzy Wróblewski, *The Judical Application of Law*, Z. Bankowski, N. MacCormick (ed.), Springer 1992.

15 G. Lakoff and M. Johnson, *Metaphors We Live By*, The University of Chicago Press 1980, p. 10.

The speaking subject puts its message in words-containers and passes them, like objects, towards the listener. On the other end, the listener takes the words-containers and pulls out the meaning. In other words, the language is like a conveyor belt. This metaphor structures the whole system of speaking about language: "passing" messages, "possessing" information, "hiding" thoughts, and so on. Communication is only possible thanks to the fact that both sides of the conveyor belt possess similar competences. The high level of conventionalization of the system causes its metaphorical fundaments to be barely visible. Lakoff and Johnson indicate that this metaphor hides contextual relations of meaning. Since meanings are physical objects, their properties are independent of the situational context. At the same time, the metaphor does not determine speaking about language completely. Thanks to it, a language user references meanings *as if* they were objects, and does not claim meanings to be *actual* objects.

Translating the above into the language of analytical theory, we see that the structure of interpretive theory or the meaning of the language of law within this theory matches the conduit metaphor. We may reformulate it into the following claims:

1) The lawmaker places the meanings – rules and norms – in a text just like objects in a container;
2) The lawyer receives the container and extracts its meanings;
3) The interpretation is the extraction of objects-meanings from containers-texts based on some rules of interpretations.

Even a cursory analysis of this metaphorical structure reveals that the legal interpretation understood in this way is measurable, acontextual and reproductive. In the interpretation process, a given lawyer can be replaced by anyone with similar knowledge, which will lead to an analogous interpretation result. This creates a three-part structure of transmission (interpretation): Lawmaker-Text-Lawyer, which fills the notion of law adopted in analytic theory. This is the basic epistemic structure of this theory, that is, a metaphor that is constitutive of the entire discourse. It defines what kind of statements (knowledge) can be expressed in a given area. Determining the way of speaking in a given area, it also establishes the ontological foundations of this area.

There are serious arguments indicating that the standard theory of meaning requires careful reconsideration. The effect of this reconceptualization is the post-analytical philosophy of language, here represented by Donald Davidson, Richard Rorty, and Stanley Fish. Davidson indicated that conventions are not necessary to communicate.[16] They undoubtedly facilitate communication, but lack of conventions does not stop communication from occurring. Let us imagine a situation in which someone twists words and, instead of saying "respecting law is important," says "respecting lewd is important." Let us assume this person uses "lewd" instead of "law" consistently. While meeting this person for the first time, we may not know the convention that replaces one word with another. However, by closely listening we may reconstruct the way that person uses specific words and adjust our previous assumptions accordingly. Davidson calls initial assumptions about the meanings "prime theory" and applies the name of "passing theory" to meanings in current use. According to Davidson, communication equals constantly changing of earlier theories into passing theories, which may then turn into earlier theories. It is a dynamic relation in which visions about the meanings of words adjust to current situations. Here, language is treated as a collection of assumptions as to how our interlocutor will behave in a given situation. If the assumed behavior does not appear, the expectations need to be altered.

Let us imagine, that a user of a language gets lost in a jungle and meets a representative of an exotic culture. That representative will behave differently than the language user would expect. He or she uses a different language. In the course of subsequent acts of communication, the lost person may come to successfully communicate with the native. This is feasible but requires time. Richard Rorty remarks that "[i]f we ever succeed in communicating easily and happily, it will be because her guesses about what I am going to do next, including what noises I am going to do next, and my own expectations about what I shall do or say under certain circumstances, come more or less to coincide, and because the converse is also true."[17]

According to Davidson and Rorty, such a situation does not qualitatively differ from everyday language use; only the amount of guesses needing verification may be larger. This causes the use of a given language like language of law to not require the knowledge of grammar, although it is essentially helpful. This agrees with the everyday language practice. At the same time, language loses its ontic status of a separate entity and ceases to bridge between consciousness and reality. In other words, (meta)language does not exist.

---

16 D. Davidson, "A Nice Derangement of Epitaphs," *The Essential Davidson*, Oxford University Press 2006.

17 R. Rorty, *Contingency, Irony, and Solidarity*, Cambridge University Press 1989, p. 14.

The difference between analytical theory of meaning, based on the conduit metaphor, and the post-analytical theory that rejects the existence of metalanguage is a difference between the foundational and the anti-foundational epistemic attitude.

Stanley Fish defines[18] foundationalism as "an attempt to ground inquiry and communication on something more solid and more stable than beliefs or unresearched practice."[19] Upon finding such point of support, one may proceed to derive a whole system of beliefs and actions out of it, therefore making beliefs and actions objective and repetitive. In order for such a foundation to serve its role, however, it needs to possess certain properties. It needs to exist, be unchanged in time, independent of cultural context, and apolitical. Fish remarks that in the long history of the development of humanity, such fundaments may be found in God, material world, rationality, logic, natural observation language, eternal values, and autonomic consciousness. Hence, foundationalism promises a recipe for objective knowledge and effective action.

In other words, a successful foundationalist project provides a "method"; a recipe with a list of ingredients which will independently create the right solution when orderly mixed according to absolutely clear principles, with clarity and explicitness as another fundamentalist premise. In linguistics, the solution will be giving structural descriptions to sentences, in literary studies, poems and novels will receive a valid interpretation, and in teaching composition "the discovery of rules which are so fundamental as to make them universal" and which simply need to be followed in order to achieve legibility, coherence, understandability, and the power of persuasion.[20]

Rejecting the conduit metaphor leads to antifoundationalism, which claims that every recipe for meaning/interpretation is context-bound. There is no metalanguage that could serve as support. This does not mean an automatic rejection of such notions as meaning, truth, or structure. Antifoundationalism, however,

---

18 Fish's translator refers to "foundationalism" as "fundamentalism." In order to differentiate between foundationalism and political fundamentalism, I opted for a less handy, but unfortunately already deeply rooted in Polish literature, notion of foundationalism. Cf. S. Judycki, "Epistemologia XX wieku: przegląd stanowisk," *Roczniki Filozoficzne*, Vol. 46/47 1998/1999, pp. 6–66.

19 S. Fish, "Antyfundamentalizm, nadzieja na teorii a nauczanie kompozycji literackiej," *Interpretacja, retoryka, polityka*, translated by M. Glasenapp-Konkol, Kraken, Universitas 2007, p. 362.

20 Ibid., p. 363.

stresses that the notions are contextual and dependent on the situation. A situation is "a bundle of silent or unspoken assumptions that at the same time introduce order to the world and change in reaction to the order that they themselves introduce."[21] Truths, patterns, and beliefs are tools that allow specified groups to cope with the world. They are always relativized to the context of a specific interpretive community. The process is more important than the final product for antifoundationalism.

Antifoundationalist attitude towards analytical philosophy does not mean abandoning this type of philosophy, but rather the limitation of cognitive claims and reserved approach to validation attitudes of declared theorems. Therefore, this philosophy will be called "post-analytical." The "post" prefix carries semantic weight. What follows the prefix is situated in a time continuum. It signifies an end and a beginning. An end, because what is post- has passed away and may not remain in its known form. A beginning, because what is supposed to leave does not want to leave and returns in a different shape. As Richard Rorty, who "betrayed" analytical philosophy in favor of the continental, puts it: "I think that analytic philosophy can keep its highly professional methods, the insistence on detail and mechanics, and just drop its transcendental project. I'm not out to criticize analytic philosophy as a style. It's a good style. I think the years of superprofessionalism were beneficial."[22]

4 The Post-Analytical Theory of Law

Together with philosophical changes of the second half of the 20th century, there can be observed a rapid inflation of law. To use the words of J. Habermas, we may say that the "life-world" became colonized with "system-world." Increasing amounts of human activity have become subject to legal regulations. Possible reasons are higher levels of complication of economic life in connection with globalization and the fall of the validity of traditional normative systems such as morality or religion. At the same time, traditional legislative process is time-consuming and cannot always adequately react to current social and political situation. These are the results of introducing general clauses or fuzzy notions in law, which may lead to questions about the scope of discretional knowledge of lawyers. At the same time, lawyers need to make increasingly more judgments

21 Ibid., p. 374.

22 E. Mendieta, *Take Care of Freedom and Truth Will Take Care of Itself: Interviews with Richard Rorty*, Stanford University Press 2005, p. 23.

based on general rules. Yet, another factor in the period under scrutiny is the constitutionalization of basic rights. This has set law, especially the system of constitutional courts, on a colliding course with that of the executive power. Law became an increasingly limiting force to political power. Politics became juridized and, at the same time, the legal system became political.

In the light of the above changes, analytical theory of law based on formal-semantic approach to language, the traditional concept of meaning, and foundational epistemic attitude loses its legitimization. Michael Sullivan indicates[23] that the space vacated by foundationalism may be occupied by one of three candidates: positivist epistemology, Rorty's irony, or Dewey's pragmatism as philosophy of reconstruction.

The first tactic is based on an attempt to find a logical minimum which would be true for any possible world. It is a foundational viewpoint which assumes the existence of the fundament of knowledge. At the same time, it is a simple continuation of the analytic theory. The consequence of searching for the said minimum is abstracting to an increasing number of new categories. Sacrificing the context causes the general categories to become useless. In another form, the tactic is based on assuming the role of an "explainer." The role of theory is to explain the served explanations and, thus, potentially make the discussion clearer. The final decision, however, remains outside of theory. As an example, we will ask whether punishment is due for religious insults. Theory might help us to describe the notion of religious freedom and freedom of speech. It will also show differences between the two. The decision on whether and how to punish, however, will be made outside theory, since this is the domain of politics. In such context, the theory of law may merely be "a servant of politics." As an example of this attitude in the field of theory of law, we can mention the post-positivist position.

The attitude of a liberal ironist goes beyond positivist epistemology. Rorty perceived pragmatism as protest against the design of philosophy as based on epistemological certainty of truth (foundationalism). In his later works, Rorty indicated that supporting the theses in their justifications is of similar structure. Justification simply replaces truth. Rorty indicates that philosophy should move on and abandon theoretical claims in favor of liberal irony inspired by literature. Theory does not improve the state of freedom to such a high degree as literature does, and, therefore, it should be more literary, use metaphors, strengthen its

23 M. Sullivan, *Legal Pragmatism*, Bloomington, Indianapolis: Indiana University Press 2007.

rhetorical message at the cost of accuracy. It is to instill in individuals the will to live their lives with respect and tolerance towards others. Theory is merely the creation of useful fictions, at the same time being the rejection of analytical theory.

In the third possibility that follows John Dewey, legal institutions are conservative. Time needs to pass for them to adapt to the social change. This is the result of courts tending to decide in accordance with previous decisions, which were frequently delivered in different social conditions. Another conserving factor is the need to call upon an authority to confirm the adopted views. It may be a verdict of a court of higher instance or that of legal scientists. Because legal institutions are inevitably determined by the past, the goal of the theory of law should be to reconstruct these institutions with the application of the temporal aspect. Pragmatic theory is directed towards solving current problems by looking at the past in search of alternative scenarios. This criticism cuts through the division of legitimization/delegitimization. Theory delegitimizes because it shows the history of an institution and simultaneously denaturalizes it. However, it also enriches the institution, broadening its horizons by new ways of actin, and simultaneously legitimizes it. After J. Dewey, the process may be called "reconstruction," which provides added value to everyday experiences. It considers them basis for any theory, since a theory is useful if it reacts to everyday challenges. Transferring the above to the theory of law, the everyday may be viewed as legal practice and education. Theory is included in a different language of problems approached by practice and the constructs conveyed by deduction. Practice and theory are bound together by the notion of "experience." Previous experience, collected in the theory, allows to shape future experience or, in other words, solve problems that can be encountered in everyday practice. Theory is not a precondition to practice's possibilities but rather a tool that allows one to act within the legal world. In this sense, if past theory is analytical, it would be a mistake to denounce it completely. The fact that a theory has been institutionalized means that it solves specific problems. On the other hand, keeping with the theory may in itself cause the problem of lack of adjustment of tools to the encountered problems. This is why I use the notion of "post-analytical theory" to denote the reconstructivist attitude to analytical theory. It will be based on a pragmatization and socialization of analytical theory.

We may enumerate the following features and assumptions of philosophical pragmatism: there are no absolute truths but merely useful ones; the best method of verification is an experiment; development depends on the environment; democracy is rooted in everydayness and states the best social policy. Based on the above, Brian E. Butler lists the following features of legal pragmatism: contextualism, antifoundationalism, instrumentalism, and perspectivism.[24] We may also add holism to the list.

Contextualism means the inclusion of context in the process of interpretation. Neither the text in itself nor the legal system/language contain sufficient information to decode meanings. The same text but in different conditions may provide different meanings. For these reasons, it is crucial to include context. In the scope of legal interpretation, pragmatism prefers the correct interpretation instead of an abstract one. Moreover, Butler states that foundationalism is associated with deductionism.[25] If we assume the existence of an identified basis for making a decision – a foundation – we may as well assume that there is a method of interpretation based on deduction, which allows for the decision to be made. Deduction becomes the preferred method, because thanks to it the decision remains in strict connection with its foundation. The foundationalist attitude will state that the legal text in itself provides a foundation for making a decision and that anyone equipped with proper methods of interpretation will reach the same conclusion. On the other hand, antifoundationalism claims that in legal interpretation the text is one of many factors. In consequence, a rule arises that binds us to consider other arguments before a decision is made. Instrumentalism means the focus of pragmatism on the future. Theory is always practical in the sense that it addresses real problems. The future becomes the basis for the verification of theoretical statements. In words of legal interpretation, pragmatism prefers functional interpretation and focuses on the consequences of potential legal decisions.[26] It moves the center of gravity from statements to experience, assuming change and liability to verification. In the legal context, perspectivism is the opposite of formalism which argues for the objectivity and stability of meaning of a legal text. Perspectivism allows for the change of meaning with the increase of experience. Holism, in turn, means a methodological rule of rejecting dualisms, such as fact/value, subject/object, theory/practice. Pragmatism does not invalidate these distinctions but abandons their ontological interpretations. Reality is not based on dichotomies, which may be useful but serve no higher purpose. They are useful hypotheses that may be falsified by future experience.

---

24 B. E. Butler, "Legal Pragmatism: Banal or Beneficial as a Jurisprudential Position?," *Essays in Philosophy* (3), Vol. 2 2002.

25 Ibid.

26 Instrumentalism in this sense can be differentiated from the rationalism of law and economics. Instrumentalism takes into account relativity. Depending on the adopted viewpoint, a decision may be deemed useful or not. Economics-inspired science of law entails a fundament of a priori economical rationality.

Regarding the socializing of theory, American philosopher George Herbert Mead indicates that the definition of laws (freedom, property, equality, etc.) should be applied to a specific social and political situation.[27] For instance, in reference to the French Constitution of 1795, this will be the context of revolution and fear of the return of absolute monarchy. For these reasons, the constitution defined laws mostly through negation: freedom as lack of outside intervention, property as lack of intervention in the use of property, and equality as lack of unjustified legal distinctions. However, after institutionally securing these negations, keeping to the negative understanding of these rights will be too abstract. Social conditions changed, as happened to the revolution. However, Mead argues that

> It is to be remembered, however, that a *working* conception can be abstract only in so far as that to which it refers for its functioning, needs only to be designated, not by analytically defined. The abstract political individual of the seventeenth and eighteenth centuries were quite concrete, every-day persons. They were pointed out by the negative definitions of those who speculated about them, and the negative definitions had reference to the hindrances to their activities which most interested the individuals.[28]

This is a somewhat different approach to defining than the one proposed by Hart. Mead considers laws as expressions of social conditions in which the people and the governments express certain truths about themselves; that is, about the obstacles they face. It is a much more dynamic picture than that showing a system of rules based on a socially constructed rule of recognition. In the moment when the conditions change, obstacles are overcome and new ones appear; also change laws and their meaning. Mead indicates that we may observe excessive institutional protection of law by judging laws themselves. We may understand it so that in the line of legal and political thought a lot more has been said and written about legal and democratic procedures than the positive contents of law. Analogically, we may say that in the theory of law also much more has been written about methodology and formal features than about the positive contents of law.

5 The Faces of Legal Theory

Concerning such a depicted post-analytical theory, we may formulate certain doubts. In a famous comment, David Luban wrote: "if legal pragmatism is only

27 G. H. Mead, "Natural Rights and the Theory of the Political Institution," *The Journal of Philosophy, Psychology and Scientific Methods* (XII), Vol. 6 1915, p. 143.

28 Ibid., p. 144.

eclectic, result-oriented, historically minded antiformalism, it turns out to be a remarkably uncontroversial doctrine. It stands free of philosophical controversy only because it stands free of all controversy, and it avoids controversy by saying very little."[29]

Similar remarks can be extended to post-analytical theory. What are then the consequences of post-analytical theory? It seems that the controversy which Luban calls for is included in the normative plane of the theory: the notions of pluralism and democracy.

The central notion of this theory is not a "norm" but "rights." Sullivan defines rights as "self-conscious social efforts to assure individual development"[30] or "the tools thanks to which the society protects citizens against unwanted intervention of the state or the tyranny of the majority."[31] This is a formal definition that does not assume a vision of the desired subject or society. It is of negative character and is not useful in the construction of the desired state of things. However, it allows us to criticize the undesirable visions of a subject or the society, which limit or exclude individual development. The notion of pluralism appears to be central here. It introduces alternative patterns of activity thanks to which it maximizes the possibilities. A society based on the rules of pluralism provides better chances of development to its citizens than a homogenous society. Development is, thus, another name for increasing pluralism.

Shifting the center of gravity from norms to rights opens legal discourse to the political. Rights are equally important in legal and political terms.[32] According to the pragmatists, the proper political vision of pragmatism is democracy. Since in their everyday environment, an individual comes across different patterns of behavior resulting from the activity of different institutions, the everyday includes a democratic potential. The question is how to institutionalize the pluralism of the everyday? How to transfer the everyday to the level of legal and political institutions? Democratic everyday also has the character of a formal

29 D. Luban, "What's Pragmatic About Legal Pragmatism?," *Cardozo Law Review* (20), Vol. 18 1996, p. 45.

30 M. Sullivan, *Legal Pragmatism*, op. cit., p. 98.

31 Ibid., pp. 98O_IT.

32 One can recall here the argument by Ronald Dworkin, that general theory of law contains a definitive part, focused in the analysis of the language of law and associated with philosophy of language, and a normative part, portraying the vision of the desired social order and therefore associated with philosophy of politics and morality. Cf. R. Dworkin, *Biorąc prawa poważnie*, translated by Tomasz Kowalski, Warsaw, Wydawnictwo Naukowe PWN 1998, pp. 4.

notion and does not include any detailed indications as to the desired social vision. As a rule, it may therefore act only negatively. Institutional expression of the function may be constitutional courts, which are "negative lawmakers" in the first place. They reject legal regulations which limit pluralism. The difference lies in that although analytical theory forces democracy to conform to the requirements of constitutional courts, pragmatism opts for the constitutional courts to conform to the requirements of democracy (pluralism). The negative approach shields jurisprudence from politics.

Such theory should lead to a shift in the model of legal education. The education should focus on the question of the genesis of legal institutions, their efficiency and limitations, with the potential of improving them in the face of new challenges. Since consciousness appears in interaction of an individual with the environment, a lawyer develops within the walls of a university or a legal firm or courtrooms. On the one hand, the process of education is controlled, while, on the other, it does not entail the emergence of instant practical effects. Legal education may therefore be seen as experimental space for attempting new solutions in the scope of legal argumentation and the sources of law. Differences between the analytical and post-analytical theory gathers the table below:

	Analytical theory	**Post-Analytical theory**
Epistemic approach	Foundationalism	Antifundationalism
Ontology of the legal world	Language (system)	Set of practices
Object of cognition	Legal norm, rule	Rights and institutions
Criteria of truth	Consistency of judgment with reality	Coherence of beliefs
Source	Lawmaker	Community
Goal	Objective cognition	Justified belief
Fundamentals of validation	Systemic	Esthetic
Model of interpretation	In abstracto	In corecto
Methodology	Set theory	Prototype and family resemblance
Approach to the past	Ahistorism	Historism
Political rule	Hierarchy	Democracy
Education rule	Monologue	Dialogue

Analytical theory is like a mirror that "reflects" the system of law. The language of theory and that of practice should correspond. Theory should be the grammar of practice. Pre-war theoretician of law, Bronisław Wróblewski, father of Jerzy Wróblewski, suggested an alternative solution when he wrote: "The language of law is not a constant and does not resemble a marble statue, as Demczenko wrote; it is rather like a changing human face reflecting life. One needs to remark that legal language is not closed in books but is in constant motion."[33]

The metaphor of the post-analytical theory as a face seems to be a valid counterpoint and alternative to the metaphor of the analytical theory as a mirror. A face reflects what is outside and is a medium of communication. Therefore, it retains the reference properties of a mirror and expands them, because the face also reflects what is "inside," it expresses current emotions and gathered experience. A face breaks the epistemological dichotomies of inside/outside, permanence/change, private/public.

33 B. Wróblewski, *Język prawniczy i prawny*, Kraków, Polska Akademia Umiejętności 1948, p. 86.

Zbigniew Pulka

Philosophical Premises of the Concept of Systemness of Law in Jerzy Wróblewski's Theory of Interpretation

1 Metatheoretical Assumptions

Jerzy Wróblewski's theory of interpretation is characterized by a philosophical attitude based on the adoption of Marxist rules as philosophical premises of theoretical activity in jurisprudence. According to Wróblewski, we may say that the relation between his theory of interpretation of people's law and the Marxist philosophy is both the relation of invocation and that of attribution. This means the connection is not only of declarative character (the relation of invocation) but also of subject-matter nature (the relation of attribution). The author formulates the following definition of the relation of attribution: "Tp theorem is attributed to Tf theorem if and only if from Tf Tp can be concluded based on the adopted directives of reasoning and potentially with the assistance of other theorems Te of analytical or synthetic character."[1] In turn, the directives of reasoning that the definition mentions are "the most broadly understood directives of logic, which encompass not only the inferring of sentences from sentences, but also of norms and evaluations."[2] In a slightly different perspective, Wróblewski characterizes the relation of attribution, indicating that it occurs when there appear "broadly understood logical connections"[3] between theoretical and philosophical claims. Stressing the heuristic function of philosophy towards the theory of law, the author indicates that in the case of the Marxist theory of law, the connections between theory and philosophy are of deductive character because the theory is inferred from a set of philosophical-methodological assumptions and may be seen as a part of the Marxist philosophical system.[4] Seeing the dependencies as having a deductive character indicates that philosophical assumptions

1 J. Wróblewski, "Filozoficzne problemy teorii prawa (Rozważania metodologiczne)," *Państwo i Prawo* Vol. 11, 1974, p. 6.

2 J. Wróblewski, "Postawa filozoficzna i afilozoficzna we współczesnej teorii prawa," *Studia Prawnicze*, Vol. 13, 1933, p. 74.

3 Ibid., p. 70.

4 Ibid., p. 82; cf. also J. Woleński, *Z zagadnień analitycznej filozofii prawa*, Kraków 1980, p. 14ff.

are the starting point when formulating theoretical theses which may be seen as logical (quasi-logical) consequences of the adopted philosophical assumptions. With such a view, the process of constructing the theory of law is a "top-down" approach. The starting point of the cognitive process are general philosophical decisions of ontological, epistemological, and axiological character, whose adoption determines the outcomes of at least part of legal questions that may be found on a lower level of generality of theory of law.[5] Looking at the relation between philosophy and theory of law as having a deductive character indicates that philosophical assumptions cognitively precede the theorems of theory of law. The notion of cognitive primacy adopted in the Marxist methodology of science indicates that the relation occurs when theorems T2 (secondary in the cognitive sense) assume a model of reality which was included in theorems T1 (primary in the cognitive sense.)[6] In the analyzed case, theorems T2 are related to theory of law, and T1 are philosophical. This would mean that the theorems of Marxist theory of law as cognitively secondary, assume a model of reality defined in the cognitively primary philosophical theorems of Marxism as a philosophical system. Agreeing with a statement that philosophy serves mainly a heuristic function to theory of law, one could assume that cognitively primary philosophical theorems serve the function of a "heuristic program" in the process of the construction of theory of law.[7] That would mean that cognitively primary ontological, epistemological, and axiological decisions determine the field for the performance of cognitively secondary decisions in the area of theory of law and thus favor (or not) the creation of valuable theories of law.

It is worth mentioning that the author, in order to characterize the relation of attribution, uses the words "broadly understood logical dependencies" or "the most broadly understood directives of logic." The use of such words indicates the existence of not only formal (deductive) relations, but also of informal relations, having an argumentative character and belonging to a group of the so-called soft argumentative strategies.[8] In my opinion, it can be especially interesting to interpret the relation of attribution as a presupposition in which theory of law

---

5 J. Wróblewski, "The Concept of Legal Philosophy," in: *Sur la Philosophie de Droit*, R. Lukić (ed.), Beograd 1978, pp. 311–312.

6 J. Kmita, "Uwagi o holizmie marksowskim jako koncepcji metodologicznej" in: *Założenia metodologiczne "Kapitału" Marksa*, Warsaw, 1970, pp. 69–71.

7 H. Eilstein, "Hipotezy ontologiczne i orientacje ontologiczne," in: *Teoria i doświadczenie*, H. Eilstein, M. Przełęcki (eds.), Warsaw, 1966, pp. 230–231.

8 P. Jabłoński (*Polskie spory o rolę filozofii w teorii prawa*, Wrocław 2014, pp. 94–97) indicates the informal character of the relation of attribution.

claims presuppose specific philosophical theses. As we know, presuppositions are divided into semantic (logical) and pragmatic.[9] In the first case, we will say that sentence A presupposes sentence B if the truth of B is the condition for the truth of A and its negation (not A).[10] In the second case: "The speaker pragmatically presupposes B in a given moment of conversation in the case when he is inclined to act linguistically as if he judged the truth of B to be evident and assumed that his listeners knew about it."[11] Both definitions of presupposition may be useful for the characteristics of the relation between the theory of law and philosophy. Nevertheless – in my opinion – in the case of the Marxist theory of law, we should consider the definition of these relations in the category of presupposition of semantic character as especially important. Let us draw the reader's attention to the fact that for the characteristics of semantic presuppositions, fundamental character is applied to the so-called resistance to negation – that is, that presuppositions are implied by a judgement as well as the negation of the judgement. It is so because these presuppositions are predefined existential judgements confirming the existence of objects (sentence B) which are judged on the grounds of their properties (sentence A). Transferring this understanding of presupposition to the relation of theory of law and philosophy, we can say that the relation occurs when the theorems of a given theory of law presuppose the existence of objects that are defined by the philosophical assumptions which it adopts. In the case of the Marxist theory of law, the theorems presuppose the existence of a world – a social reality – described on the basis of the adopted philosophical assumptions. Transferring these considerations into the realm of Jerzy Wróblewski's theory of interpretation, which reflects the Marxist philosophical attitude, we may say that this theory presupposes the existence of a world whose fundamental features are defined by the theorems of dialectical and historical materialism. It is worth adding that both the existence of such a world and its basic features are determined already at the level of philosophical assumptions, which constitute the starting point of any activity in the field of theory of law. In that sense, they also cognitively precede theory of law.

9 M. Smolak, *Wykładnia celowościowa z perspektywy pragmatycznej*, Warsaw, 2012, p. 224ff.

10 J. Woleński, *Z zagadnień...*, pp. 51–52.

11 M. Smolak, *Wykładnia...*, p. 227; cf. also: R. Sarkowicz, *Poziomowa interpretacja tekstu prawnego*, Kraków, 1995, p. 136; pragmatic character of presupposition is indicated by J. Wróblewski, "Presupozycje rozumowań prawniczych," *Studia Prawno-Ekonomiczne*, Vol. XXXVII, 1986, pp. 8–9.

2 The Level of Philosophical Assumptions and Their Consequences in Theory of Law

Jerzy Wróblewski's theory of interpretation is the theory of interpretation of "people's law"; that is, the socialist-communist law. It means that, in the semantic (logical) sense, its theorems presuppose the existence of an object to which "people's law" applies. I would like to stress that, in my opinion, "people's law" designates a philosophical category, that is, that the fundamental features of the designate of the term are already defined at the level of Marxism's philosophical assumptions. A question arises: what features of legal phenomena, called "people's law," are in the scrutinized case determined by the adoption of Marxism's philosophical assumptions?

Without going into details of the assumptions of Marxist philosophy, it needs to be said that it is a dialectic philosophy; that is, one whose program is set to break traditional oppositions, such as those of being and thinking, being and duty, and cognition and evaluation.[12] The fundamental philosophical resolution of Marxism is a thesis saying that history is a purposeful process and, as such, it is a process of progress based on a transition from a lower-level being (marked by alienation in class societies) to a being of a higher rank (free of alienation in a Communist people's society). According to the Marxists, the thesis unites cognition and evaluation. It is of cognitive, descriptive sense because it describes the process of evolution of a social being, and in this sense, it is an ontological thesis, defining the fundamental principle of a social being. It also holds evaluative meaning because it is equal to considering an alienated being as the prime evil, with parallel consideration of alienation-free being the highest good; in this sense, it is an axiological thesis that defines a hierarchy of values. In consequence, the being of a lower rank contains within itself the obligation of having it destroyed, and a being of a higher rank the obligation of having it created – therefore we are looking at the unity of being and obligation. Marxist theory of social development is simultaneously a theory of ethical progress, that is, it contains the ethics of development by formulating fundamental primary (unrelativized) evaluations and the related directives of acting (normative ethics). Accepting the eschatology of the final unity of being as the ultimate solution in Marxist system of dialectic knowledge decides the image of "people's law" whose main features are defined at the level of philosophical assumptions. For this reason, the notion of "people's law" is a philosophical category, that is, one that is devoid of

12 I am indicating the Marxist properties of the model of dialectic knowledge in *Legitymizacja państwa w prawoznawstwie*, Wrocław 1996, pp. 13–32.

empirical meaning. In Jerzy Wróblewski's theory of interpretation, philosophical theorems defining the image of "people's law" function as cognitively primary philosophical presuppositions. I am using the notion of presupposition in the strong semantic meaning, which means that the philosophical theorems in question are of existential character, stating the existence of an object with specified properties. These theorems are as follows:

1. People's law is to be an efficient tool whose application will facilitate the objective historical process of the emergence of the higher form of social existence – Communism, seen as being free of alienation in which a person is fully socialized.[13] In the condition of higher form of social being, people's law ceases to be a form of mediating conflicting class interests and becomes a tool of creating social unity. This means the adoption of instrumental concept of law as a tool in the hands of political powers – lawmakers. People's law is the tool of global social reconstruction, which is based on the creation of higher-level being, of a Communist society. Cognitively privileged lawmaker who has the special knowledge of the ultimate goals of law at his disposal, by defining intermediate goals he does not proceed in a random fashion because the selection of intermediate goals is subordinated to the ultimate goal, defined by the eschatology of the final unification of being. The ultimate goal is specified by historical logos which takes the form of objective truths of social development. Teleological unity of the system of people's law is based on the role of this law as an efficient way of delivering the ultimate goal marked by historical reason.[14]
2. Of close connection with the instrumental vision of law is the adoption of the thetic concept of the binding force of law. The fundament for the binding force of people's law is an act of making law by cognitively privileged lawmaker. As a consequence, in order to classify a legal norm as binding, its formal features are important, that is, the accordance of the law-creating act with the norms of lawmaking competence and lawmaking procedure. This leads to adopting the concept of systemic binding force of the norm as conclusive when solving validating problems in systems of people's law.[15]
3. The content of people's law is to reflect the will of the ruling class, articulated by the cognitively privileged avant-garde of the class – the lawmakers. This is the

13 W. Lang, J. Wróblewski, "Aksjologia prawa socjalistycznego," in: *Prawo socjalistyczne*, H. Rot (ed.), Ossolineum 1989, Chapter 3, passim.

14 W. Lang, J. Wróblewski, S. Zawadzki, *Teoria państwa i prawa*, Warsaw 1986, p. 390.

15 Ibid.

fundament for the sociological unity of the system of people's law.[16] Therefore, the content of people's law is of top-down character established by cognitively privileged lawmaker and does not have any discursive character, that is, it may not be specified in a legal discourse, especially in an axiological discourse on the understanding of justice, fairness or due process of law. All axiological questions of people's law are decided upon top-down, by the socialist ideology, that is, cognitively primary philosophical assumptions which contain the formulation of the system of unrelativized primary evaluations.[17] Primary values, specified at the level of philosophical assumptions are coded as a coherent system of internal values of people's law.[18]

4. The coherent system of internal values of people's law defines a new form of life, whose universal acceptance by the interpreters is assumed by the ideology of people's law interpretation.[19] According to this ideology, there is an imperative of formulating evaluations relativized to the system of values defined by ethics of progress in legal discourse.[20] In the process of defining contents of law, cognitively privileged policymakers – the lawmaker – are not limited by the existing morality of the lower form of being, the capitalist one. People's law is the tool of creating the new, higher, morality defined by ethics of progress.[21] As a consequence, fundamental axiological issues in law are decided upon by the lawmaker, not the legal discourse. Rejecting the discursive concept of law is the consequence of its instrumentalisation. If law is to be an efficient tool for creating social unity, the fundamental elements of its content, especially axiological, cannot be subject to never-ending debates in doctrine and jurisdiction.
5. According to the instrumentative and non-discursive concept of people's law, deciding what is and what is not binding law is reserved for the lawmaker,

16 Ibid.

17 W. Lang, J. Wróblewski, S. Zawadzki, *Teoria…*, p. 32.

18 J. Wróblewski, Wartości a decyzja sądowa, Ossolineum 1973, p. 47ff.

19 W. Lang, J. Wróblewski, S. Zawadzki, *Teoria…*, p. 485.

20 On the subject of ethics of progress, cf. J. Wróblewski, "Rozumność rzeczywistości w Heglowskiej filozofii prawa a dualizm bytu i powinności," *Zeszyty Naukowe Uniwersytetu Łódzkiego, Nauki Humanistyczno-Społeczne*, Series I, Vol. 52, Łódź 1957, pp. 16–17; cf. also J. Wróblewski, "Relatywistyczne teorie prawa," *Państwo i Prawo* Vol. 8–9 1963, pp. 218–219; cf. also J. Wróblewski, *Teoria racjonalnego tworzenia prawa*, Ossolineum 1985, pp. 227–230.

21 J. Wróblewski, Zagadnienia teorii wykładni prawa ludowego, Warsaw 1959, p. 389; cf. also J. Wróblewski, "Stosunki między systemami norm," *Studia Prawno-Ekonomiczne* Vol. 6, 1971, pp. 31–32; J. Wróblewski, *Relatywistyczne teorie…*, passim.

that is, the cognitively privileged policymakers. Specifically, these issues may not be decided upon by subjects applying the law or interpreting legal texts. Marxist concept of people's law therefore entails radical separation of making and applying law. The role of law applicators, the interpreters, in the scope of determining the contents of law ought to be minimal, because the monopoly on determining the contents of the law lies with the cognitively privileged lawmaker. This is accompanied by the assumption that the content of people's law is sufficiently precisely determined in the act of making law. From this results the radical critique of court lawmaking and the exclusion of the possibility of making praeter or contra legem decisions by those that apply law.[22] As a consequence, interpretation of law is not a creative but rather a reproductive act. In Marxist theory of people's law, law is not an interpretative fact, but an imperative one, issued by the superior lawmaker.

6. Law as the tool of global social change is a system, that is, an ordered collection of legal norms perceived as language utterances which specify binding patterns of behavior. People's law, as a system, is characterized by a high level of social coherence – the expression of the will of the ruling class – and teleological (creating the higher form of being) as the ultimate goal of the law. In consequence, the system of people's law is characterized by axiological cohesion, where internal values of the law create an internally coherent system defined by the ethics of progress, as well as a high level of formal coherence – vertical bonds resulting from the hierarchy of the policy-making authorities, as well as material cohesion (norms are usually textually in accordance with the capital norms).[23] The consequence of adopting instrumental image of law as the tool of global social reconstruction is the adoption of systemic character as an immanent feature of people's law. This means that law does not become a system in the process of optimizational exegesis of legal texts, but it is given as a system as the result of the lawmaker's activity. In other words, the system of law is the work of the lawmaker, not the interpreter who performs the systematization of law. It is worth mentioning that in Marxist theory of law, systemic character of law is of decidedly ontological connotation, not an epistemological one. The system is a necessary form of the existence of people's law, that is, law exists as a system or may exist only within a system

22 J. Wróblewski, "Modele systemów norm a system prawa," *Studia Prawno-Ekonomiczne*, Vol. 2, 1969, pp. 46–47; J. Wróblewski, "Sądowe stosowanie prawa a prawotwórstwo," *Państwo i Prawo*, Vol. 6, 1967, passim; cf. also J. Wróblewski, "Interpretatio secundum, praeter et contra legem," *Państwo i Prawo*, Vol. 4–5, 1961, passim.

23 W. Lang, J. Wróblewski, S. Zawadzki, *Teoria...*, pp. 389–390.

> of norms. The category of a system describes the way of existence of law, and unlike the epistemological category is not the method of cognizing law or a necessary assumption in the process of optimizing it. Systemic character of law in Marxist theory and philosophy of law holds realistic interpretation instead of an instrumental one.[24]

I think that adopting these fundamental elements of Marxist theory of law as cognitively primary philosophical assumptions (presuppositions), decides the way of perceiving of systematic character of people's law in Jerzy Wróblewski's theory of interpretation of law.

3 The Level of Theory of the Interpretation

Adopting the above assumptions as cognitively primary philosophical presuppositions makes Jerzy Wróblewski's theory of interpretation of law characterized with strong drive towards objectivization of law. In the theory of interpretation in question, it is assumed that the "people's law" category, defined based on cognitively primary philosophical assumption points at objectively existing social reality characterized by the features enumerated above. I understand the term "objective existence" as existence independent of the cognitive subject, in this case the interpreter. Specifically, the author assumes that the legal rule formulated in a language exists objectively and as such is not identical to its meaning, which is the pattern of behavior.[25] Therefore, the norm – the law – is something more than a pattern of behavior identified in the process of comprehending the norm. In consequence, a change of meaning resulting from interpretation is not identical to change of norm as an objective being, determined as a derivative of

---

24 J. Wróblewski, "Pojęcie systemu prawa a informatyka prawnicza," *Studia Prawno-Ekonomiczne*, Vol. XXV, 1980, passim; J. Wróblewski, "Modele systemów norm a system prawa," *Studia Prawno-Ekonomiczne*, Vol. 2, 1969, passim; J. Wróblewski, "Stosunki między systemami norm," *Studia Prawno-Ekonomiczne*, Vol. 6, 1971, passim; J. Wróblewski, "Decyzja sądowa a koncepcja systemu prawa," *Acta Universitatis Lodziensis, Zeszyty Naukowe Uniwersytetu Łódzkiego, Nauki Humanistyczno-Społeczne*, Series I, Vol. 28, 1978, passim; J. Wróblewski, "Concepts of Legal System and Conceptions of Validity," *Acta Universitatis Lodziensis, Folia Iuridica*, 24, 1986, passim; J. Wróblewski, "Ustawa o tworzeniu prawa a pojęcie prawa i prawoznawstwa," *Państwo i Prawo* Vol. 8–9, 1977, passim; J. Wróblewski, "Obowiązywanie systemowe i granice dogmatycznego podejścia do systemu prawa," *Studia Prawno-Ekonomiczne*, Vol. XXXVI, 1986, passim; J. Wróblewski, "Nieostrość systemu prawa," *Studia Prawno-Ekonomiczne*" Vol. XXXI, 1989, passim.

25 J. Wróblewski, Zagadnienia…, p. 140.

the lawmaker's activity. This means that the norm as an objective being which came to life by an act of the lawmaker exists independently of the acts of interpretation of law. What is more, the author maintains, consistently in all the phases of the establishment of his theory of interpretation, that also the meaning of the norm as a pattern of behavior is always, at least to a degree, independent of the interpreter.[26] Law is not an interpretative fact defined in the process of interpretation, but an imperative fact, defined in the acts of establishing law by the lawmaker. Similarly, to a rule of law, also the system of law as an ordered collection of the rules exists objectively, that is, independently of the acts of interpretation of legal texts. Also, just like the meaning of the norm, the level of systemic order of norms is determined by the acts of establishing the law by the lawmaker, not by interpretations of law performed by the interpreter. In consequence, the assumption of objective existence of the system of law is a fundamental existential presupposition of interpretation activities, adopted at the level of cognitively primary philosophical assumptions. This means the systemic character of law is not the result of interpretation as an optimizing activity, that is, an activity that maximizes the value of the object of interpretation – the legal text. In fact, it is just the opposite: the assumption of the systemic character of law is the starting point for interpretation activities as the basic ontological characteristics of people's law. The assumption of the systemic character of law is therefore the conclusion of the way of the existence of law, not a notional tool to cognize law in the process of interpretation as an optimizing activity. According to the cognitively primary philosophical assumptions that describe law as a tool of the creation of the higher form of social existence, in the case of Jerzy Wróblewski's theory of interpretation, the category of system of law functions as an ontological category, that is, defining the way of existence of law, not as an epistemological category, defining the way of cognizing law. In consequence, on the grounds of the theory of interpretation which is being analyzed, norm as a meaningful language utterance needs to be always perceived as belonging to the system of law. Systemic character is a defining feature of a norm because a norm is defined as a meaningful language utterance belonging to the system of law. A single norm is therefore a systemic being because its existence is impossible outside of the system of law. It is the result of adopting the systemic concept of the binding force of the norm.[27] In consequence, the perception of a norm as a systemic being determines the activity of the interpreter not only in the process of the strictly

---

26 J. Wróblewski, *Rozumienie prawa i jego wykładnia*, Ossolineum 1990, pp. 111–112.
27 Ibid., p. 11.

systemic interpretation but also in the process of functional and linguistic interpretation. In other words, the characteristic feature of the theory of interpretation described here is that it takes into account the systemic context also when in the process of establishing the meaning of the norm the interpreter refers to the linguistic and functional context of the norm. This means the assumption of the systemic character of the norm is always present in the process of establishing its meaning, as a pattern of behavior.

On the grounds of the theory of interpretation described here, in the scope of linguistic interpretation, the assumption of the systemic character of a norm finds its expression in the form of a postulate of semantic coherence of a legal text. In the case of linguistic interpretation, the interpreter in the process of establishing the meaning of the norm follows the linguistic context of the norm, that is, refers to more or less obvious properties of the legal language. According to Jerzy Wróblewski's theory of interpretation, one of the most obvious features of legal language is a defined level of its semantic coherence, that is, it is assumed that phrases of the same shape in a legal text carry the same meaning. This assumption is found in the form of a postulate according to which phrases of equal shape ought to be understood identically. The postulate of semantic coherence of a legal text is expressed in most of the directives of linguistic interpretation proposed by the author. It can be assumed that the postulate of semantic coherence is expressed in the directives either directly or indirectly. In the direct way, it is expressed by a directive that may be described as prohibition of homonymic interpretation and which is based on an assumption that there are no homonyms in a legal text. In Wróblewski's theory of interpretation, this prohibition may be either narrow or wide. In the former case, the scope of prohibition is restricted to a given act of law: "Identical linguistic phrases within the same legal act must not be assigned the different meaning."[28] In the latter case, there is no limit of a single legal act and the prohibition reads: "Without good reason, different meanings should not be assigned to the same phrasing within legal regulations."[29] We may assume that in this version, the prohibition of homonymic interpretation is related to a legal text understood as the collection of all legal texts in binding force at a given time and place – to a specific system of law.

In the indirect form, the postulate of the semantic coherence of a legal text is expressed in two fundamental directives of linguistic interpretation – in the

28 J. Wróblewski, *Zagadnienia…*, p. 247; cf. also K. Opałek, J. Wróblewski, *Zagadnienia teorii prawa*, Warsaw 1969, p. 247; cf. also, W. Lang, J. Wróblewski, S. Zawadzki, *Teoria…*, p. 443.

29 J. Wróblewski, *Rozumienie…*, p. 79.

described case, these are directives named conjecture of common language and conjecture of legal language. They prohibit the assignment of specific legal meaning to interpreted utterances "without sufficient reason" in case when the meaning is determined by common language (conjecture of common language) or by legal language, for example, legal definition (conjecture of legal language). Let us notice that deviation from these conjectures is only possible under the condition of "sufficiently wide consideration of the meaning of equally-shaped utterances in norms belonging to one system of law or part thereof."[30] The common element of the two directives is the drive towards limiting the freedom of the interpreter in creating new meanings if these meanings are already established in common language (conejecture 1) or legal language (conjecture 2). Let us also notice that the meaning of the two conjectures is not identical for maintaining the semantic coherence of a legal text. This is because the level of defining of directives of meaning in common language is significantly lower than in legal language, where a part of these directives is defined in the form of legal definitions. Assuming that the fundamental method of defining meanings in legal language is the use of legal definitions, the second directive is to be understood as a conjecture of the universal scope of usability for legal definitions, that is, we need to assume that the scope of usability of legal definitions covers the whole system of law. However, Jerzy Wróblewski does not develop this issue, but it seems that we may differentiate between the radical (maximal) and moderate (realistic) variants of conjecture of legal language. In the first case, the postulate of the universal scope of the usability would refer to each legal definition. In this understanding, it is not acceptable by either legal doctrine or legal practice, because it is not a realistic postulate. In the latter case, the postulate would only refer to the so-called source legal definitions, that is, definitions contained in those provisions that are the source for a given institution of law, such as the definition of "firearms" contained in the provisions of the Guns and Ammunition Act.[31]

As already mentioned, in the theory of interpretation under discussion, the assumption of the systemic character of law intervenes into the process of establishing the meaning of the norm in case of interpretation that references linguistic, systemic, and functional contexts. At the level of linguistic interpretation,

30 J. Wróblewski, *Zagadnienia…*, p. 246; cf. also, W. Lang, J. Wróblewski, S. Zawadzki, *Teoria…*, p. 443; cf. also, K. Opałek, J. Wróblewski, *Zagadnienia teorii…*, p. 247.

31 More on this matter, cf. Z. Pulka, "Zagadnienie spójności semantycznej systemu prawa w klaryfikacyjnej teorii wykładni," in: *Postanalityczna filozofia prawa*, M. Jabłoński, M. Paździora (eds.), *Przegląd Prawa i Administracji*, Vol. CII, Wrocław 2015, passim.

the assumption of the systemic character of law is evidenced in the form of the postulate of semantic coherence of a legal text. At the level of systemic and functional interpretation, the assumption of systemic character of law encompasses the following: (1) Elements of the legal system and its scope, (2) The issue of consistency and completeness of the legal system.

Specific solutions to both these issues are found in the fundamental directive of systemic interpretation: "The interpreter ought to establish the meaning of the interpreted norm in a way which is not followed by technical contradiction between the interpreted norm and any other norm belonging to the same system of law."[32] This directive assumes the idea of a norm which belongs to a legal system, which is to be understood as synonymous with the notion of a binding norm. Therefore, this directive assumes a specific understanding of the system of binding law which is the subject of interpretation. A crucial question arises: what understanding of system of binding law is assumed by the fundamental directive of systemic interpretation which requires that interpretation of a norm be conducted in such a way as to avoid technical contradictions with the other norms constituting the system of binding law? On the grounds of the described theory of interpretation, a norm belonging to the system needs to meet two conditions: (1) It is a general and abstract norm, (2) A general norm needs to meet the criteria set by the notion of systemic binding force of law.

The first solution is important, because it excludes these norms that are the effect of application of law (individual and specific norms) outside of the system of law. It is associated with the characteristic for the theory in question radical differentiation between the creation and application of law.[33] It also results in the rejection of Kelsen's concept of a dynamic system, which relativizes the creation and application of law and assumes that subject-matter norms created as the result of the applying of norms of lawmaking competence are elements of the dynamic system. As a consequence, the radical version of the system of operational law (LSOP, sometimes also LSOL) is considered unacceptable, because it includes norms which rose as a consequence of the decisions of application of law into the legal system. The reasons are ideological – ideology of lawful and rational court decision implies radical separation of lawmaking and application

---

32 W. Lang, J. Wróblewski, S. Zawadzki, *Teoria…*, p. 444; cf. also, J. Wróblewski, *Zagadnienia…*, p. 298.

33 J. Wróblewski, *Modele systemów norm…*, pp. 46–47; J. Wróblewski, "Sądowe stosowanie prawa a prawotwórstwo", *Państwo i Prawo*, 1967, z. 6, s. 865 i n.

of law – and operative, where there is no possibility of determining the borders of the legal system.[34]

The second solution assumes that the belonging of a norm to the legal system is decided by the criteria established by the notion of systemic binding force of the norm. According to this notion, the norm is binding if: (a) it has been established in accordance with the norms that are binding in the system and entered into force, (b) or is a consequence of norms that belong to the system and was accepted because of the rules of the system, (c) was not formally derogated, (d) is not contrary to any binding norm in the legal system, and if it is contrary, it does not lose its binding force on the basis of adopted collision directives or does not change its meaning by adopting directives of interpretation (in another version, was interpreted in such a way in which it is not discordant with any rule which is binding in the system).[35]

The adoption of the concept of systemic binding force of law assumes that the legal system is characterized by "completeness of the binding force," that is, that we can state, in reference to any norm, whether it belongs to the system or not. It is possible because we assume that the legal system contains only such norms that have been established on the basis of norms that already belongs to the system and which gained and not lost its binding force. The criteria established by the notion of systemic binding force create the rule of recognition which ought to contain unambiguous premises of deciding upon validation issues. Let us point out, however, that in H. L. A. Hart's concept, the rule of recognition is a constant practice of judging norms to be binding, of deciding upon validation issues, which means it is a social fact.[36] We may say that in Hart's concept, the rule of recognition exists in the factual understanding, that it is binding because it is applied in practice.[37] In turn, in Wróblewski's concept, the rule of recognition, at least in its basic part – criterion a – is binding in the thetical understanding, that is, as a consequence of an act of establishing of law. In other words, the fundamental element of the rule of recognition, created by the norms of lawmaking competence and lawmaking procedures (element a) are binding

---

34 J. Wróblewski, *Decyzja sądowa a koncepcja systemu prawa*, p. 23 and ff.; J. Wróblewski, *Ustawa o tworzeniu prawa a pojęcie prawa i prawoznawstwa*, pp. 28–31; J. Wróblewski, *Sądowe stosowanie prawa a prawotwórstwo*, passim.

35 J. Wróblewski, *Rozumienie…*, p. 11; cf. also W. Lang, J. Wróblewski, S. Zawadzki, *Teoria…*, p. 390.

36 H. L. A. Hart, *Pojęcie prawa*, Warsaw 1998, p. 140ff.

37 J. Woleński, "Obowiązywanie prawne w ujęciu H. L. A. Harta," *Zeszyty Naukowe Uniwersytetu Jagiellońskiego, Prace Prawnicze*, p. 51, 1971, passim.

on the basis of being established by the lawmaker. It is therefore the lawmaker, not social practice, that decides on the criteria for deeming the norm binding, or belonging to the system of law. It is worth mentioning that according to Jerzy Wróblewski's theory of law the fundamental element of the rule of recognition created by norms of competence and lawmaking procedures decides on the identity of the legal system. As long as these rules are maintained, the legal system maintains its identity and we cannot speak of revolutionary changes within it, at least in the plane of legality.[38]

Criteria of systemic binding force (a), (c), and (d) define the LSLE system, a system of norms legitimizing themselves through thetic justifications, that is, resulting from lawmaker acts. Adding the criterion (b) defines an LSFC system, a system that encompasses formal consequences of established norms, apart from the norms plainly established themselves. In Wróblewski's theory of interpretation, it is the LSFC system that makes up the system of binding law.[39] The characteristic feature of such conceived binding law in this interpretation is not only "completeness of binding" but also maintaining the lawmaker's monopoly on determining what law is binding. Let us draw the attention to the fact that such conceived "binding law" assumes the monopoly of the lawmaker on the following: (a) determining the criteria for the effect of the law, as well as (b) undertaking lawmaking activity in accordance with the defined criteria making up the rule of recognition. This means the need to exclude the rules of the LSIC system outside of the scope of the binding law – with the LSIC system encompassing the interpretation consequences of the established norm. The same is true of the LSOP system – operational law encompassing rules that are binding in the factual understanding, and LSPP – the system that encompasses the rules which are binding in the factual and axiological meaning. The inclusion of the rules that are defined by the LSIC, LSOP, and LSPP systems into the system of binding law would be equal to the deprivation of the lawmaker of monopoly on deciding what is binding law and what is not, by deciding that the criteria for the binding force of the law may be included in the decisions of application of law. Such solution is unacceptable for Wróblewski because of ideological reasons. The ideology of "lawful and rational court decision," accepted by the author, assumes radical separation of making and applying law. Directival concept of system of law is accordant with this ideology – it is a concept in which criteria of binding force

38 J. Wróblewski, "Zmiany prawa, rewolucja a zmiany społeczne," in: *Prawo i prawoznawstwo wobec zmian społecznych*, H. Rot (ed.), Wrocław 1990, passim.

39 J. Wróblewski, *Rozumienie...*, p. 16.

are defined by the rules of the system. Decisive concept of the system, where criteria of binding force are defined in the decisions of law applying cannot be reconciled with the postulate of legality of making law. Additionally, with LSIC and LSPP concepts, their rejection is also supported by operational premises, that is, lack of possibility of defining a norm that would close up the system and indicate unambiguous criteria for binding force of norms within the system. This makes it impossible to define the borders of the legal system. The notion of binding, encompassed only by the LSFC system, contains a vision of law system which is unambiguously determined by acts of making law performed by the lawmaker. With such defined binding law, the lawmaker retains the monopoly not only on setting the rule of recognition but also on undertaking lawmaking actions in accordance with this rule.

Determining the borders of binding law requires an analysis of the LSFC system, which contains formal consequences of established norms that make up the LSLE system. The notion of "formal consequences" relates to logical (deductive, L-consequences) as well as consequences defined on the basis of the rules of reasoning which are "interpretations" of specific formulae of logical calculus, for example, *a fortiori*, reasoning from the goal to the means, *exceptiones non sunt extendendae*. Consequences based on these rules of reasoning are of quasi-logical character, because they are the result of "proper" application of the rules of logic to the normative utterances (QL-consequences). The category of formal consequences may contain consequences defined in the analogia legis and a contratio reasoning, but only if their application is legally regulated, because only then will the result of the reasoning be deemed as systemic consequences of established norms (S-consequences).[40]

As an example, legal prohibition of *analogia legis* equals the order of *a contrario* reasoning, then the result of the reasoning leads to the establishment of an S-consequence of the binding norm. If, on the other hand, the application of *analogia legis* or *a contrario* reasoning is not legally regulated, it is based on evaluation, that is, is an issue of the choice of the interpreter, not determined by the lawmaker, which causes the consequences based on such application are of illusory character (P-consequence) or, in another version, alleged consequences (D-consequence). Then, the results of the reasoning are not of systemic character and cannot be considered elements of binding law.[41]

40 J. Wróblewski, *Zagadnienia...*, p. 392 and ff.; cf. also, K. Opałek, J. Wróblewski, *Zagadnienia teorii prawa*, pp. 80–87.

41 J. Wróblewski, *Zagadnienia...*, pp. 86–87.

As can be seen, the LSFC legal system contains only consequences of the type L, QL, and S, which can be described on the basis of logical rules (L-consequences), the "proper" application of the rules of logic (QL-consequences) or based on the rules of the system of law (S-consequences). If considering as consequences of binding norms is the question of evaluation and is based on the decision of the interpreter, the consequences acquires an "illusory" or "alleged" character and may not be considered part of the binding legal system.[42] It is worth adding that the way to determine the formal consequences that belong to the system is not the *analogia iuris*, which is brought down by the author to an order of deciding all the unforeseen cases on the basis of the "entirety of the binding norms."[43] According to the author, in this shape this directive gives no precise premises of deciding, in the form of a norm or a group of norms. In another understanding, the *analogia iuris* is "assigning specific legal consequences to the facts which did not have such consequences according to the binding legal norms and consequences thereof."[44] According to the author, the subject who performs the *analogia iuris* changes its position from law applying to law-making agent.[45] Even in cases where the application of *analogia iuris* is legally ordered, the consequences resulting from it create illusory consequences of binding norms.[46] As a result, the reason behind rejecting the *analogia iuris* as a reasoning determining the binding consequences of norms, is on the one hand its lawmaking character, and on the other lots of freedom in defining the premises of such reasoning. It seems there is a close relation between these reasons for rejecting *analogia iuris* as a way of determining binding consequences of norms. It is because evaluative character of the interpreter's activity in the area of determining the premises of reasoning leads to these activities acquiring lawmaking character. In any case, the indeterminacy of the premises excludes the possibility of accepting the results of the *analogia iuris* as QL-consequences and even if its application would be legally ordered, evaluative character of the reasoning is decisive for recognizing its consequences as illusory (conjectured).

Let us draw attention to the fact that in such interpretation, formal consequences encompass two categories: (a) determined by rules of logical thinking, that is, deductive rules and their "normative" counterparts applied to normative utterances, (b) defined by rules/norms of the system of law. In both

42 Ibid., p. 308.
43 Ibid., pp. 305–306.
44 Ibid., pp. 311–314.
45 Ibid., p. 311.
46 Ibid.

cases, the level of determination of these consequences is very high because that their definition is not the result of more or less free conjectures of the interpreter. With some simplification, we may say that in both the former and the latter case these are consequences that have been indirectly (L- and QL-consequences) and directly (S-consequences) determined by the lawmaker. In other words, F-consequences in the LSFC model which form part of the binding law system are such consequences whose acceptance is a necessity – either of logical character, determined by the rules of thinking that function as (quasi-)deductive rules of legal language or of normative character, determined by the norms of the system of law, determining the terms of use of reasonings such as *analogia legis* or *a contrario*. Where there is lack of logical or normative determination, consequences are of illusory or alleged character and are not elements of binding law. This is related to *analogia iuris*, because of its lawmaking character, and also to *analogia legis* and *a contrario*, in which the application of such reasonings is not normatively determined and, consequently, whether this type of reasoning will be conducted or not is decided upon the evaluations of the interpreter. This fact is worth exposing because based on the theory of interpretation under scrutiny, the LSFC model, the so-called established law, and its formal consequences create the idea of binding law, which is subject to interpretation.[47]

As already mentioned, the fundamental directive of the systemic interpretation contains an order to conduct interpretation in such a way as to avoid technical discrepancies within the system of law. In the described theory of interpretation, the contradiction of norms is understood as a situation in which realization of norm N1 excludes the realization of a second norm N2.[48] Such conceived contradictions may be of abstract character and are then identified already at the stage of language analysis, for example, behavior in N1 is described as a negation of behavior in N2. They may also be of a specific character – a situation of the so-called confluence of norms in a specific case, excluding simultaneous realization of N1 and N2.[49] Such a contradiction is a technical one if it is not intended by the lawmaker and may be considered an effect of erroneous legislation technique. In other words, it is not a contradiction that exists in the deep structure of the law, on the level of lawmaker's intentional activity, but

47 J. Wróblewski, *Rozumienie…*, p. 16.
48 J. Wróblewski, *Zagadnienia…*, p. 283ff.
49 W. Lang, J. Wróblewski, S. Zawadzki, *Teoria…*, pp. 400–401.

it occurs in the surface sphere of law, on the level of norm formulation.[50] The author considers technical discrepancies as inevitable in the process of development of law. They occur if during a rapid development of social relations "law does not keep pace with life."[51] Progress in the area of legislation technique may lead to the reduction of these discrepancies. On the one hand, the author shows the inevitability of legislative process faults, while on the other, he expresses his belief in the inevitability of progress within this process.[52]

On the grounds of the described theory of interpretation of law, an original solution to the perception of gaps in the legal system is considering technical gaps as a specific form of technical contradictions. A technical gap is defined as a situation when "rules that define positive consequences of a fact are not complete, because they do not regulate some element of the institution without which ascertaining positive consequences is not possible."[53] The author interprets this situation as a technical discrepancy between the order of decision of positive consequences as resulting from the general order of decision-making and prohibition of deciding upon the consequences on the grounds of the lack of legal basis. In such a situation, the application of *analogia legis* may lead to the definition of S-consequences, which are systemic consequences included in the system of law, or D-consequences, which are alleged consequences that do not belong to the system of law, depending on the level of normative determination applied to the reasoning.[54]

Considering the acceptance of the consequences of *analogia legis* as binding norms, the position of the author is ambivalent. In the primary version, where because of lack of normative determination the application of this reasoning leads to alleged consequences, dependent on the conjectures of the interpreter, these are not considered binding norms belonging to the system of law.[55] In the latter, more moderate, version, the author concludes that of the reasoning, including the *analogia legis*, because of lack of logical or normative determination leads to alleged consequences, its legitimacy ought to be measured by the legitimacy of evaluations that decide upon its application.[56] This would mean

50 J. Wróblewski, "Zagadnienie niesprzeczności i zupełności systemu prawa," *Zeszyty Naukowe Uniwersytetu Łódzkiego*, Nauki Humanistyczno-Społeczne, Series I, Vol. 9, Łódź 1958, pp. 5–6.

51 J. Wróblewski, *Zagadnienia…*, p. 284.

52 Ibid.

53 W. Lang, J. Wróblewski, S. Zawadzki, *Teoria…*, p. 407.

54 J. Wróblewski, *Zagadnienia…*, p. 314.

55 Ibid., p. 282ff.

56 K. Opałek, J. Wróblewski, *Zagadnienia...*, p. 87.

that we may consider alleged consequences as describing binding norms, that is, that belong to the LSFC system if this is justified by the evaluations adopted when formulating of these consequences. *Analogia legis* consequences could be therefore considered F-consequences, even if because of lack of normative determination, the effects of the application of reasoning could not be considered S-consequences. Such a viewpoint seems to be confirmed in the thesis stating that on the grounds of the postulated ideology of lawful and rational court decision it is permitted not only evaluative determination of technical contradictions but also their evaluative settlement by means of *analogia legis*.[57] As a consequence, this would mean that the inclusion of a norm consequence to the system of law as an F-consequence is decided upon, on the one hand, the logical and normative necessity (L-, QL-, S-consequence) and on the other hand the validity of applied evaluations. The latter would occur if the application of *analogia legis*, because of lack of normative determinacy, may not be said to lead to S-consequences, and still there are strong axiological reasons behind conducting such reasoning. Let us add that the validity of evaluations is to be decided upon on the grounds of the postulated ideology of lawful and rational court decision which assumes complete identification of the interpreter with the system of internal values of people's law, defined through socialist ideology. Let us also point out that the ideology of lawful and rational court decision excludes the freedom of the interpreter within leeway of making evaluative choices. An integral part of this ideology is the postulate of the interpreter completely internalizing the system of internal values of people's law. It also needs adding that in the author's understanding, the system of internal values of people's law is characterized by a high degree of axiological coherence, which makes it possible to treat this system as defining a universally acceptable form of life. With the assumption that the coherent system of internal values of people's law is defined by socialist ideology, the form of life defined by this system of values can only be one, namely a communist society free of alienation. Let us add that the author regards the assumption of the existence of a universally acceptable form of life or a universally acceptable system of values, whose compulsory internalization is the source of axiological choices of the interpreter, as the fundamental axiological presupposition of legal interpretational reasoning.[58]

---

57 W. Lang, J. Wróblewski, S. Zawadzki, *Teoria...*, p. 408.

58 J. Wróblewski, *Presupozycje rozumowania prawniczego*, pp. 12, 18–19. Cf. also J. Wróblewski, *Rozumienie...*, p. 108 ff., in which the author formulates the postulate of the rationality of material interpretation decisions understood as consistency of interpretation decision with commonly accepted form of life defined through the

On the grounds of the discussed theory of interpretation, the fundamental assumption deciding the image of the system of people's law is accepting technical discrepancies as illusory ones. The illusory character assumes that: (a) they are not intended by the lawmaker and therefore are of random nature, (b) their emergence is connected with the dynamic development of law and errors of legislation technique which are inevitable in this context, (c) they are not contradictions of law, but of formulations of law, that is, they are not intended discrepancies of norm in the deep structures of law, but surface random discrepancies on the level of formulation of norms, (d) they are prima facie contradictions, which disappear when the meaning of the norm is sufficiently deep determined in the process of interpretation or when collision rules are applied.[59] Identification of such conceived technical contradictions is based on the assumption that that are results of errors on the level of lawmaking technique. Because of this, they may be removed during interpretation activity which in this case does not carry the stigma of lawmaking activity. What is more, we are justified to claim that such activity is in accordance with the intentions of the creator of the imperfect legal text, who simply used a wrong expression within the said text. Such an understanding of the interpretation activity connected with the existence of technical discrepancies is the consequence of perceiving these as prima facie contradictions, that is, as contradictions that occur on the level of the formulation of the law. It is important that while removing the technical discrepancies of the law the interpreter does not enter the role of the lawmaker but remains in the area defined by the role of an interpreter. Many take for granted that removing technical contradictions is the interpretation of law, not the creation of law.

The author confronts illusory technical discrepancies with real political discrepancies. Political discrepancies in the system of law are of real character because they are the consequence of the existence of class conflicts. Their existence is intended, as the result of a game of political powers. Referring to the works of Marxist classics, the author indicates an example of political discrepancies – a situation in which constitutional norms which are a political compromise assign some rights, which are afterwards limited by norms of lower rank. This situation consists in the programmatic character of constitutional norms that assign some rights, which, however, are not realized due to limitations or exclusions at the lower level of the legal system. The author points out an

internal values of law. Cf. also J Wróblewski, "Poziomy uzasadnienia decyzji prawnej," *Studia Prawno-Ekonomiczne*, Vol. XL, 1988, p. 29ff.

59 J. Wróblewski, *Zagadnienie niesprzeczności...*, passim.

especially radical form of such contradictions, a specific legal gap (the so-called realizational contradiction) which is based on the lawmaker not issuing norms required in order to realize the program norms.[60] The real character of political contradictions causes that these discrepancies cannot be removed in the process of interpreting the law – only as the result of the lawmaker's activity. With the assumption that these discrepancies are characteristic of class societies, their existence in the system of people's law is impossible. The author states clearly: "The assumptions of the workings of a socialist political system do not allow for such discrepancies to occur."[61]

It is worth highlighting that the LSFC construction of people's law, which makes the base of the described theory of interpretation, is not only a theoretical construct that excludes the existence of real discrepancies in the system of law, but also one that eliminates gaps in the system of law. Many assume that the system of people's law is not only actually internally coherent but also complete in reality. In this theory of interpretation, the effect of real completeness of the system of people's law is achieved by the inclusion of the incompleteness of legal regulations in the category of illusory technical discrepancy, eliminated by *analogia legis* or – similarly to typical technical discrepancies – by interpretation activity. Hence, the elimination of a technical gap by means of interpretation is not a lawmaking activity, that is, it does not hold the character of creating new normative acts by filling in legislative blanks but is an act of eliminating illusory imperfections at the level of the formulation of legal acts. Understanding a technical gap as a technical contradictions means that we are not facing a situation of real lack of legal regulations which may only be removed by lawmaking activity, but merely a situation where an existing regulation is formulated imperfectly, and which can be removed by interpretation activity that in itself does not hold any lawmaking character.

In my opinion, the influence of ideological assumptions on the adopted concept of real coherence and completeness of the system of law is evident. The ideology of lawful and rational court decision is based on the radical opposition of making versus applying law, which results in the equally radical negation of court lawmaking.[62] A fundamental assumption of the ideology is the acceptance of the unquestioned monopoly of the lawmaker on the process of making the law, which is the consequence of the decisions made on the philosophical

60 J. Wróblewski, *Zagadnienia...*, p. 286.

61 K. Opałek, J. Wróblewski, *Zagadnienia...*, p. 99.

62 J. Wróblewski, *Sądowe stosowanie prawa a prawotwórstwo*, passim.

level and related to the ontology of people's law. According to the philosophical decisions of Marxism, people's law is a tool of global social reconstruction, based on creating a higher-level being, within a communist society free of alienation. In turn, according to the epistemological assumptions of Marxism, the cognition of a higher-level being is accessible only to socially privileged political representatives of the class of progress, an ascending class that represents an objective process of historical progress. So, cognitive privilege predestines to act as a people's lawmaker. In consequence, no one else – especially the interpreter who applies the law – may be legitimized to undertake lawmaking activities, which could break the legislative monopoly of the epistemologically privileged lawmaker. The theoretical constructions, suggested by the author, of coherence and completeness of people's law system that exclude court lawmaking, need to be therefore considered consequences of adopting the above philosophical decisions as cognitively primary premises for theoretical activity, that is, cognitive activity realized on the level of theory of law.

As far as the role of the principles of the legal system in the process of establishing the meaning of a legal text is concerned, the author's viewpoint is ambivalent. In the primary version, Wróblewski assumes a subsidiary role of the principles, that is, adopts a viewpoint according to which the interpreter may appeal to the principles only when the application of other linguistic directives does not lead to unambiguous results. In other words, subsidiary character of the principles means that they serve to solve interpretation conflicts which arose as the consequence of the application of other directives of interpretation, for example, linguistic directives. An example of such a viewpoint is a directive: "If, on the grounds of linguistic directives, doubts arise as to the meaning of a legal norm, a solution is to be chosen which is in accordance with the principles of a part of the legal system and the legal system that the interpreted norm belongs to."[63] In the latter version, which can be considered more representative, principles play an independent role in the process of establishing the meaning of a norm. An example here can be the following directive: "If a norm is contradictory to a principle of the system of law, the meaning of the interpreted norm is to be established so that it is consistent with this principle."[64] Another is: "The interpreted legal norm is to be assigned meaning with which it is most coherent with the adopted principle of law."[65]

---

63 J. Wróblewski, *Zagadnienia...*, p. 281.

64 W. Lang, J. Wróblewski, S. Zawadzki, *Teoria...*, p. 445; cf. also, K. Opałek, J. Wróblewski, *Zagadnienia...*, p. 250.

65 J. Wróblewski, *Rozumienie...*, p. 83.

According to Wróblewski's theory of interpretation, of fundamental importance for the comprehension of the principles of a system of law is the rejection of positions that the author calls "legal nihilism." In his words, "legal nihilism" is any viewpoint that assumes different existence of principles than as the consequence of acts of making law. In consequence, "legal nihilism" consist in not only perceiving the principles from a "natural law" point of view, where higher normative order is identified on the basis of axiological criteria, but also in adopting the realistic point of view, where principles of law are treated as social facts.[66] In short, what is the principle of law is decided only by the lawmaker in the process of making law. In consequence, the author makes a fundamental notional and terminological distinction, differentiating the principles of the system of law from the postulates of the system of law.[67] Principles are binding norms or their formal (logical) consequences which, based on their contents, are of fundamental importance to the whole legal system or part thereof. Principles are elements of binding law, that is, they are thetically binding, in accordance with the rules of systemic binding, and as such are elements of the LSFC system that encompasses the established norms (LSLE) and their formal (L- or QL-) or systemic (S-) consequences. On the other hand, postulates belong to the system of law if adopting wide and decisive concept of the LSPP system, composed of, apart from established rules, also of "principles, policies, and other standards" – rules that are binding in the axiological and/or factual meaning, that is, not being the result of lawmaking.[68] The concept of the LSPP system is a decisive concept of a system because the norm considered binding is decided upon by the law applying bodies (interpreters) who form their decisions on axiological and/or factual criteria. The concept of the LSPP system in this form is definitely rejected by Wróblewski who indicates that it assumes that there may be some rules that belong to the system but which fail to meet the rule of recognition defined by the notion of systematic binding force of a norm. At the same time, the author unambiguously supports a narrow and directive-based concept of the legal system (LSFC) in which the rule of recognition says that only these rules are binding which have been plainly established by the lawmaker and their formal consequences, justifying this choice with the need to differentiate between *lex*

66 J. Wróblewski, *Zagadnienia...*, p. 258; cf. also, K. Opałek, J. Wróblewski, *Zagadnienia...*, pp. 116–120.

67 W. Lang, J. Wróblewski, S. Zawadzki, Teoria..., pp. 398–400.

68 J. Wróblewski, *Rozumienie...*, p. 14.

lata and *lex ferenda*, that is, binding law and postulated law.[69] The concept of the LSPP system, as defined by R. Dworkin, is conceived as a concept removing free recognition in the case of the lack of an established rules because in such a case the judge is obliged to apply "principles, policies, and other standards" that are legitimized with proper axiological justification and "institutional support" in the form of being included in the decision practice so far. Wróblewski criticizes the LSPP system's fuzziness of the borders as well as illusory character of overcoming decisional leeway in the process of applying law due to fuzzy criteria of deeming the existing standards binding in the factual and axiological meaning by the institutions that apply law.[70] However, it needs to be clearly stated that what decides on the abandoning of the LSPP system is the fact that this concept entails breaking of the monopoly on deciding what is and what is not binding law – according to the Marxist philosophical assumptions adopted in this theory of interpretation such monopoly is the exclusive feature of the cognitively privileged lawmaker that represents the class of progress. Let us add that the adopted concept of binding law, in the LSFC system, assumes the monopoly of the lawmaker in regards to the binding law, hence it is coherent with the vision of law based on the cognitively primary assumptions of the Marxist philosophy. I would like to remind that according to these assumptions, only the avant-garde of the class of progress is epistemically legitimized to conducting lawmaking activity, that is, to act as a lawmaker because it possesses distinguished knowledge on the higher form of social being, of Communism, that is supposed to be created with the help of people's law.

The consequence of adhering to the adopted philosophical assumptions is referring the directive of systemic interpretation that forces the coherence of the meaning of the norm with the principles of law only for the principal rules that are binding on the premises of an act of lawmaking or are derived from these norms with logical necessity (LSFC). Therefore, the next directive of systemic interpretation reads: "If a principle of the system, or part thereof, is invoked, it needs to be specified by pointing out a rule of law or a group of rules that contain the principal rule; alternatively, a rule or a group of rules that it is undoubtedly derived from (L- or QL-consequences)."[71]

Holding true to the adopted philosophical assumptions also causes the principles, policies, and other standards to be, on the grounds of the addressed

69 Ibid.; cf. also, W. Lang, J. Wróblewski, S. Zawadzki, *Teoria...*, p. 400; cf. also, J. Wróblewski, *Decyzja sądowa a koncepcja systemu prawa*, pp. 17–20 and 22–23.

70 J. Wróblewski, *Rozumienie...*, p. 14.

71 J. Wróblewski, *Zagadnienia...*, p. 278.

theory of interpretation, included in the extra-legal functional context created by "extra-legal evaluations and social rules" and as such are applied in the framework of functional interpretation. These standards constitute a dynamic category of rules, such as rules of social coexistence, where the dynamics is often stimulated by the lawmaker.[72] Based on Wróblewski's theory of interpretation, it is law that stimulates the development of extra-legal evaluations and norms because they are to be consistent with the goals and tasks of people's state. One of the tasks is the creation of higher socialist/Communist morality.

It is characteristic that Wróblewski recognizes only these directives that drive towards maintaining the axiological coherence of the system of law as the only universal directives in the functional context.[73] In the directives of functional interpretation, the order to maintain axiological coherence of the system of law may be expressed hypothetically or categorically. In the former case, the interpretation directive reads as follows: "If extra-legal goals, values, and rules are applied in the establishment of the meaning of the interpreted legal rule, they ought to be equally applied to all the rules that constitute the institution to which the interpreted rule belongs."[74] It is worth pointing out that the limitation of axiological coherence found in this directive is restricted only to the limits of the institution containing the interpreted norm. This limitation is removed if the directive takes the categorical form: "Interpreted rule is to be assigned a meaning with which it is most coherent with the accepted evaluations of the axiological system or the evaluations of an accepted axiological system."[75] It may seem that the adoption of the hypothetical formula in the former case and the categorical one in the latter case is not contingent. Let us point out that in the former case we are referring to "extra-legal evaluations and social rules," that is, such that are not internal evaluations and values of people's law. In this case the interpreter may recognize them or abandon them. The latter case refers to "accepted axiological system" without specifying whether it is related to the system of internal values of law or extra-legal standards. It is worth recalling that on the basis of this theory of interpretation the assumption of the existence of a universally accepted system of values, next to the assumption of the existence of universal interpretational directives is suggested as the necessary element of justifying the interpretation decisions.[76] It can be said that the "accepted axiological system" is a system

72 Ibid., p. 392.

73 J. Wróblewski, *Rozumienie...*, p. 84.

74 Ibid.

75 Ibid., p. 85.

76 J. Wróblewski, *Presupozycje...*, pp. 18–19.

of values that defines the universally accepted form of life that the interpreter refers to when justifying the axiological choices in the process of interpretation. It is natural that the postulate of the interpreter referring to the "accepted axiological system" or the universally accepted form of life entails cultural relativization of the system of values which justifies the interpretation decision.[77] It needs to be stressed, however, that the ideology of lawful and rational court decision, as accepted by Wróblewski, posits an absolute postulate of material rationality of the interpreter. This means that according to the postulates of the said ideology, the interpreter may not justify the axiological choices by calling upon any system of values that defines any form of life. The postulate of material rationality of the interpreter, defined by the ideology of lawful and rational court decision, assumes that the only system of values whose inclusion is the absolute duty of the interpreter is the system of internal values of people's law defined by socialist ideology. The system declares a higher form of life, the Communist society, defined by objective laws of historical progress.[78] In consequence, it needs to be accepted that on the grounds of the ideology of lawful and rational court decision, the only "accepted axiological system" may be no other than one dictated by objective laws of social progress, identified at the level of cognitively primary philosophical assumptions of Marxism. Let us add that on the grounds of the ideology of lawful and rational court decision the "extra-legal evaluations and social rules" that are referenced in the hypothetical variant of the functional directive may be included in the scope in which they are consistent with the internal values of people's law, whose inclusion is the absolute duty of the interpreter. This duty is expressed by the categorical form of the directive that commands the drive towards maintaining of the axiological coherence of the system of law in the process of interpreting it.

4 Conclusions

Jerzy Wróblewski's theory of interpretation of law is one that represents a philosophical attitude in which fundamental philosophical assumptions of Marxism are accepted as cognitively primary premises for theoretical activity in jurisprudence. Using the author's terminology, the relation between Wróblewski's theory of interpretation and the fundamental assumptions of Marxism is that

77 Ibid., p. 18.

78 J. Wróblewski, *Zagadnienia...*, pp. 181–182; Cf also ibid., p. 199; cf. also, W. Lang, J. Wróblewski, S. Zawadzki, *Teoria...*, p. 486; cf. also, J. Wróblewski, *Wartości a decyzja sądowa*, pp. 87–93.

of both invocation and attribution. In consequence, the way of perceiving the systemic character of law in Wróblewski's theory of interpretation is prejudged by the adoption of cognitively primary philosophical assumptions of Marxist philosophy. This is so because this theory of interpretation is the theory of interpretation of the people's law. This concept of the people's law is a philosophical category, not an empirical one, that is, the fundamental traits of people's law are defined by cognitively primary philosophical assumptions. This means that the theorems of the theory of interpretation presuppose in the strong semantic sense the existence of people's law as a philosophical category. The existence of people's law is the fundamental ontological presupposition of this type of theory of interpretation. Thus, theoretical theorems are consequences of cognitive primary philosophical assumptions. The relations of logical primacy is one of semantic presupposition which occurs between the existential judgements on social being which is people's law (formulated on the level of philosophical cognition) and theorems on the interpretation of people's law formulated on the level of the legal-theoretical cognition. In the case of the theory of interpretation elaborated here, the assumption of the systemic character of law may be therefore analyzed at the level of cognitively primary philosophical assumptions, as well as at the level of cognitively secondary theorems of the theory of law related to law and interpretation thereof, as well as at the level of interpretation directives defined by these theorems.

Paweł Jabłoński

Towards Post-Analytical Theory of Law. On the Consequences of Richard Rorty's Metaphilosophy

1 Introduction[1]

The goal of this article is to attempt to relate to a general reflection on law of the manner of perceiving philosophy as recommended by Richard Rorty. It attempts to answer the question of what model of philosophy of law can be proposed on the basis of the metaphilosophical position of the author of *Contingency, Irony, and Solidarity*, the most influential American thinker of the second half of the 20th century and the first decade of the current century. As Rorty rarely spoke on the subject of philosophy of law, this endeavor will be based not only on fishing for explicitly stated viewpoints on the matter under scrutiny but also on deriving consequences from the "general" metaphilosophy of the American thinker.[2]

As one of the leading representatives of neopragmatism, Rorty is sometimes also called a "postmodernist," "soft postmodernist," "neopragmatically-oriented ally of postmodermism,"[3] and "postanalytical thinker."[4] Even though there are

1 The Polish version of this essay was previously published in M. Jabłoński, M. Paździora (ed.), "Postanalityczna filozofia prawa," a monographic issue of *Przegląd Prawa i Administracji*, 2015, Vol. 102 pp. 101–120.

2 A similar endeavor was undertaken by Douglas E. Litowitz in his *Postmodern Philosophy and Law* (University Press of Kansas, 1997), devoting a separate chapter to "Rortian jurisprudence." The author focuses primarily on the above-mentioned "fishing out" of Rorty's statements on law and theory of law, performing an interesting critical analysis thereof, while he treats the other areas of the American "classic" as background. Litowitz indicates the two highlights of Rorty's philosophy-of-law viewpoint: critique of formalism and recommendation of Dewey's experimentalism (p. 145). Andrzej Bator undertook an endeavor which is closer to my own intentions, where he makes strong rerefences to Rorty's philosophy, but not so much in the context of legal practice, as the theory of law itself. He, however, focuses chiefly on only one aspect within my area of interest, see A. Bator, "Polityczne interpretacje analitycznej teorii prawa," in: M. Zirk-Sadowski, B. Wojciechowski, T. Bekrycht (eds.), *Integracja zewnętrzna i wewnętrzna nauk prawnych. Cz. 1*, Łódź 2014.

3 J. Kmita, "*Rorty i Putnam wobec relatywizmu kulturowego*," in: A. Szahaj (ed.), *Między pragmatyzmem a postmodernizmem. Wokół filozofii Richarda Rorty'ego*, Toruń 1995, p. 219.

4 See A. Głąb, "Postanalityczność – nowa kategoria?," "*Znak*," May 2007, Vol. 264. As Tomasz Szubka aptly points out, Rorty – despite an opinion of being the most widely

good reasons to call Rorty each of these names, this chapter will portray him in a still slightly different theoretical context, as a thinker who belongs to a broadly understood hermeneutic tradition. While I am not fond of too much devotion to assigning individual authors their specific places on the map of philosophy, I still think that such declarations and decisions may be to some degree useful, since they give clues as to the way of reading texts. Although Rorty's connections with the hermeneutic tradition could be a topic for a thick volume, I will make things brief. Let us point out two aspects.

First, it seems that such an affiliation would not meet Rorty's opposition. The author not only encourages to perform redescriptions of philosophical tradition, but also in an introduction to one of his texts hints that they "should be read as examples of what a group of contemporary Italian philosophers have called weak thought."[5] Referring to "weak thought," he brings up a term which was coined and with some success popularized by an Italian hermeneutist, Gianni Vattimo. In few other places, Rorty describes the recommended form of practicing philosophy simply as "hermeneutical."[6]

Second, this way of perceiving Rorty's achievements is nothing new. For instance, Vattimo lists him among hermeneutic thinkers.[7] He is also cited as a representative of broadly understood hermeneutics by Nicolas Smith, by assigning him the status of a "weak hermeneutist" Smith differentiates between two more forms of hermeneutics: "strong," in which he places Hans-Georg Gadamer, Paul Ricoeur, and Charles Taylor; and deep, in which he positions affiliated philosophers like the "early" Jürgen Habermas.[8] Rorty's proximity to

---

known apostatę and critic of analytical philosophy – found a lot of recognition and sympathy for this tradition till he stopped publishing. He praised it for making it easier to recognize blurry and pretentious thinking – see: R. Rorty, *Achieving Our Country: Leftist Thought in Twentieth Century America*. Cambridge, MA: Harvard University Press, 1998.

5 R. Rorty, *Essays on Heidegger and Others. Philosophical Papers*, Cambridge University Press 1991, II, p. 6. In yet another text, Rorty indicates his closeness to hermeneutic "post-Nietzchean tradition," see R. Rorty, *Philosophy and Social Hope*, London 1999, p. xvi.

6 See, for example, R. Rorty, *Philosophy and the Mirror of Nature*, Princeton.

7 G. Vattimo, *Beyond Interpretation. The Meaning of Hermeneutics for Philosophy*, translated by D. Webb, Stanford 1997.

8 N. H. Smith, *Strong hermeneutics. Contigency and Moral Identity*, London and New York 2002, pp. 10–34. An advantage of Smith's typology is providing the perspective-making room for exhibiting the similarities of the philosophical projects belonging to the "hermeneutical family" and the differences between them.

hermeneutics is also found in Polish literature, such as the monograph on the birth of contemporary hermeneutics by Leszek Kleszcz.[9] The philosopher from Wrocław, while reconstructing the most crucial indicators of widely understood hermeneutical tradition enumerates the following: consciousness of limited and assuming character of thinking bound into historic and linguistic character, putting much attention to the figure of conversation, considering the experienced world a non-reducible basis of reflection, primate of practical attitude over theoretical one.[10] These features, also visible in Rorty's metaphysical project, will play a major role in this attempt of applying the American author's works to philosophy of law.[11]

2 Public Character of Philosophy of Law

One of the major features of Rorty's philosophy is attaching major importance to differentiating between what is public and what is private.[12] This postulate from the liberal tradition translates into the perception of the work of the humanities. In *Contingency, Irony, and Solidarity*, Rorty differentiates two types of books and correspondingly two types of authors.[13] Books of the first type, written by "self-creation thinkers," with some examples being Friedrich Nietzsche and Martin Heidegger, are associated with individual self-development and as such may support becoming one's best version of oneself. They are related to individual decisions and projects that normally do not need – at least in liberal societies – any wide-scale arrangements. All is situated in a more or less intensive

9 L. Kleszcz, *Boczne drogi. Z genealogii filozofii hermeneutycznej*, Wrocław 2004, p. 461. See also: W. Lorenc, *Hermeneutyczne koncepcje człowieka. W kręgu inspiracji Heideggerowskich*, Warsaw 2003, pp. 321–340. An interesting synthetic comparison of Rorty's and Gadamer's philosophy which reveals the similarities and differences can be found in: A. Szahaj, *Ironia i miłość. Neopragmatyzm Richarda Rorty'ego w kontekście sporu o postmodernizm*, Wrocław 2002, pp. 69–73.

10 L. Kleszcz, *Boczne drogi. Z genealogii filozofii hermeneutycznej*, Wrocław 2004, p. 32.

11 Setting aside the complicated metaphilosophical discussion on the relations between the terms "general reflection on law," "theory of law," and "philosophy of law," for the purpose of this text I will adopt the regulating definition according to which the terms are used interchangeably. I address this problem in a different publication (P. Jabłoński, *Polskie spory o rolę filozofii w teorii prawa*, Wrocław 2014) and the relevant subject literaturę may be found there.

12 In Rorty's autobiographical essay "Trotsky and the Wild Orchids" (in: R. Rorty, *Philosophy and Social Hope*) we may trace the personal path of Rorty reaching this idea.

13 R. Rorty, *Contingency, Irony, and Solidarity*, Cambridge 1989, pp. 13–16, 217–225.

sphere of individual meaning-creative personal activity in its varied levels of self-consciousness. Books of the second type, written by "thinkers of justice," with the examples being John Rawls and Jürgen Habermas, are related to widely understood social cooperation. They thematize the effects that private activity has on others as well as social practices and institutions.

Private and public dictionaries are two different universes, constructed with different goals in mind.[14] The goal of the former dictionary is self-creation, while the latter is a tool in social benefit. Similar division can be found in Rorty's another work, *Philosophy as Cultural Politics*,[15] although here he stresses the difference between "projects of individual self-development" and "projects of social cooperation" and he proposes that the paradigmatic example of the latter is law. Let us add further that social cooperation is perceived in a wider meaning, reaching beyond the issues of justice and encompassing the areas of natural sciences.

The chief lesson from the above typology of books and projects, according to Rorty, is a warning of the possibility of blending the two types of discourse, and Rorty considers a situation where an author of a self-creation (individual) project, falls in for the "temptation of attempting to find pubic, political, counterpart to the other, private, search"[16] to be especially undesirable. As he says, "The vocabulary of self-creation is necessarily private, unshared, unsuited to argument. The vocabulary of justice is necessarily public and shared, a medium for argumentative exchange."[17] Nietzsche or Heidegger – as Rorty claims – read as authors of private philosophical endeavors may invoke great awe and provide gripping fruitful read, but read as thinkers of public life become "at best useless and at worst dangerous."[18] Conversely, Habermas or Rawls as participants of public debate on the workings of the society deserve attention, while read as authors that are to inspire private life they will most likely seem bland and boring. The warning not to blend the two types of discourses results not only from esthetics but also from ethics. In general, in the public sphere one has much smaller freedom than in the private sphere, and Rorty sees the fundamental borders in

14 A very good description of this dichotomy that takes into account its evolution – characterized by increasing levels of appreciation of private philosophy – can be found in: M. Kwiek, *Rorty i Lyotard. W labiryntach postmoderny*, Poznań 1994, pp. 54–66.

15 R. Rorty, *Philosophy as Cultural Politics*, in: *Philosophical Papers*, Vol. 4, Cambridge 2007.

16 See R. Rorty, *Moral Identity and Private Autonomy*, Cambridge 1987.

17 R. Rorty, *Contingency, Irony, and Solidarity*, p. xvi.

18 Ibid., p. 68.

the need to protect democratic institutions (in this context he speaks for the primacy of democracy over philosophy)[19] and in the solidarity with others. Here, it is worth mentioning that the said solidarity is not seen as the abstract postulate of identifying with "people as such" which Rorty criticizes, but rather as the attention to social consequences of the activity of various institutions, developed in the societies of the West.

Referring to this division to law, Rorty assigns law – as has been already mentioned and as is rather obvious – to the sphere of social cooperation. It seems that the first postulate related to theory of law can be derived here; that is, expectation that philosophy of law be of public character. More specifically, a philosopher of law ought to differentiate philosophy as their own project from philosophy as activity for the public. Using Wittgenstein's categories, we may say that these are two different games that, although they can inspire one another, ought not to be blended.[20] There seem to be no reasons for private philosophical projects could not be related to law, since they can be related to anything, but we need to differentiate between private practicing of philosophy from practicing of public philosophy reflection in philosophy of law. What would be the features of this publicly practiced philosophy of law? At first, let us mention three that we can call utility, inclusivity, and responsibility.

Utility is understood here as taking into account the functions and the resultant specifics of the social practice of applying law. An important element of Rorty's perspective is taking into account that "social practice needs to block the road of inquiry, halt the regress of interpretations, in order to get something done."[21] Undoubtedly, law is one of the spheres where weighing of arguments and recontextualization performed on different theoretical levels ought to take place on the one hand, but on the other hand, in a suitable moment ought to be cut off. Negotiating this moment in individual situations may be the subject for a fascinating cooperation between a philosopher of law and a representative of a specific jurisprudence or practical legal profession. The acceptance of the indicated need seems to be a necessary element of philosophy of law perceived as "a project of social cooperation." As Rorty writes: "In a liberal society, we do not expect our political behavior amidst other citizens to be romantic or full of

19 R. Rorty, "The Priority of Democracy to Philosophy", in: R. Rorty, *Objectivism, Relativism, and Truth*, Cambridge 1991.

20 See M. Kwiek, "Zdrada we krwi. O sokratejskim charakterze intelektualistów postmodernistycznych," *Czas Kultury*, MarchApril 1992, Vol. 3 (38), p. 42.

21 R. Rorty, *Consequences of Pragmatism. Essays of 1972–1980*, Minneaoplis 1982, p. xli.

ideas – it is to be characterized by a clearly defined and comprehensive character of the market or the courtroom."[22]

Inclusivity is here understood as the drive to utilize such arguments which – adopted – do not amount to the adoption of a defined philosophical concept or a religion. Marek Zirk-Sadowski's remarks are useful in specifying this postulate: he stresses the difference between the theoretical and the practical forces of an argument[23] as well as indicates that he took into account "philosophical costs" when assessing individual projects in general reflection on law.[24] Let us notice that a cost is not something one does not perform, but rather something performed rationally, while preparing the profit and loss sheet, all the time remembering the former need to be justified by the latter. One of the fundamental ways of minimizing philosophical costs could be attempts to transpose the results, worked out on the basis of some specific philosophical tradition, into more inclusive language. Generalizing, we may say that we are not giving up particular arguments, in the philosophical or worldview understanding, but rather that we are reformulating them into the language of public debate, so as they do not cut off of social conversation but rather enrich and enliven it.

The third of the consequences of adopting the general reflection on law as public is taking into account the practical consequences of the promoted ideas. Rorty himself seems to be far distanced from disregarding the influence of philosophers' impact on reality as well as from overrating it. On the one hand, he stresses that philosophy nowadays does not count as the center of culture, but on the other, he grants that ideas sometimes carry real social consequences. For these reasons, although in private projects, "fiery and idiosyncratic errors" may be more educational than "calm and useful truth," in the public space the "calm and useful truth" is preferred. As an example of a philosophical project entering into public issues without due restraint Rorty provides the writings of Michel Foucault. Unilaterality and bias of the analyses of the French thinker, who combines uncovering and dramatizing on the internal threats of liberal society with concealing pro-freedom assets and changes, are the source of disdain not only from Rorty but also such "freedom thinkers" as Michael Walzer, Jürgen Habermas, or Charles Taylor.[25] Rorty recognizing the need of

22 R. Rorty, *Moral Identity and Private Autonomy*, p. 21.

23 M. Zirk-Sadowski, *Wprowadzenie do filozofii prawa*, Zakamycze 2000, pp. 150–151.

24 Marek Zirk-Sadowski's opinion in the discussion as part of the XX Jubileuszowy Zjazd Katedr Teorii i Filozofii Prawa (6–9 September 2012, Łódź).

25 See: R. Rorty, *Moralna tożsamość a prywatna autonomia: przypadek Foucaulta*; Ch. Taylor, *Foucault o wolności i prawdzie*; M. Walzer, *Samotna polityka Michela Foucaulta* –

specific reserve in the discourse on public matters is also visible in his critique of Jean-François Lyotard. The American philosopher blames the author of *The Postmodern Condition* with carelessness on interpreting social-political processes,[26] expanding the reservations to a large part of contemporary French philosophy, and – in consequence – with trying to "make philosophical hay out of current events."[27] which does not invoke trust. Yet, another charge that Rorty puts forward to the same circle, related to the above-mentioned postulate of inclusivity, is lack of care for notional continuity of discourse in public matters. Here, we can read: "We Anglo-Saxons suspect that French philosophy could profit from realizing that adopting a new vocabulary only makes sense if you can say something about the debilities of the old vocabulary for the inside, and can move back and forth, dialectically, between the old and the new vocabulary. It seems to us as if our French colleagues are too willing to find, or make, a linguistic islet and then invite people to move onto it, and not interested enough in building causeways between such islets and the mainland."[28]

3 Philosophy of Law as Conversational Philosophy

Another crucial division of Rorty's perspective is that he distinguishes two types of philosophy which depend on the demands they make. The division results from Rorty's adoption of epistemological and axiological antifoundationalism along the related antirepresentationalism.[29]

According to the first type – typical of the thought of Immanuel Kant – philosophy serves a privileged role in relation to the other areas of culture because all these other areas are founded on it. With this way of thinking, it is a discipline that verifies and grounds their demands.[30] One needs to add that Rorty sees Kant's elevation of philosophy also in many later traditions of thought, including in analytical philosophy.[31] The second approach is characterized by treating

all the texts trans. M. Kwiek, [w:] Idem (ed.), in, „*Nie pytajcie mnie kim jestem…" Michel Foucault dzisiaj*, Poznań 1998. See also: Rorty, *Contingency, Irony, and Solidarity*, p. 61–69.

26 R. Rorty, *Objetivity, Relativism, and Truth*, p. 220.

27 Ibid, p. 221.

28 Ibid., 221.

29 See R. Rorty, *Philosophy and Social Hope*, pp. 23–46. Cf. A. Szahaj, *Ironia i miłość. Neopragmatyzm Richarda Rorty'ego w kontekście sporu o postmodernizm*, Wrocław 2002, p. 15ff.

30 R. Rorty, *Philosophy and the Mirror of Nature*, pp. 3–7.

31 Ibid., p. 8. In this text we can read: "As I see it, the kind of philosophy which stems from Russeli and Frege is, like classical Husserlian phenomenology, simply one more

philosophy as one of many equal cultural activities. It can be said that vertical relations are replaced with horizontal. A philosopher is not situated in the role of cognitively privileged arbiter, competent to judge any fundamental difference of opinions, but rather as a representative of one of fields of culture who can sometimes bring something useful into some discussions. Rorty tells it straight, stating that "philosophy, as a discipline, makes itself ridiculous,"[32] when it claims that it is able to provide a neutral, privileged foundation for solving the problems of other disciplines. In the second approach to philosophy, recommended by the American thinker, the position it develops is therefore only one of the many equal perspectives.[33] Therefore, subject literature aptly notes that "[i]nstead of traditional philosophy, Rorty postulated a hermeneutic approach to cognition, granting the inability to discover absolutely believable, universally binding, objective truths, limiting himself instead to raising the level of discussion and interpretation … Philosophy can still exist, not as cognition and vision, but as voice and conversation, and especially as 'conversation of the humanity.' "[34] Even though philosophy has no privileged status among other areas of culture, in some situations it may be useful.

Conversational character and the resultant weakening of the claims of philosophy of law does not mean abandoning argumentation and convincing. Public philosophy of law, as opposed to private philosophical projects, ought to attempt to influence the course of public affairs. However, the rationale it puts forward do not so much have the status of a domineering proof that reaches to the bottom of the issue, but rather that of a persuasive reason bound in narration.[35] Conversational character of philosophy of law is also excluded by dogmatism, and this is regardless of whether it is of open character or whether it hides under pretenses of objectivism or critique.

---

attempt to put philosophy in the position which Kant wished it to have – that of judging other areas of culture on the basis of its special knowledge of the 'foundations' of these areas. 'Analytic' philosophy is one more variant of Kantian philosophy, a variant marked principally by thinking of rep resentation as linguistic rather than mental, and of philosophy of language rather than 'transcendental critique,' or psychology, as the discipline which exhibits the 'foundations of knowledge.' "

32 R. Rorty, *Contingency, Irony, and Solidarity*, p. 51.

33 See M. Kwiek, *Rorty i Lyotard. W labiryntach postmoderny*, Poznań 1994, pp. 72–74.

34 J. P. Diggins, *Iluzje pragmatyzmu. Modernizm oraz kryzys poznania i autorytetu*, translated by M. Filipczuk, Warsaw 2010, p. 557.

35 The opposition *reason-proof* was adopted from the article by Lech Witkowski, "Przygodność, ironia, solidarność i …? (Ku nowej estetyce pedagogii w

According to Rorty, the main assets of philosophers are their interdisciplinary nature and knowledge of philosophical tradition. Philosophy of law practiced in a conversational style would therefore not much in the way of reaching to some deeper, more fundamental truths, inaccessible directly to other disciplines, but broad view and the resultant easiness of moving between different discourses.[36] A philosopher of law acts here as an interdisciplinary translator, undertaking hermeneutical tasks of stimulating dialogue and integrating different areas of science and culture. The analogy that comes to mind, that of a widely discussed program of internal and external integration of legal sciences, requires pointing out a major difference. Rorty does recommend a way of practicing philosophy that leads to its integration with other areas of culture[37] but this interaction is perceived differently than would result from the mentioned naturalistic program of integration of legal sciences. Specifically, it is not to take the form of constructing a single, large, and durable theory encompassing the whole of phenomena of our interest, but rather be a dialogue that reacts to specific needs that arise "here and now," an act of social cooperation leading to solving or at least clarifying a problem. Philosophy of law in such practice does not try to provide or thematize fundamentals of other disciplines but involves itself in object discussion, representing its own point of view.[38] As Andrzej Bator aptly remarks, when accepting Rorty's approach, the distance between general reflection of law and specific sciences is greatly shortened.[39] Therefore, also the distance between law and legal practice ought to get shorter. Let us make two remarks on the last issue, though.

First, the key moment in this case is major weakening of the claims of one of the sides, based on the acceptance of what has been already defined as a shift from vertical to horizontal perspective. In the dispute with the contemporary

---

post-pedagogice)," in: A. Szahaj (ed.), *Między pragmatyzmem a postmodernizmem. Wokół filozofii Richarda Rorty'ego*, Toruń 1995.

36 See W. Throop, "Neopragmatyzm po piętnastu latach," translated by P. Gutowski and T. Szubka, in: A. Bronk (ed.), *Filozofować dziś. Z badań nad filozofią najnowszą*, Lublin 1995, p. 364.

37 R. Rorty, *Philosophy as Cultural Politics*, pp. 9–10.

38 See A. Bator, "Polityczne interpretacje analitycznej teorii prawa", in: M. Zirk-Sadowski, B. Wojciechowski, T. Bekrycht (eds.), *Integracja zewnętrzna i wewnętrzna nauk prawnych. Cz. 1*, Łódź 2014, p. 25.

39 A. Bator, "Polityczne interpretacje analitycznej teorii prawa," in: M. Zirk-Sadowski, B. Wojciechowski, T. Bekrycht (eds.), *Integracja zewnętrzna i wewnętrzna nauk prawnych. Cz. 1*, Łódź 2014, p. 31.

American philosopher of law, David Luban, Rorty undermines the image of philosophy as something that provides to lawyers the necessary fundament in the process of applying law.[40] In short, the author of *Contingency, Irony, and Solidarity* has no doubt as to the fact that judges ought to be well read and of wide mental horizons but denies that the knowledge of traditional philosophical disputes is of any usefulness to judges in the performance of their daily routines. While writing with high esteem about American court system, Rorty highlights that efficiency and justice of the system depends not on the securing in some theory, but rather on the elemental decency of judges and their courage and readiness to talk. Does it mean, then, that the history of philosophical and theory of the many of law disputes is not needed? Here, we reach the second of the remarks. It seems that the issue of the meaning of philosophical and theory-of-law tradition leads to one of the many breaking points between two social practices, namely, applying law and practicing philosophy of law. Seeing them close to one another does not mean seeing gravity towards identity, but rather closing of the cooperation. In other words, what is not essential in one practice may prove the fundament for the other. As already mentioned, according to Rorty apart from the interdisciplinary character, the most vital feature of a philosophy is the knowledge of the history of widely understood theoretical disputes.

4 "Doing Philosophy Historically"

In the mid-1980s, in Anglo-Saxon literature works on the subject of the idea of "doing philosophy historically" started to appear. They analyze the specifics of scientific approach, different from reconstructing the history of philosophy as well as from "normal" solving of contemporary philosophical problems.[41] There is no agreement as to the details, but the researchers in the field are unanimous in that in the late 20th century, a number of influential philosophical works appeared that escaped the traditional division of reconstructing the history of ideas and practicing philosophy. In his 2009 book, *The Uses of the Past from Heidegger to Rorty. Doing Philosophy Historically*, Robert Piercey, returning to the reflection on doing philosophy historically accentuates Rorty's alignment with the scientific train of thought. Let us take a closer look at what Rorty's involvement of history of thought is based on.

---

40 See R. Rorty: "Pragmatism and Law: A Response to David Luban", in: R. Rorty, *Philosophy and Social Hope.*

41 See R. Piercey, *The Uses of the Past from Heidegger to Rorty. Doing. Philosophy Historically*, Cambridge, Cambridge University Press 2009, pp. 2–5, 9–15.

Indicating the knowledge of philosophical tradition is, according to the American philosopher, the most sensible answer to the question on what a philosopher actually has to offer if he or she does not offer Plato's cognition of "the real world," Husserl's "insight into the essence" or positivist metascience. Let us quote Rorty as he addresses the knowledge of tradition as the actual workshop of a philosopher: "To drop the notion of the philosopher as knowing something about knowing which nobody else knows so well would be to drop the notion that his voice always has an overriding claim on the attention of the other participants in the conversation. It would also be to drop the notion that there is something called 'philosophical method' or 'philosophical technique' or 'the philosophical point of view' which enables the professional philosopher, ex officio, to have interesting views about, say, the respectability of psychoanalysis, the legitimacy of certain dubious laws, the resolution of moral dilemmas, the 'soundness' of schools of historiography or literary criticism, and the like. Philosophers often do have interesting views upon such questions, and their professional training as philosophers is often a necessary condition for their having the views they do. But this is not to say that philosophers have a special kind of knowledge about knowledge (or anything else) from which they draw relevant corollaries. The useful kibitzing they can provide on, the various topics I just mentioned is made possible by their familiarity with the historical background of arguments on similar topics, and, most importantly, by the fact that arguments on such topics are punctuated by stale philosophical cliches which the other participants have stumbled across in their reading, but about which professional philosophers know the pros and cons by heart."[42] In yet another passage we read: "Stories of the history of philosophy belong among the most efficient tools of persuasion that philosophers have at their disposal."[43]

Rorty's recommended method of making use of tradition can be described as adaptive and redescriptive. By adaptability, I understand such use of the history of ideas that it serves current debates. The goal of reaching for tradition is not recreating the ways of thinking of the past, but rather better consideration

42 R. Rorty, *Philosophy and the Mirror of Nature*, p. 392ff.

43 R. Rorty, "Emancypacja naszej kultury," in: J. Niżnik (ed. and translation), *Habermas, Rorty, Kołakowski. Stan filozofii współczesnej*, Warsaw 1996, p. 41. See also, in the same volue: J. Habermas, "Kłopoty z przygodnością: powrót historyzmu" p. 13. Cf. A. Szahaj, *Ironia i miłość. Neopragmatyzm Richarda Rorty'ego w kontekście sporu o postmodernizm*, Wrocław 2002, p. 61.

and clarification of current problems. Application is therefore a valid moment of referencing the inherited achievements. Rorty calls upon a rule coined by Hegel that orders notions be thought of as people – just like the history of an individual allows to better understand their current behavior, so the history of a notion helps to understand its current possibilities and threats.[44] With such an understanding of using the history of thought comes inevitable selectivity. Rorty himself admits to selectively using tradition, relying more on "rational" rather than "historical" reconstruction.[45] For example, encouraging to use Heidegger's works, he references them as "a toolbox containing some splendid things lying next to a lot of outdated junk."[46]

The adaptive character of reaching for tradition comes closely with redescriptivity. If the way of reading is conditioned by specific issues that we are facing, the above-mentioned clarification is of mutual character – the developed tradition allows to reconsider current problems anew, but the current issues also allow to rethink tradition anew. Indicating such historicizing approach to philosophy, Rorty stresses that it is sometimes also called hermeneutic philosophy, whereas "the term 'hermeneutic' signals a shift of interest from what can be gotten right once and for all to what can only be reinterpreted and recontextualized over and over again."[47] A philosopher, drawing on the experience of his discipline tries not to construct a theoretical puzzle which could claim to be able to definitely answer the question of how things are, but rather constructs extending or perspective-reconstructing narrations that can bring something useful into the researched matter. As one of the commentators wrote: "Such redescriptions often take the form of narration on the history of thought in an area, therefore we observe Rorty's susceptibility … to tell stories of how we got to the place we currently are."[48]

Let us note further that this recontextualization of tradition which falls easily into the hermeneutic thinking apart from gains in the form of enriching public

44 R. Rorty, *Philosophy as Cultural Politics*, p. 163. See also: M. Kwiek, *Rorty's Elective Affinities. The New Pragmatism and Postmodern Thought*, Poznań 1996, pp. 159–184.

45 See J. Grygieńć, "Rortiańska nadzieja na lepsze społeczeństwo. Rzecz o zachodniej pysze i pragmatycznej pokorze", in: R. Rorty, *Filozofia a nadzieja na lepsze społeczeństwo*, translated by J. Grygieńć and S. Tokariew, Toruń 2013.

46 R. Rorty, *Philosophy and Social Hope*, p. 192.

47 R. Rorty, *Philosophy as Cultural Politics*, p. 182.

48 W. Throop, "Neopragmatyzm po piętnastu latach" translated by. P. Gutowski and T. Szubka, in: A. Bronk (ed.), *Filozofować dziś. Z badań nad filozofią najnowszą*, Lublin 1995, p. 364.

discourse also play a major autcreation role.[49] The choice of one's own philosophical heroes defines an author's workshop and self-portrait.[50]

The way of historical practicing of philosophy characterized above may bring various doubts. Let us point out two. First, it is very easy to raise claims of discrepancy between the indicated public character of philosophy of law and the resultant postulate of inclusivity on one side and encouraging the application of different philosophical traditions on the other. This issue has been clarified to some degree already, but let us restate that the postulate of inclusivity is not about abandoning the application of different particular sources of inspiration about but the way it is done. We may put it this way: when applying a philosophical tradition for heuristic means, it is worth to attempt to translate the intuitions and developed results into a more inclusive language and search for better support of these activities. When a philosophical tradition is applied to rationalizations, it is good to perform the above-mentioned profit and loss sheet that are the result of exclusive (here: excluding those that do not share the praise of a given philosophical tradition) character of the claim. We also need to remember the weak, conversational status of the philosophy-of-law claim. It bears no demands decree to decree any solution based on allegedly deeper vision but is merely one of the voices in the dispute.

The second doubt is related to the redescriptive approach to tradition. A question arises as to whether such handling of the history of ideas is followed by agreeing to unhampered and disorienting narration, the "academic fantasizing" that Tadeusz Szubka claims is the domain of some of Rorty's commentators but – significantly – not to the author of *Contingency, Irony, and Solidarity.*[51] Optionally, lessening the doubt a little, we may ask whether the redescriptive way of treating philosophy ought to be reserved for private projects instead of being

---

49 Suffice it to recall the figure of the fusion of horizons by H. G. Gadamer; along Gadamer's "conversational" approach to the history of philosophy, which is criticized by many according to P. Dybel, "Wstęp,", in: H.-G. Gadamer, *Teoria, etyka, edukacja. Eseje wybrane*, Warsaw 2008, pp. 8, 16–17; P. Ricoeur's refiguration in his *Czas i opowieść. Tom 1. Intryga i historyczna opowieść*, translated by M. Frankiewicz, Kraków 2008, pp. 98–106; or O. Marquard's "renewing of old buildings in the country of the spirit" in his *Rozstanie z filozofią pierwszych zasad. Studia filozoficzne*, translated by K. Krzemieniowa, Warsaw 1994, pp. 132–133.

50 M. Kwiek examines this more closely: see M. Kwiek, *Rorty i Lyotard. W labiryntach postmoderny*, Poznań 1994, p. 79.

51 T. Szubka, *Neopragmatyzm*, Toruń 2012, p. 10.

realized within public philosophy. While giving a negative answer to this question, I am also providing two arguments to support it.

First, of quasi-empirical character, is more than indicating successfully realized philosophical projects practiced in the redescriptive way, such as the writings of Rorty or authors as Paul Ricoeur, Alasdair MacIntyre, and many others. Let us point out that Rorty, praised by the commentators for his ease of navigating throughout the history of Western thought and contemporary philosophy,[52] thanks to the redescription of the works of Charles Sanders Peirce, William James, and John Dewey, made Americans recall the contents and value of their philosophical achievements as well as revived the seemingly condemned tradition of pragmatism. Selectivity, recontextualizing, reworking was not an attack on the achievements of the past but a way to preserve it.

The second argument refers to the way of reading, indicated at the beginning, that treats Rorty as a representative of the broadly understood hermeneutics. Even though with Rorty the ontological status of the text is weaker than in Gadamer's hermeneutics, both authors preferred similar methods of drawing upon tradition, at least in the aspect that we are discussing here. Gadamer's remarks are educative in this area; they are related to language and they claim that speech ought to avoid two poles, both of which are threats to its sensibility. One is a trap of excessively individualized speech – whoever speaks an incomprehensible, private language, does not speak at all. The other extremity is also dangerous, that is, using a language completely conventionalized in choice of words, syntax, and style.[53] Here, speech is also feigned, or simply hollow. Living language is such that is capable of avoiding either of these threats. Hermeneutic approach to tradition is similar, where the moment of freedom is equally important to the moment of determination. As Gadamer writes: "hermeneutical activity, where comprehension would mean the reconstruction of the primary state would convey a dead sense"[54] so "a text is comprehended only if it is understood in a different way

52 Tadeusz Szubka thus wrote about the author of *Contingency, Irony, and Solidarity*: "Following him, however, is not that easy, as it requires equally in-depth and versatile knowledge of contemporary philosophy as Rorty had at his disposal, both in the analytical and the continental stream; I dare say that in this scope Rorty was the most erudite among the most recognized thinkers of the last century." (T. Szubka, *Neopragmatyzm*, Toruń 2012, pp. 136–137).

53 H. G. Gadamer, *Rozum, słowo, dzieje. Szkice wybrane*, translated by M. Łukasiewicz and K. Michalski, Warsaw 2000, p. 122.

54 H. G. Gadamer, *Prawda i metoda. Zarys hermeneutyki filozoficznej*, translated by B. Baran, Warsaw 2004, p. 243.

each time"[55] which, however, is no agreement to arbitrariness.[56] With Rorty, similarly, encouraging redescription is no agreement to arbitrariness. In reference to private philosophical projects, the area of freedom is wide and its borders seem to be defined only by esthetics (it suffices to mention Rorty's praise of Derrida's refined play with tradition),[57] in public practicing of philosophy the author of *Contingency, Irony, and Solidarity* is much more restrictive – this, however, does not abolish us of the need to redescribe. This restrictive character can be seen in the above-mentioned reservations that Rorty voices towards Foucault and Lyotard.

Setting up a relation of doing philosophy historically and general reflection on law we get an image of a discipline which is deeply rooted in history of philosophy and tradition of the broadly understood theory of law. In the Polish context, this, on the one hand, means reaching towards different philosophical streams, and on the other, enriching the consideration of contemporary legal problems with extensive and inspiring achievements of Polish theory of law – both in the context of pre-war works and later texts.

5 Anti-Scientism

Yet, another aspect of Rorty's metaphilosophical project is anti-scientism. For the purpose of presenting it, I am going to indicate three aspects of the anti-scientism of the said viewpoint: method, scientific character, theory.

The first aspect is overestimating the notion of the method. Rorty indicates the validity of this issue to theory of law.[58] As he highlights, doubts as to the scientific method expand to cover the methodic approach at large which is of high importance in the world of law. At the same time, bearing in mind the relation of pragmatism to legal practice, Rorty ascertains contemporary triviality of the stream, because its associated theorem of informal and unmethodical character of the application of law does not raise any reservations nowadays, according to Rorty. He also claims that, not only with narrow understanding of formalism, defined after Richard A. Posner as the conviction of the answers to legal questions being answerable on the basis of inter-notional connections, but also with the wide understanding it is difficult nowadays to find a "good

55 Ibidem, p. 423.

56 Ibidem, p. 181.

57 R. Rorty, *Contingency, Irony, and Solidarity*, pp. 122–137.

58 R. Rorty, "The Banality of Pragmatism and the Poetry of Justice", in: R. Rorty, *Philosophy and Social Hope*.

formalist" among theoreticians of law. Wide understanding is based on Roberto M. Unger and presents formalism as the theorem of the existence of a specific method of legal justification, different from the argumentation from outside the area of legal disputes.

The second aspect of Rorty's anti-scientism is the overestimation of the scientific character. The author points out that rejecting the fixed border between what is scientific and what is not, deeply rooted in Kuhn's image of science, or rather evidencing its relative character in every case to the society of researchers slightly weakens the dears of science maintaining its character. This does not mean that each method of conducting scientific research is equally sensible and reasonable – Rorty considers tackling some theory-of-law matters, such as the problem of the nature of law, as empty and devoid of goal. Rorty rather tries to say that the claim of the lack of scientific character transposed from the epistemological categories to sociological ones loses some of its weight. The part that remains is related to the requirements of usability, reliability, and social-institutional conditions.

The third aspect is based on the rejection of the postulate of constructing a single large theory as the goal of research practice. Overestimating such formulated theory is associated with the above-mentioned idea of anti-representationalism. It therefore negates the understanding of cognition as reaching towards the natural image of reality. As Rorty says, although there exists an external reality, there is no external, "natural" description thereof. Antirepresentationalism is combined with "replacing the metaphor of reflection with the metaphor of usage"[59] – according to Rorty, cognition and comprehension is rather based on better handling reality rather than mirroring its true image. Constructing theory is therefore replaced with solving actual problems. In other words, the measure of cognition and comprehension lies not in presenting the general image of the whole but referring to a specific situation.[60] We would like to easily tackle the

59 R. Rorty, "Odpowiedź Kołakowskiemu," in: J. Niźnik (ed. and translator), *Habermas, Rorty, Kołakowski: Stan filozofii współczesnej*, Warsaw 1996, p. 84.

60 In order to gain some distance to understanding the goal of doing philosophy as reaching single, unchanging truth or – in other words – to differentiate the true image of reality, Rorty proposes the following thought experiment: "Let's imagine – to change the example – that in a few years we will take an issue of *The New York Times* just to read that philosophers gathered on a congress decided unanimously that values exist objectively, science is rational, and truth is an issue of accordance with reality, etc. Following recent breakthroughs in semantics and metaethics, as we read on, the last remaining opposition to cognitivism in ethics put down their weapons. Analogous achievements

thought of the American philosopher if we were to assume that he is falling into thoughtless relativism or that he is abandoning the usage of the word "truth." As Andrzej Szahaj aptly points out, with favorable interpretation Rorty's point of view needs not be perceived as relativistic but rather as anti-antirelativistic.[61] We are not facing some philosophically novel answer to the question concerning the nature of truth; rather, what we are faced with is the reevaluation and abandoning this question. We are no longer dealing with any – even relativistic – concept of truth, but we are dealing with the negation of the idea of anything in the shape of the concept of truth.[62] As Rorty remarks, philosophers are the only group that requests such a theory, while in everyday context the word "truth" is not a problematic one.

6 Philosophy of Law as Practical Philosophy

We thus reach the last postulate formed towards philosophy of law based on Rorty's perspective, that is, the expectation that it be of practical character. The indicated "practicality" may be opposed to "unpracticality" as well as "theoreticality."

In reference to the first aspect, the mentioned T. Szubka expresses Rorty's metaphilosophical postulate in this way: "Philosophy ought to primarily either be of practical character or be capable of skillfully combining the theoretical dimension with the practical one. It may not, however, serve to satisfy its own esoteric interests by a small group of researchers removed from real life."[63] These words need to be supplemented with one clause according to which the postulate

---

philosophy of science led to Kuhn officially renouncing his belief that there is no way in which, independently of theory, we may interpret claims as to the 'things that are out there.' All the new disfunctionals renounced their earlier beliefs. In order to cover the damages caused by mental havoc from the philosophical circles, philosophers adopted a short, substantial collection of standards of rationality and morality. It is expected that next year's congress will accept a report from a commission who received a task of formulating standards in the scope of esthetic good taste. People would most likely not comment such news with 'We're saved!' but would rather ask 'Who the hell do these philosophers think they are?' " (R. Rorty, *Objectivity, Relativism, and Truth*.

61 A. Szahaj, *Ironia i miłość. Neopragmatyzm Richarda Rorty'ego w kontekście sporu o postmodernizm*, Wrocław 2002, pp. 35–37.

62 See L. Kołakowski, "Uwaga o stanowisku Rorty'ego," in: J. Niźnik (ed.), *Habermas, Rorty, Kołakowski: Stan filozofii współczesnej*, Warsaw 1996, p. 77.

63 T. Szubka, *Neopragmatyzm*, Toruń 2012, p. 288.

is related only to public philosophy, not the private "philosophical laboratory" which is so much valued by Rorty with his liberal and romantic mood.[64]

An important element of the metaphilosophical project of the American thinker is the unwillingness to close humanities in the boundaries of specific scholastics and the resultant excessive professionalization, exhibited by conducting highly complicated specialist debates, results of which are the subject of interest of only the participants.[65] Falling into such form of scholastics in one of the most serious charges that Rorty makes towards analytical philosophy. This remarkable researcher does not call for barbarization of academic philosophy in the name of naïve postulates of truth and easy cognitive accessibility but rather accentuates the need to cooperate with other areas of culture, as well as highlights the necessity of honest evaluation of the real wager of individually conducted disputes. Rorty does not attempt to convince us in favor of "philosophy of acting" which, while abandoning "intellectual puzzle games" would call – just like history has called repeatedly – for replacing reflection with action. Just the opposite – he warns us against exaggerated ambitions and revolutionary character of philosophy when he writes that despite ethical involvement it should not attempt to become the engine of social changes.[66]

---

64 See A. Szahaj, "Między romantyzmem a pragmatyzmem. Richarda Rorty'ego postmodernistyczny humanizm i jego etyczno-polityczne implikacje," in: A. Szahaj (ed.), *Między pragmatyzmem a postmodernizmem. Wokół filozofii Richarda Rorty'ego*, Toruń 1995; M. Kwiek, *Rorty i Lyotard. W labiryntach postmoderny*, Poznań 1994, pp. 70–72; M. Kwiek, *Rorty's Elective Affinities. The New Pragmatism and Postmodern Thought*, Poznań 1996, pp. 238–256. Andrzej Szahaj and Marek Kwiek aptly remark that there are two intertwining trends in Rorty's writing – pragmatic and romantic. The fascinating game played between these two trends does not allow to simply assign the former one to the public sphere and the latter – to the private one. On the issue of the meaning of the romantic trend to the public sphere, see R. Rorty, "The Banality of Pragmatism and the Poetry of Justice". Cf. the comments of: R. A. Posner, *Law, Pragmatism and Democracy*, Harvard Univeristy Press, Cambridge, Massachusetts, London, 2003, pp. 46–49; D. E. Litowitz, *Postmodern Philosophy and Law*, University Press of Kansas, 1997, pp. 145–146. We may, however, risk the weaker claim, namely that in reference to public philosophy Rorty's thought primarily reveals its pragmatic aspect. This occurs for the price of some simplification, as in Rorty's perspective pragmatism permeates romanticism – see R. Rorty, *Philosophy as Cultural Politics*, pp. 27–41.

65 See M. Żardecka-Nowak, *Wspólnota i ironia. Richard Rorty i jego wizja społeczeństwa liberalnego*, Lublin 2003, p. 80.

66 R. Rorty, "Filozofia i przyszłość," *Przegląd Filozoficzny – Nowa Seria*, 1996, R. V, No. 1. See also: R. Rorty, "Putnam a groźba relatywizmu," translated by A. Szahaj, in: A. Szahaj

The second aspect of the postulate of practicality may be extracted in reference to theoreticality. In short, Rorty is reluctant towards practicing philosophy as building a single holistic image of reality in the form of disputing its fundamental rules or constructing new theoretical tiers walked by only the builders. "Somewhere we all know that philosophically sophisticated debate about whether human nature is innately benevolent or innately sadistic, or about the internal dialectic of European history, or about human rights, or objective truth, or the representational function of language, is pretty harmless stuff."[67] What is, therefore, the practical character of public philosophy since it is not to construct the "large" theory? In this context, Rorty relates to solving actual problems and it seems we can distinguish three features of such philosophical work on problems – corresponding with the aspects that have already been discussed in this article. Forst, a public philosopher – hence like a lawyer – ought not to construct problems, but rather to react to problems that praxis encounters.[68] Second, Rorty strongly highlights limiting claims and promises made by philosophy. He states that theoretical reflection can often be of little help not only to solve social problems but also to describe them better. A complicated philosophical dictionary, upon being submitted to "the whole self-deceiving sophism"[69] rarely brings something new that a philosopher would not already have known.[70] Where philosophy is actually useful, its input into social cooperation is mainly based on setting specific matters in focus,[71] for example, through exposing the alternative approaches at our disposal or be revealing the consequences of the adopted solutions, as well as proposing unifying ordering narrations, so important to culture. In Rorty's metaphilosophy, the big theory is replaced with small stories – which I perceive as the third aspect – that draws on

(ed.), *Między pragmatyzmem a postmodernizmem. Wokół filozofii Richarda Rorty'ego*, Toruń 1995, p. 74; M. Żardecka-Nowak, *Wspólnota i ironia. Richard Rorty i jego wizja społeczeństwa liberalnego*, Lublin 2003, p. 81.

67 R. Rorty, *Contingency, Irony, and Solidarity*, p. 183.

68 R. Rorty, "Filozofia i przyszłość," *Przegląd Filozoficzny – Nowa Seria*, 1996, R. V, No. 1, p. 88.

69 R. Rorty, "Filozofia jako nauka, jako metafora i jako polityka," translated by A. Grzeliński and A. Szahaj, in: A. Szahaj (ed.), *Między pragmatyzmem a postmodernizmem. Wokół filozofii Richarda Rorty'ego*, Toruń 1995, p. 35.

70 R. Rorty, "Filozofia jako nauka, jako metafora i jako polityka," translated by A. Grzeliński and A. Szahaj, in: A. Szahaj (ed.), *Między pragmatyzmem a postmodernizmem. Wokół filozofii Richarda Rorty'ego*, Toruń 1995, pp. 35–36.

71 R. Rorty, "Racjonalność i różnica w kulturze: ujęcie pragmatyczne," translated by L. Witkowski, in: A. Szahaj (ed.), *Między pragmatyzmem a postmodernizmem. Wokół filozofii Richarda Rorty'ego*, Toruń 1995, p. 52.

the history of thought to try different possibilities of understanding of contemporary problems and optimizing language which is constantly in shift.[72] Just as philosophy fed on the faith in the possibility of ultimate cognition and description of the ever-changing reality, with Rorty the rationale behind the existence of philosophical reflection is contingency and change. "In free societies, there will always exist a demand for the services of philosophers, because such societies undergo constant change, so old vocabularies get outdated."[73]

7 Final Remarks

Metaphilosophical perspective developed by Rorty provides an image of general reflection of law as a discipline: opposed to private practicing of philosophy, conversation-oriented and antiscience-oriented, drawing upon philosophical and theory-of-law tradition, and focusing on recognizing and undertaking problems of practice rather than on constructing next tiers of theoretical issues.

To sum up my considerations, let us point out two more short remarks on the status of the perspective offered on the basis of Rorty's work. First, it ought to be clear that such considerations cannot and may not replace the proper, subjective, philosophy-of-law work. Rorty, referencing Posner's remark, indicates that the real actual profit from pragmatism's "excursions" towards jurisprudence may be a "change of philosophical outlook"[74] and therefore preparing the ground for the main work. Second, the proposed perspective is nothing but an attempt to develop one of the possible approaches to philosophy of law. Treating Rorty's affiliation to the tradition of so-called "weak thought" seriously, we may quote him as follows: "weak thought … philosophical reflection which does not attempt a radical criticism of contemporary culture, does not attempt to refound or remotivate it, but simply assembles reminders and suggests some interesting possibilities."[75]

---

72 See: R. Rorty, "Filozofia i przyszłość," *Przegląd Filozoficzny – Nowa Seria*, 1996, R. V, No. 1, pp. 88–89, 92; R. Rorty, "Filozofia jako nauka, jako metafora i jako polityka," translated by A. Grzeliński and A. Szahaj, in: A. Szahaj (ed.), *Między pragmatyzmem a postmodernizmem. Wokół filozofii Richarda Rorty'ego*, Toruń 1995, p. 34; M. Żardecka-Nowak, *Wspólnota i ironia. Richard Rorty i jego wizja społeczeństwa liberalnego*, Lublin 2003, pp. 261–264.

73 R. Rorty, "Filozofia i przyszłość," *Przegląd Filozoficzny – Nowa Seria*, 1996, R. V, No. 1, p. 88.

74 R. Rorty, *Philosophy and Social Hope*, p. 228. See also: D. E. Litowitz, *Postmodern Philosophy and Law*, Lawrence, University Press of Kansas, 1997, p. 155.

75 R. Rorty, *Essays on Heidegger and Others. Philosophical Papers*, Cambridge, Cambridge University Press 1991, II, p. 6.

Przemysław Kaczmarek

Legal Culture as Praxis: Towards Interactionalism

1 Legal Culture as Praxis – Why?[1]

Legal culture understood as praxis exposes the category of causative activity of jurists in institutional practice.[2] For what reasons is it advisable to consider legal culture as praxis? To answer this question, I would like to point out three phenomena: organized irresponsibility, anonymity of action, and culture of impunity. They are not the only ones that may serve as a basis to show the potential costs of excluding causation and moral responsibility from activity, but they suffice in illustrating the angle of argumentation in favor of treating legal culture as praxis.

Let us start by invoking the play *Ubu and the Truth Commission* by Jane Taylor and William Kentridge in cooperation with a puppet theater.[3] It focuses on the character of Ubu, a greedy king from Alfred Jarra's *Ubu Roi ou les Polonais* transferred to the time of transformation in the Republic of South Africa. Ubu, who in literature serves as the model of abuse of power, is a representative of Afrikaners who have been just removed from power. As a police officer, he is presented to the Truth and Reconciliation Commission. In order to avoid being punished, he first considers destroying the documents and photographs which can put the blame on him, calling upon the syndrome of stress, and blaming his faults on someone else. Finally, Ubu justifies his action in front of the Commission with his duty and states: "These things were done by those above me, below me,

---

1 This article is an altered version of a text: "Kultura prawnicza jako praxis: o sprawczym działaniu," *Przegląd Prawa i Administracji*, M. Jabłoński, M. Paździora (eds.), 2015, Vol. 102, pp. 85–100.

2 I use the notion of legal culture to denote the activity performed by lawyers within their professional activity. On the differentiation between legal culture and culture of law, see e.g. K. Pałecki: "O użyteczności pojęcia kultura prawna," *Państwo i Prawo* 1973, Vol. 2, p. 74. Culture as praxis is described by Zygmunt Bauman, see *Culture as praxis*, London 2000.

3 After Ewa Dynarowicz, see: "Komisja Prawdy i Pojednania w kulturowym repertuarze nowej RPA: Południowoafrykański dramat po apartheidzie (1996-2002)," in: *Kalejdoskop Afrykański. Problematyka tożsamości w literaturach Afryki przełomu XX-XXI wieku*, R. Diaz-Szmidt, M. Szupejko (eds.), Warsaw 2012, p. 210ff.

beside me. I have been betrayed! I knew nothing."[4] In the last scene of the play, Ubu with his accompanying characters sails away towards the setting sun. Ubu symbolizes both the South African police officers asking for amnesty as well as representatives of the oppressing power.

The play is recalled in subject literature in the context of the critique of the Truth and Reconciliation Commission. The fundamental charge is that of the way of serving justice to those who were responsible for apartheid. Within legal discourse, Scott Veitch formulates a definitely critical opinion towards the Commission.[5] According to Veitch, the image of law as a system that creates responsibility is a mistaken one. It is especially visible in cases of violation of human rights. The analysis of the Scottish philosopher is moving – actions according to law may lead and usually do contribute to human suffering.[6] One of the examples offered by Veitch is the process of transformation in the RSA. The goal of the Truth and Reconciliation Commission was to settle the accounts with the regime of those responsible for apartheid. Many of them, according to Veitch, evaded consequences of their actions as the result of the Commission's work. This was the effect of, for example, legal discourse that shaped methods of activity in an institution that blurs responsibility for the undertaken decision.[7] The reason for which responsibility disperses is, for example, locating it in complex organizational structures. This causes a shift in responsibility from the person – performer of a role to the legal norm.[8] According to Veitch, this practice leads law to produce organized irresponsibility, that is, a situation which disperses responsibility and gives it an impersonal dimension.[9]

Peter Cane formulates similar diagnoses – according to him, the reasons for the working of the mechanism described above can be sought in legal discourse, focusing the attention on responsibility in retrospective understanding.[10] Let

---

4 J. Taylor, W. Kentridge & The Handspring Puppet Company, "Ubu and the Truth Commission 1997," in: *Postcolonial Plays: An Anthology* H. Gilbert (ed.), London 2001, p. 45.

5 S. Veitch, *Law and Irresponsibility: On the Legitimation of Human Suffering*, Routledge Cavendish 2007. See also R. Cover, "Violence and the Word," *The Yale Law School* 1986, Vol. 95, pp. 1601–1629.

6 S. Veitch, *Law and Irresponsibility: On the Legitimation of Human Suffering*, pp. 12–24.

7 Ibidem, pp. 29–34.

8 Ibidem, pp. 85–95.

9 Ibidem, p. 143.

10 P. Cane, *Responsibility in Law and Morality*, Hart Publishing Oxford-Portland Oregon 2002, p. 30.

us recall that responsibility can be assigned two meanings. One of them is retrospective, connected with sanctions, and directed towards the past, while the other is prospective – it exposes moral obligations connected with being responsible for something or someone.[11] Retrospective responsibility bears negative character, while prospective responsibility is positive and directed towards the future. According to the Australian researcher, in legal discourse there ought to be place for responsibility in both the retrospective and prospective understanding. On one side, legal responsibility looks back and assumes (potential) prosecution for actions. On the other side, responsibility can be understood as an idea which sets obligations and duties for the future. Arguing in favor of this solution, P. Cane states that associating responsibility only with sanctions "tends to conceal the importance, both within the law and elsewhere, of what I shall call 'prospective responsibility.' "[12]

Peter Cane's viewpoint corresponds with those of Larry May.[13] In her *The Socially Responsive Self. Social Theory and Professional Ethics*, May argues in favor of the thesis that legal institutions become problematic when they reduce the activities of an individual to a common denominator. "What is lost in anonymity is the sense of personal responsibility that will counteract the possible willingness to contribute to harm.… In this respect, we should be suspicious of anonymity of institutions. For anonymous interactions, the face of evil is not easy to identify."[14]

Costs of excluding objectivity from institutional actions may also be traced with the help of what Ryszard Sarkowicz called the culture of impunity.[15] The author describes it thus: "spreading, both in the society and its organs, institutions, and public functionaries the attitude of passivity, silent acceptance or even consent to recurring breaches of law in various aspects of life."[16] Among potential costs of the culture of impunity we may enumerate lack of the feeling of responsibility for the undertaken decisions and lack of respect to law as a system

---

11 J. Filek, *Ontologizacja odpowiedzialności. Analityczne i historyczne wprowadzenie w problematykę*, Kraków 1996.

12 P. Cane, *Responsibility in Law and Morality*, p. 30.

13 L. May, *The Socially Responsive Self. Social Theory and Professional Ethics*, Chicago/London 1996.

14 L. May, *The Socially Responsive Self. Social Theory and Professional Ethics*, pp. 79 and 84.

15 R. Sarkowicz, "Kultura bezkarności" in: *Consul est iuris et patriae defensor. Księga pamiątkowa dedykowana doktorowi Andrzejowi Kremerowi*, F. Longchamps de Béreir, R. Sarkowicz, M. Szpunar (eds.), Warsaw 2012.

16 R. Sarkowicz, *Kultura bezkarności*, p. 343.

in which we act. This remark brings to memory an apt thought formulated by Jerzy Leszczyński, related to the lawyers acting within the system and justifying their decisions as if they were not part of the system.[17] To explain the meaning of the act of forgetting, we will quote a Łódź theoretician of law: "The forgetting is something very important to lawyers' activity: that is, it is a condition for making law positive, and in consequence a condition for lawyers to play their professional roles."[18]

Remembering the social-institutional costs which are revealed by the three above-mentioned phenomena, that is, organized irresponsibility, anonymity of action, and culture of impunity, I am going to present legal culture as a praxis. In order to achieve this, first I am going to use the claims of Zygmunt Bauman presented in his *Culture as praxis* (Section 2). I am going to attempt to refer, with the help of the text, to the jurisprudential discussion of the meaning of legal culture. In the process, I will indicate two interpretations. One of them assumes that Bauman's definitions of culture may be related to the meanings of legal culture as formulated in jurisprudence (Section 3). The second interpretation suggests that individual definitions of legal culture are bound by a category of action and differentiated by ways of performing the research (Section 4). The last accent of the text will be showing culture as praxis in the light of such notions as objectivity, responsibility, and trust (Section 5).

2 Bauman's Culture in Three Types of Discourse

Zygmunt Bauman, when plotting the meaning of culture, states that it is researched as a concept, a structure, and praxis.[19]

Culture as a concept is a collection of norms that serve to differentiate an area of social practice, separate from the remainder of the sphere of social reality. It is also indicated that culture understood as a collection of norms is a communication tool within a given social practice. It is a sort of medium for communication

---

17 J. Leszczyński, *Pozytywizacja prawa w dyskursie dogmatycznym*, Kraków 2010, p. 16.

18 Ibidem.

19 Z. Bauman notes: "Thirty years ago, I tried to disentangle the incoherences evident in the usages of 'culture' through separating three distinct discursive contexts in which the concept was entangled, while drawing different meanings from each of the contexts. I still think that keeping apart the three discourses which offer three related, yet different, meanings to the idea of culture remains a preliminary condition of any attempt to clarify the subject of disagreement, but I no longer believe that this operation will eventually remove the ambivalence which the discourse of culture necessarily contains." See *Culture as praxis*, p. xxii.

among the members of a culture. According to Bauman, culture understood as a concept was introduced "into three separate *univers du discours*. In each of the contexts the term orders a different semantic field ... suggests different sets of cognitive questions and research strategies. Which means that in each case the term, though keeping its form intact, connotes a different concept."[20] The three universes reveal culture as hierarchical, differentiating, and specific.

Culture as a hierarchical concept, according to Bauman, "is so deeply ingrained in the common pre-scientific layer of the Western mentality, that everybody knows it well, though sometimes unreflectively, from his own everyday experience. We admonish a person, who has failed to live up to the group standards, for his 'lack of culture.' "[21] To be sure, such an understanding of culture carries a hidden evaluation with itself, and is conductive to differentiating people between the members of a culture and those that do not belong. This differentiation helps construct the identity of the social group. A similar aspect can be found when considering culture as a differentiating concept. In this understanding, "the term 'culture' is employed to account for the apparent differences ... between communities of people."[22] For this reason, "cultural differentiation is not, conceptually, at odds with the assumption of essential pre-cultural unity"[23] and for this reason we understand it as "a self-contained system of traits which distinguishesone community from another."[24]

We can say that the differentiating approach (similarly to hierarchical one) assumes an image in which culture equips its members with a relatively fixed set of rules. On this foundation, an understanding of the autonomy of one community relative to others is formed.

The specific understanding of culture faces another problem. "The more successive the differential concept [of culture] is in splitting the human scene into a multitude of unrelated, self-sufficient enclaves, the more strongly the need is felt to tackle the problem of the essential unity of mankind."[25] This draws the attention to the dichotomy between "culture" and "nature" as well as exposes the problems of human condition.

When describing the above-mentioned understandings of culture as a notion, Bauman highlights: "If the hierarchical notion of culture puts in the limelight the

20 Z. Bauman, *Culture as praxis*, p. 4.
21 Ibid., p. 5.
22 Ibid., p. 13.
23 Ibid., p. 29.
24 Ibid., p. 26.
25 Ibid., p. 29.

opposition between 'refined' and 'coarse' ways to live as well as the educational bridge between them; if the differential notion of culture is an offspring of, and a bolstering to, concern with the countless and endlessly multipliable oppositions between the ways of lifes of various human groups, the generic notion is construed around the dichotomy the human and the natural world … The generic concept is about the attributes which unite mankind in the way of distinguishing them from everything else."[26]

The second understanding presents culture as a structure. Bauman makes this distinction on the grounds of factual relations in social practice. These relations are determined by a structure that the Polish sociologist understands as a relatively fixed and ordered set of interconnected rules. "The structure sought by the structuralist understanding of culture is the set of generative rules, historically selected by the human species, governing simultaneously the mental and practical activity of the human individual viewed as an epistemic being, and the range of possibilities in which this activity can operate. Since this set of rules precipitates into social structures, it appears to the individual as transcendental law-like necessity."[27] Construed in this way, structure will ensure the state of order and communication within a set of elements.

The third understanding sees culture as praxis. This proposition does not do away with the structural dimension as one that influences the actions of an individual but abandons the structuralist notion which underestimates the individual dimension.[28] Culture as a praxis is characterized by drawing attention to the concept of action and the personality of a person who participates in social practice. In this context, Bauman observes that "contrary … to Durkheim's absolutization of the community, communal praxis would hardly be possible were not human beings, as members of the human species, capable of producing creatively potent communities."[29]

If I am reading Bauman right, culture as a notion requires the differentiation between social practice and other public traits of human activity. Presenting culture as a hierarchic, chronological, and differentiating notion, we may answer the question of who is the participant of culture and indicate the rules that are binding within this culture. Such an approach to culture has a sort of "differentiating power" for distinguishing one culture from another, participants of culture from those that do not belong. On the other side, culture as structure and praxis

26 Ibid., pp. 29–30.
27 Ibid., p. 30.
28 Ibid., p. 94.
29 Ibid., p. 95.

describes the way humans act within culture. In both these approaches, attention is paid to the character of the relation between the culture and the individual – with, however, different views on it. In one case, the notion of structure defines the way of participating in culture, in the other, this activity is seen in the light of both the structural and subjective factors.

The three definitions of culture, according to Bauman, thematize the following aspects, respectively:

1) cultural rules that are means of communication and are to ensure autonomy towards other social practices;
2) structure that equips the participants of a social practice with a relatively fixed set of rules of ontological and epistemological character;
3) interactions of the subject in institutional structure as well as self-awareness of the individual as the participant of the interactions.

3 Legal Culture from the Perspective of Zygmunt Bauman

I would like to relate the three meanings assigned to culture to the Polish jurisprudence's considerations of legal culture. This can be justified with a diagnosis of Włodzimierz Gromski: "Increasingly frequent reaching for the notion of legal culture in the deliberations on jurisprudence does not mean that we are facing a singular, commonly accepted way of comprehending it. It is just the opposite, difficulties of jurisprudence and other sciences that use the notion of legal culture with exactly this notion resemble to a high degree the above-mentioned difficulties with the way culture in general ought to be viewed."[30] Bearing this in mind, we will attempt to look at legal culture in the light of the three understandings of culture.

According to Sławomira Wronkowska, legal culture "relates to the commonly accepted within a community, especially a legal community, set of beliefs what law should be like, what goals it is to serve, etc. – how it ought to be created, interpreted, and applied. The beliefs are accompanied by a set of systematized rules and directives that indicate how the goals of law are to be reached and what methods are to be abandoned in reaching the goals of law."[31] Similar understanding, related to the normative concept, is proposed by Maria

30 W. Gromski, *Autonomia i instrumentalny charakter prawa*, Wrocław 2000, p. 49. Similar remarks can be found in Maria Borucka-Arctowa, see "Kultura prawna na tle myśli filozoficznej i społecznej o kulturze," *Studia Prawnicze* 2002, Vol. 1, p. 5ff.

31 S. Wronkowska, "O stanowieniu i ogłaszaniu prawa oraz o kulturze prawnej," *Państwo i Prawo* 2007, Vol. 4, p. 9.

Borucka-Arctowa, defining legal culture as "a set of norms and the resultant values accepted and adopted as models for those who perform the so-called legal professions … as well as lawyers employed in public administration – those whose views and activity are of special importance to the application of law."[32]

Understanding legal culture – as a set of rules and values – can be interpreted as a form of communication competence.[33] Tomasz Gizbert-Studnicki, describing this notion, says: "communication competence in the area of legal texts is composed of not only the knowledge of specified types of rules but also the skill of practical application thereof … Sometimes the necessary condition of the skills … is possessing specific subject knowledge. The subject knowledge in this case encompasses e.g. the knowledge of the system of values adopted by the lawmaker or accepted by the community subject to the given system of law, knowledge of the general shape of legal regulation, knowledge of social facts, processes and regularities, etc."[34]

Acquiring communication competences entails equipping the members of the institution with something that T. Gizbert-Studnicki describes as an interpretation paradigm through which he means "currently acceptable within the legal culture set of models of interpretation activities."[35] "The existence of the interpretation paradigm is evident in some interpretations and inference directives are commonly accepted and applied … as well as in common acceptance of specific values and beliefs that are the basis for the application of these interpretation directives … The existence of the interpretation paradigm is sign of acceptance within the legal culture of some common set of beliefs and values."[36]

The presented understanding of legal culture is characterized by the sort of "differentiating power" that differentiates legal practice from other areas of human activity. This property may be viewed from subjective as well as objective angle. On the one hand, the presented definition of legal culture answers the question of who participates in it (subject aspect) and on the other assumes some common object knowledge. Using this understanding of legal culture, we expose

32 M. Borucka-Arctowa, *Kultura prawna na tle myśli filozoficznej i społecznej o kulturze*, p. 18.

33 T. Gizbert-Studnicki, "Język prawny z perspektywy socjolingwistycznej," *Zeszyty Naukowe Uniwersytetu Jagiellońskiego DCCLXXVII. Prace z nauk politycznych, zeszyt 26*, Warsaw-Kraków 1986, p. 114.

34 T. Gizbert-Studnicki, *Język prawny z perspektywy socjolingwistycznej*, p. 114.

35 T. Gizbert-Studnicki, *Wieloznaczność leksykalna w interpretacji prawniczej*, Kraków 1978, p. 11.

36 T. Gizbert-Studnicki, *Język prawny z perspektywy socjolingwistycznej*, p. 89.

the problem of (1) communication between a lawyer, judges and a layman, between lawyers, judges and the society, (2) communication competence in the area of understanding legal texts. Developing of the interpretation paradigm as an element of legal culture can be assigned repair and protective functions.[37] The former relies on correcting "errors made by the lawmaker."[38] It is realized through exegesis rules whose role is not really the description of law, but rather optimization thereof.[39] In turn, when referencing the protective function, we draw attention to legal culture as the factor shaping the law. The mentioned functions may be supplemented with further two: integrating and relieving. Legal culture assists in the construction of common rules, standards of acting that can be referenced to the process of interpreting a legal text and solving moral dilemmas in professional activity. The last dimension, especially present in professional ethics codes, also serves a relieving function. Legal culture, relieving the lawyer and the judge from deciding moral dilemmas, at the same time facilitates integrity understood as shaping common standards of activity.

Apart from the presented definition of legal culture, we may also distinguish such an understanding of this notion in jurisprudence that highlights the role of a lawyer and judge, the way a lawyer and judge participates in culture. In this area, the researched matter is the position of a lawyer and judge in an institutional structure that may be plotted using the notion of objectivity in structural and subjective understandings. Exposing of the first term is of key importance in researching culture as structure, however, in terms of culture as praxis an important aspect is to notice subjective agency and the (prospective) responsibility of the performer of a role for his actions.

The meaning of legal culture as a structure also seems to have found its place in Artur Kozak's writings.[40] Legal practice is founded on culture which is to secure solid ontology of law.[41] This is one of the key ideas of juriscentric model of legal practice, the research project of the described author. In describing this project, let us quote A. Kozak: "In truth, the subject exists in institutions (and only to the degree allowed by the institutions) while institutions manifest their existence

37 Qtd. after Sławomira Wronkowska, see *O stanowieniu i ogłaszaniu prawa oraz o kulturze prawnej*, pp. 9–10.

38 S. Wronkowska, *O stanowieniu i ogłaszaniu prawa oraz o kulturze prawnej*, p. 9.

39 Z. Pulka, "Prawoznawstwo: opis czy optymalizacja prawa?" *Przegląd Prawa i Administracji*, Vol. XLIII, Wrocław 2000, p. 84ff.

40 A. Kozak, *Granice prawniczej władzy dyskrecjonalnej*, Wrocław 2002, pp. 162–166.

41 A. Kozak, *Myślenie analityczne w nauce prawa i praktyce prawniczej*, prepared for print by M. Pichlak, introduction by A. Bator, Wrocław 2010, Part 2, Chapter 1.

through what we have grown to call the subject."[42] "This whole reality, including the perceiving subject, is a result of the functionally specialized social institutions that have lasted for centuries and reproduce in the mechanism of socialization."[43] Similarly to the understanding of culture as structure, in juriscentrism we also are facing the exposition of ontological and epistemological problematics.

In turn, the understanding of culture in the light of subjective agency may be referred to the considerations of Marek Zirk-Sadowski related to the three models of lawyers' participation in culture.[44] Presenting the way of this participation, let us quote the viewpoint of Marek Zirk-Sadowski: "Participating in culture is … a relation between an acting subject and the normative patterns of behavior … the relation can be based on purely 'instinctive,' 'mechanical' application of the patterns, and on the other hand – on fully conscious application, interpretation or even creation of the said patterns."[45]

Zirk-Sadowski's recommended model of participating in culture allows to plot the role of lawyers and judges in the following ways: positivist (in two versions: primary and refined) and hermeneutic. Abandoning the positivist approach in favor of hermeneutic is accompanied by exposing the creative aspect of human activity. Institutional structure ceases to play the role of an external factor in reference to the subject, and instead becomes a framework within which the interactions may be assigned productive and reproductive meaning.

Using the proposal of Zygmunt Bauman, which plotted culture within three frameworks of discourse, we may distinguish two methods of researching legal culture within Polish jurisprudence. The first one presents legal culture as a form of communication competence, encompassing, for example, knowledge of and possibility of applying interpretational directives. The second sees legal culture in the perspective of jurists participating in culture. In the former case, we look at legal culture as a set of rules which create an interpretation paradigm, in the latter the presenting of the role of a lawyer within the institutional structure becomes of key importance.

---

42 A. Kozak, "Trzy modele praktyki prawniczej" in: *Studia z filozofii prawa, S 2*, J. Stelmach (ed.), Kraków 2003, p. 146.

43 A. Kozak, "Homeostaza prawa," in: *Z zagadnień teorii i filozofii prawa. Autonomia prawa ze stanowiska teorii i filozofii prawa*, J. Helios (ed.), Wrocław 2003. p. 147.

44 M. Zirk-Sadowski, *Prawo a uczestniczenie w kulturze*, Łódź 1998, Chapters 3 and 5; M. Zirk-Sadowski, "Wykładnia prawa a wspólnoty sędziów," in: *W poszukiwaniu dobra wspólnego. Księga jubileuszowa Profesora Macieja Zielińskiego*, A. Choduń, S. Czepita (eds.), Szczecin 2010, p. 78ff.

45 M. Zirk-Sadowski, *Prawo a uczestniczenie w kulturze*, p. 36.

4 Legal Culture: Analytical, Structural, and Interaction Understandings

The above-mentioned legal culture research in Polish jurisprudence may be perceived from the perspective of the category of agency in its analytical, structural-functional, and interaction understandings.[46] These correspond to three understandings of culture, according to Z. Bauman.

Analytical approach is conducted largely under the influence of Ludwig Wittgenstein, from the time of his *Philosophical Investigations* as well as of John L. Austin. Both authors centralize the category of acting. For Austin, the key thought states that each language utterance is an action.[47] This position combines language with acting, which is highlighted by the follower of Austin's line of thought, John R. Searle. In turn, Wittgenstein extrapolates the category of acting in the notion of a linguistic game. Speaking is acting, and the understanding of the act requires taking into account the situational context.[48] This leads Wittgenstein to perceiving language as a "form of life" which comprises the sets of practice of a given language community. In legal discourse, this is highlighted by Tomasz Gizbert-Studnicki when he relates the issue of understanding of legal texts: "Situational context is therefore assigned to utterances, understood as parole act results, i.e. individualized acts of language use."[49]

Category of acting is also thematized in the theory of acts of speech.[50] According to Austin, the use of language is a form of action. We may observe this in the locutive act (uttering a sentence with specified meaning), illocutive act (making a declaration, a promise), and perlocutive act (exerting influence by the author of the utterance over his audience). Analytical approach puts the

46 A. Giddens links agency to praxis, see: *New Rules of Sociological Method: A Positive Critique of Interpretative Sociologies*, London 1993 (1976), p. 81.

47 See J. L. Austin, *How to Do Things with Words*, Cambridge 1962.

48 T. Gizbert-Studnicki, "Język prawny a obraz świata," in: *Prawo w zmieniającym się społeczeństwie*, lead editor G. Skąpska, Toruń 2000. See also: M. Paździora, "Uprzywilejowanie praktyki, czyli o tzw. zwrocie praktycznym w teorii i jego konsekwencjach," in: *Z zagadnień teorii i filozofii prawa. Ponowoczesność*, M. Błachut (ed.), Wrocław 2007, pp. 188–193.

49 T. Gizbert-Studnicki, *Język prawny z perspektywy socjolingwistycznej*, pp. 43–44.

50 See T. Gizbert-Studnicki, "Język prawny a obraz świata," in: *Prawo w zmieniającym się społeczeństwie*, pp. 158–160; M. Matczak, *Summa Iniuria. O błędzie formalizmu w stosowaniu prawa*, Warsaw 2007, pp. 97–110; A. Bator, *Użycie normy prawnej w regulacji stosunków gospodarczych*, Wrocław 2000, Section 3.3; S. Czepita, *Reguły konstytutywne a zagadnienia prawoznawstwa*, Szczecin 1996.

language in the place of the object of reflection, and in case of legal practice this will be legal language and language of law. For the analytical approach, the undertaking of problematics of the communication dimension is also characteristic. This aspect is associated with the research stream in its analytical approach that is related to sociolinguistics.[51]

The functional-structural approach exposes the meaning of structure as a constraining frame for agency.[52] Here, culture is understood as a system. This is expressed by presenting culture as providing of the acting subject with a relatively fixed set of rules which direct their action and structure the system of comprehending reality. In the described approach, we may differentiate two streams which reduce culture to the language dimension and social structure. The first reaches towards structural linguistics as presented by Ferdinand de Saussure and Roman Jakobson, subsequently developed by Roland Barthes. The latter stream draws from the sociology of Émile Durkheim and Talcott Parsons.[53] According to Patrick Baert and Filipe Carreira da Silva, the first stream focuses on the role of language, language utterances. Culture is understood as a system of signs. The latter stream highlights the "way social structures impose on one another and exert influence on causality. Social structures are treated as limiting because they shape the actions or thoughts of people and that it is difficult, if at all possible, for one person to reshape these structures."[54]

Despite there being differences between the two streams, we can point out their common features.[55] The first is the adoption of a holistic point of view which entails that "the various parts of the system should not be investigated independently of each other."[56] The holistic theory suggests that "the meaning of signs, concepts or practices depends on the broader structure or context in

51 A. Bator, "Analityczna teoria prawa," in: *Wprowadzenie do nauk prawnych. Leksykon tematyczny*, A. Bator (ed.), Warsaw 2012, p. 13. Andrzej Bator writes more on the subject in: "Polityczne interpretacje analitycznej teorii prawa," in: *Jurysprudencja. Integracja zewnętrzna i wewnętrzna nauk prawnych, cz. I*, 2014, Vol 2, p. 20ff.

52 P. Baert, F. Carreira da Silva, *Social Theory in the Twentieth Century and Beyond*, London 2010 (1998), p. 66.

53 P. Baert, F. Carreira da Silva, *Social Theory in the Twentieth Century and Beyond* p. 12.

54 Ibidem p. 23.

55 Ibidem p. 12.

56 Ibidem p. 12.

which they are embedded."[57] This means that the understanding of an utterance depends on the situational context. According to de Saussure, language is to be perceived as a structure, within which the meaning of notions depends on the connections between the individual elements of the structure. Durkheim assigns a similar meaning to the notion of social structure which, as a social fact, shapes the individual. The price paid for objectivity is the elimination of the subjective dimension, in the form of emotions, intentions, or desires of an individual. The second common feature of the structuralist stream is assigning primacy to the things that are unchanged, objective, and putting the ephemeral and subjective in the background. This stability is to be provided by social structures that are composed of a plethora of elements with their interrelations. The third feature is the explanation of things, actions of individuals through a deeper layer of reality, offered by structures (in the linguistic or social form). The fourth feature is looking at social structures and seeing limitations for individual actions. This means the acceptance of a belief that "people's actions and thoughts are heavily constrained and determined by underlying structures."[58]

Interaction approach proposes to abandon the depiction of action as something conditioned by the category of a system or structure. Instead, it researches interactions between individuals. Action is described with the use of intersubjective categories, also taking into account the individual factor – both in reference to the acting subject and to the situational context in which action is performed. This is why the category of agency encompasses the structural dimension but also the subjective one. This means that the factor that shapes the way of acting and the undertaken actions is not only the institutional structure but that it is also vital who participates in the structure. Also, the understanding of legal culture allows to assign a double meaning to actions: systemic (reproductive) and subjective. It is also worth highlighting here that interactionism not only focuses on the problem of interaction, the situation of action, but also the self-awareness of the acting subject.

These approaches: analytical, structural (structural-functional), and interactive, may be seen as individual types of research that reveal a different aspect of social agency of lawyers: participating in culture.

---

57 P. Baert, F. Carreira da Silva, *Social Theory in the Twentieth Century and Beyond*, p. 12–13

58 P. Baert, F. Carreira da Silva, *Social Theory in the Twentieth Century and Beyond*, p. 14.

5 Legal Culture as Praxis: Subjectivity, Responsibility, Trust, Historicity

I would like to describe legal culture as praxis using the notions of subjectivity, responsibility, trust, and historicity.[59] To justify these choices, I will use three arguments. First, from among the phenomena presented in the first section that marginalize responsibility and subjectivity we can derive an argument in favor of shaping legal practice in the light of the presented notions. Second, interaction understanding of legal culture allows to discuss the relations between an individual and an institution not only in the context of the individual's retaining their autonomy in the world of the institution but also the consciousness of involvement and the need to expose the axiologically important moments that make the involvement dangerous for the individual and for the functioning of the system. Third, the proposed understanding of legal culture may be related to Piotr Sztompka's project of the culture coming into reality.[60] The Polish sociologist's project is referenced in the legal discourse of Julian Webb and Donald Nicolson.[61] In their *Institutionalising Trust: Ethics and the Responsive Regulation of the Legal Profession*, they introduce the role of the lawyer by adopting, for example, Sztompka's ideas of trust.

The indicated arguments justify the attempt to plot legal culture as praxis in the light of the notions of trust, subjectivity, responsibility, and historicity.

Subject literature often references two types of trust.[62] The first is defined as personal trust and is of interpersonal character. The latter understanding is social trust directed towards institutions acting in the public realm. According to P. Sztompka, the difference between the two mentioned types of trust – personal and social – is not as radical as is commonly presented. In order to justify this claim, the researcher provides the example of trust in social roles: "personal trust towards specific performers of roles does have bearing on the maintaining, strengthening or weakening of positional trust, it may even transform into trust towards an institution as a whole."[63] Using the thoughts of P. Sztompka, we

---

59 Here, I am using the conclusions of the text: "Społeczna rola prawników: odpowiedzialność, podmiotowość, zaufanie," *Filozofia Publiczna i Edukacja Demokratyczna*, 2016, Vol. 5, No. 1, pp. 63–85.

60 P. Sztompka, *Zaufanie. Fundament społeczeństwa*, Kraków 2007, Chapter VI.

61 J. Webb, D. Nicolson, "Institutionalising Trust: Ethics and the Responsive Regulation of the Legal Profession," *Legal Ethics* 1999, Vol. 2, p. 158ff.

62 P. Sztompka, *Zaufanie. Fundament społeczeństwa*, p. 104.

63 Ibid., p. 114.

may say that trust towards legal professions depends both on the condition of institutional practice as well as the attitude of the individuals performing their professional roles.

The presented understanding of legal culture entails subjectivity, both in the structural and the subjective aspects. From the perspective of structural agency, the image of legal culture, for both the lawyers (and judges) and public opinion, is influenced by the condition of the individual institutional practices, for example, professional roles, as well as institutions such as the Constitutional Tribunal or the Ombudsman. Structural agency is to assure a degree of autonomy of legal agency from (a) political practice, (b) morality, in social and individual understanding. In turn, subjective agency is expressed in a thought according to which the shape of law depends also on the human factor, that is, on decision makers. Subjective agency allows to perceive the situational character of agency and at least potential for individuality of the undertaken decision.

Showing the agency of lawyers (and judges) in the institution world through subjectivity has the consequence of revealing the notion of responsibility. If we assume that the actions of an individual may influence the image of legal culture, a question arises on the responsibility of the decision maker. The responsibility can be plotted in the individual as well as the institutional meaning. I am responsible for a decision I make, and this decision in turn may influence the image of law in the public sphere. In jurisprudence, this issue was the subject of interest of Herbert Hart.[64] The notion of the responsibility of the role, proposed by Hart, is reinterpreted by Peter Cane.[65] The Australian philosopher of law presents the responsibility of the role of a lawyer (and judge) in three aspects. The first is protective responsibility which is founded in the retrospective notion of responsibility. The two remaining aspects, productive and preventive responsibility, encompass the prospective approach.[66] Productive responsibility is directed at creating good results, preventive responsibility serves to prevent bad ones. Cane describes the difference between protective and preventive duties by indicating that there is a difference between doing harm to somebody and being responsible for it on the one hand and not taking an action that could prevent someone being hurt on the other.[67] In his proposal, the responsibility of the role is directed towards creating good results, that is, both the productive aspect and

64 H. L. A. Hart, *Punishment and Responsibility. Essays in the Philosophy of Law*, Clarendon Press, Oxford 1968.

65 P. Cane, *Responsibility in Law and Morality*, p. 30.

66 Ibid., p. 31ff.

67 Ibid., pp. 31–32.

the prevention of negative results – in other words the preventive aspect – with the responsibility for the wrought evil or the protective aspect.

Historicity assumes that acting in the light of an institution (with the example being legal practice) is defined by two pillars. The first reveals the notion of continuity which states that the action is bound by fixed factors that influence the way of acting. The notion of change – the second pillar – suggests that the factors undergo transformations through the actions of an individual. Presenting legal culture in the light of the two pillars we may see the process of culture coming into reality. In the perspective of continuity and change, legal culture equips the participants of legal practice with specific standards, which, nevertheless, undergo change through the actions of the lawyers and judges. The action may therefore be assigned the reproductive and subjective dimensions.

From this view, we may derive legal culture as a form of moral bond encompassing the participants of institutional practice. According to the presented view, moral bonds receive the status of a social fact in Émile Durkheim's understanding. Its force depends on: first, the normative character of a given culture –the extent to which it binds the participants of the practice, shaping the framework of the institution's activity – and second, it depends on other social practices that influence the image of legal practice in the public sphere.

Andrzej Bator, Zbigniew Pulka and Adam Sulikowski

Is It the End of the Theory of Law? A View from the Polish Perspective

This question hides a presupposition that there existed something we may call or used to call "(Polish) theory of law" and what seemed to be in a good condition before a new time or new circumstances arose and good existence of theory of law is over or at least is endangered. There is a different possible diagnosis: that maybe theory of law has been touched by the syndrome of crisis from its onset, building programs – at least some of them may result in this conclusion – for which there was no social need. Speaking of need, we primarily look at dogmatics of law and professional legal practice.

The first element of the presupposition – the assumption of the presence of "theory of law" in legal academic practice – could become a subject of debate in itself, and as we know this has already happened. Jerzy Stelmach, when characterizing the founding myth of 19th-century positivist philosophy, wrote, in reference to jurisprudence, about the search for "a method that allows to construct a truly scientific theory of law, free of metaphysics, formulating verifiable theorems."[1] Abandoning earlier, speculative theory of legal philosophy it became an inspiration for the construction of a "scientific" research program for which the legitimization lay in the "theory of law." The founding myth of the philosophy of positivism was well suited to the aspirations of the legal environment. It attempted to make jurisprudence of the time into a science that realized the idea of constructing "a legal method" to serve as the weapon in the fight against the thesis of randomness and intuitiveness of legal reflection (Kirchmann, Hutcheson).[2] Currently, we may ask if we were facing an irrational myth from the very beginning or if this was an expression of sensible expectations which today – maybe temporarily – have fewer supporters.

In positivist philosophy, we may find a second idea, also relevant to theory of law, that of scientific universalism. The rule of universalism demands the identification of a single, primary model for numerous existing scientific practices. Natural sciences that research facts, equipped with specific analytical tools – sets

1 J. Stelmach, "Spór o metodę we współczesnej nauce ogólnej o prawie," in: *Prawo i polityka*. Warsaw 1988, p. 283.

2 See J. Stelmach, B. Brożek, *Metody prawnicze*, Zakamycze 2004, pp. 11–12.

of notions grounded in mathematics or linguistics – have become an inspiring source, also for jurisprudence, of meeting the second expectation, that is, the construction of a singular "theory of law." Doubts arose as to whether the research problems undertaken in jurisprudence has the features of theory in the methodological meaning[3] but also – if this doubts were set aside – if there is reason in a rule that allows empirical and analytical research to be combined within a "singular program."[4] This type of distinction is necessary in itself, but it seems that it is impossible for the natural science model of relation between the object (fact-checking) and constructing of scientific tools of describing and explaining (theory) to be copied into jurisprudence. The role normally assigned to analytical philosophy in natural sciences was openly subsidiary. It did not serve to construct an alternative or even supplementary description of the world apart from that evidenced in empirical sciences – hence, analytical philosophy has never had a research subject of its own. Analytics was of primarily critical character, that is, was a tool for ordering the language of description of facts and discourse within natural sciences.[5] In this respect, jurisprudence shaped in the culture of binding law was closer to linguistics, for which language as a means of communication is of secondary concern. Primarily, it is a specific and relatively autonomous research subject, evoking its own syntactic and semantic problems. Analytical theory of law, therefore, had its own research object – legal language – and only on this ground could it face problems that are typical for analytical philosophy, dictated by the need to order its "own" language. It is therefore difficult to speak of a singular "program" or "research programs" that would be common to the theory of law. If we did so, we would need to treat empirical and analytical theory of law endeavors separately.[6] This is what we want to do in this text.

3 J. Woleński claimed that professional activity practiced within the discipline of "theory of law" has little in common with "scientific theory in the methodological sense" – see J. Woleński, "Możliwe światy teorii prawa," in: *Szkice z teorii prawa i szczegółowych nauk prawnych*, S. Wronkowska, M. Zieliński (eds.), Poznań 1990, pp. 28–29.

4 J. Woleński, "Empiricism, Theory, and Speculation in the General Study of the Law," *Archivum Iuridicum Cracoviense*, 1970, Vol. III, p. 38.

5 "The unity of analytical philosophy is obtained not through its specific subject, because there is none such subject, but through the method of analysis that does not lead to discovering of new truths about the world but rather illuminates what we already know about the world." T. Szubka, *Filozofia analityczna. Koncepcje, metody, ograniczenia*, Wrocław 2009, p. 21.

6 K. Opałek used to separate "empirical theory of law" and "analytical philosophy of law" from "general jurisprudence," noting that in the later period "theory of law recognized the necessity of analytical studies" and nowadays all the terms are blurry in

1 The Naturalist Program in the Humanities and Polish Theory of Law

1. The naturalistic program of practicing social sciences and humanities contained the following postulates:[7]

First, the realm of social phenomena ought to be subject to objective regularities in the degree analogical to that of objective regularities determining the course of natural phenomena. The program of methodological naturalism, however, makes no necessary assumption of ontological naturalism. The thesis stating that social reality follows objective regularities does not mean that these regularities are a specific example of regularities observed in the world of nature.

Second, in the process of cognizing the regularities among humans and societies, it is possible to apply patterns of natural science in the area of cognitive tasks and methods. These are methodological patterns offered by nomological natural sciences, such as physics, whose goal is to formulate and justify theorems called laws of science. A law of science is understood as a non-analytical theorem characterized by generality (no proper names) and empirical understanding (possibility to verify or falsify the theorem by calling upon experience in the form of observational sentences). The goal of social sciences is also to construct scientific theories understood as a systematized set of laws of science and characterized by syntactic coherence – of logical consequences bound by relations – as well as semantic coherence – notions existing in the theorems are mutually definable. Theory is characterized as a set of theorems that can serve the explanatory and prognostic functions. This means that the

---

their meaning, "there is havoc" in their use – see K. Opałek, *Zagadnienia teorii prawa i teorii polityki*, Warsaw 1983, p. 64ff. Finally, Opałek in the quoted work introduces a differentiation of the described matter, relating directly to the division into "analytical and empirical theories of law" – see p. 79 and following. In a yet more obvious way, this division is seen in Z. Ziembiński, whose part of the work "Budowa teorii zjawisk prawnych" is divided into sections on "legal phenomena in their linguistic aspect" and "legal phenomena in their real aspect" – see *Metodologiczne zagadnienia prawoznawstwa*, Warsaw 1974, p. 197ff. This thought can be seen in its strongest form in J. Woleński, who claims that legal empirical research "in the non-metaphorical sense" may appear only in sociology of law (op. cit. pp. 38 and 41).

7 See Z. Pulka, *Struktura poznania filozoficznego w prawoznawstwie*, Wrocław 2004, Chapters 1 and 2.

goal of social sciences is not merely to describe the facts but also to explain and forecast of social phenomena.

Third, the naturalistic option assumes that cognizing social phenomena corresponds in the descriptive version, or ought to correspond in the normative version, to the assumptions of the general model of empirical science. According to this model, scientific cognition is based on axiologically neutral description, explanation and forecasting of objective facts, that is, those that exist objectively, independently of the cognizing subject. In the general model of empirical science, utterances that are sentences are characterized as being true or false in the understanding of the classical definition of truth – coherence of the formulated theorems with the objectively existing extra-linguistic reality. This means the utterances may not be considered binding because of the adopted epistemic or axiological premises. Therefore, we may not for example, justify the binding force of the formulated theorems by calling upon the fact that they were formulated by cognitively privileged subject – one whose ontological status (form of life) predestines then to creating true knowledge according to the epistemic premises. We also may not consider specific utterances as binding as consequence of adopting specific values (assessing utterances) or norms (utterances that state as things should be). In general, we may say that adopting the empirical criteria of validity of knowledge excludes the adoption of specific utterances as true because of the acceptance of other utterances that do not undergo empirical control.

Fourth, in the radical variant the naturalist program assumes that formulating of the laws of nature and scientific theories ought to follow the assumptions of a specific model of empirical science that describes the research practice of natural sciences, that is, inductionist, anti-inductionist or idealist. In the more relaxed variant, the naturalist program requires that the researcher of social phenomena adopts specific research approach that corresponds with the assumptions of the general model of empirical sciences.

Fifth, and finally, the naturalist program assumes that cognition is of practical meaning, that is, it equips the cognizing subject with tools of control over reality. This assumes instrumentation of knowledge as the transferability of the effects of cognition into technical directives. Theoretical cognition is the fundament of practical command of cognized reality.

In Polish general jurisprudence, the program was delivered in the form of psychological and Marxist theory of law.

2. All the elements of the naturalist program can be found in L. Petrażycki's psychological theory of law.[8] In this case, the assumptions of the naturalist program are enriched with the postulate of the creation of adequate theory of legal phenomena. In Petrażycki's understanding, the postulate of the construction of adequate theory is strictly connected with the concept of creating class notions.[9] The class notions, useful in the creation of the adequate theory, need to be created through referencing an objectively existing common feature for the given class of items. It is important that this feature points at a specific difference, that is, being common to all the elements of a given class could help to distinguish it from different classes of objects. Having at our disposal a properly constructed class notion, we can create the adequate theory through formulating theorems pointing at the necessary logical or causal connections that exist between having the specific trait and the remaining features of all the elements of the given class of items.[10] The theory is adequate if it is composed of adequate theorems, that is, in which the class of objects distinguished by specific difference – the subject – is identical to the class of objects for which we assume another feature – the predicate. In other words, "A is B" is adequate if the denotation of A, based on specific difference (subject) is equal to a denotation of B with the use of a different specific difference (predicate). The proper procedure for the identification of the necessary causal connection is elimination induction. We may therefore say that the concept of adequate theory is a variant of the inclusionist model of empirical science.

L. Petrażycki indicates the uselessness of hermeneutic notions created for practical, extra-legal, reasons. In his opinion, such notions are faulty because they either refer to non-homogenous classes, that is, they encompass objects of different specific features (vegetables, meats) or the feature that is to be the specific difference is not objective, that is, its existence is derived as an

8 J. Wróblewski, "Filozofia, metodologia i antypozytywizm prawniczy Leona Petrażyckiego," *Studia Filozoficzne*, 1981, Vol. 5, pp. 15–32.

9 J. Woleński, "Prawdziwość, fałszywość, adekwatność (Na marginesie idei Leona Petrażyckiego)," in: *Prawo i polityka*, A. Bodnar, J. Wiatr, J. Wróblewski (eds.), Warsaw 1988, passim, J. Woleński, "Metodologiczne dążenia Petrażyckiego a współczesna teoria nauki," in: *Z zagadnień teorii prawa i teorii nauki Leona Petrażyckiego*, K. Opałek (ed.), Warsaw 1969, passim.

10 L. Petrażycki, *Wstęp do nauki prawa i moralności*, Warsaw 1959, p. 185, cf. also J. Wróblewski, "Metodologia etyki Leona Petrażyckiego," *Studia Filozoficzne*, 1960, Vol. 2–3, pp. 267–278.

estimate, not a description. According to Petrażycki, the latter situation is characteristic in jurisprudence which uses the name of "law" for practical purposes in reference of the binding norms. The notion of law as "a set of norms that are binding in a state" may not be the basis for the construction of an adequate theory because the feature of binding is not exhibited in a descriptive way, but rather in assessing one. The thesis is in complete accordance with the naturalist postulate of axiological neutrality of cognition in social science. Instead, the author proposes the notion of law as an empirical fact, that is, as ethical emotions of imperative-attributive character.

Petrażycki's adoption of the notion of law as imperative-attributive emotion is connected with radical critique of "law in the legal understanding," that is, the notion of law applied by dogmatics of law. The critique focuses on two issues: (1) the way of comprehending the legal norm, (2) limiting the considerations to only a defined subclass of legal phenomena.

Ad. 1: According to Petrażycki, "legal norm in legal understanding" is a duty-type utterance with a sanction, therefore equipped with a feature of authority described as being binding.[11] It is worth noting here that Petrażycki's "binding" does not denote an objectively existing property but is decided following an evaluation, such as things are judged "good" or "nice." Such understood norm is, according to the author's terminology – a "projective being" or an "emotional phantasm." This means that a norm as an obligatory utterance equipped with a binding feature is an ideal being, non-existent, which arises as the result of projections of actually existing attributive-imperative emotions. The projection is a process of creating illusions which is based on treating what is psychic as an extra-psychic being. In consequence, naïve understanding of things ideal as things real leads the dogmatics of law to identify the binding of the norm with the actual existence thereof. Petrażycki's treating of the norm, free of illusions and realistic, assumes that the norm is the contents of a practical judgment, that is, a judgment that defines the action. A normative utterance of "X ought to behave in the way described by Z" is a form of a practical judgment but it is not a norm. A legal norm, in other words the contents of a practical judgment, is a specific psychic feeling of legal character. This means that a legal norm is a psychic feeling of attributive-imperative character associated with the

11 K. Płeszka, "Dwie koncepcje normy w psychologicznej teorii prawa Leona Petrażyckiego," *Zeszyty Naukowe UJ, Prace z Nauk Politycznych*, 1979, Vol. 12, p. 31ff.

imagining of specific behavior. Since a legal norm is a specific emotion, there are as many legal norms as there are imperative-attributive experiences.[12]

Ad. 2. Critique of "law in legal understanding" apart from the charge of naivity in terms of comprehending the norm encompasses the charge of covering only a fragment of a vast class of legal phenomena with the considerations. This class covers positive law (imperative-attributive emotions associated with the imagining of a normative act) as well as intuitive law (legal experiences that are not accompanied by the imagining of a normative act). The notion of a normative act is very broad and covers not only acts of making the norm by the organs of the state but also the opinions of authorities, constant practice of applying a specific norm, and so on. In consequence, the notion of positive law does not match the notion accepted in dogmatics of law that assumes the existence of only one type of normative facts, which causes the limitation of the area of consideration to only the so-called statutory law. In the area of positive law, Petrażycki speaks not only of statutory law but also common law, law of court practice, as well as other types of positive law in which imperative-attributive emotions are accompanied by the imagining of normative facts as opinions of legal, ethical or religious authorities.[13]

According to Petrażycki's theory, empirical understanding of law as emotion and the thesis of the multitude of normative regularities that make up positive law are accompanied by a concept of social ideal that is an assumption of politics of law. The ideal is understood in two ways, as an ending point of historical evolution or as an axiom of practical reason.[14] In the first case, the thesis of the ongoing ethical progress is treated as an empirical thesis which is to be justified by the observation of the hitherto prevailing course of the evolution process of legal psychics. In the second case, the adoption of the policy is an aprioric assumption. Independent of the justification, such a state of social relations is ideal, therefore, the altruistic attitude ceases to be a moral (imperative) experience and becomes the contents of the universally experienced feelings of legal (imperative-attributive) character. Lawmaking is to facilitate the spontaneous process of ethical progress which drives towards reaching the goal of full socialization of individuals.

12 K. Płeszka, J. Woleński, "Ontologia Leona Petrażyckiego," *Studia Filozoficzne*, 1981, Vol. 5, p. 78.

13 S. Tkacz, "O 'pozytywności' i 'oficjalności' prawa w teorii Leona Petrażyckiego," *Ruch Prawniczy, Ekonomiczny i Socjologiczny*, 2005, Vol. 1, p. 82ff.

14 L. Petrażycki, *Wstęp do nauki polityki prawa*, Warsaw 1968, p. 25.

3. All the elements of the naturalist program can be also found in the Marxist concept of constructing an empirical theory of law. In Polish theory of law, the program was most commonly associated with the idealizing model of empirical sciences.[15] There was an accompanying assumption that since Marxism is an idealizing theory, the theory of law constructed on the fundaments of Marxism ought to match the assumptions of the idealizing model of empirical sciences. Another characteristic assumption was that of ontological complexity of law which on the one hand led to the adoption of a multi-layer program of researching legal phenomena, while on the other hand it brought the postulate of external and internal integration of legal sciences. In consequence, the empirical theory of law constructed on Marxism was to integrate knowledge of law from the logical-linguistic, sociological, psychological, and axiological planes into one logically coherent system of theorems that served not only a descriptive but also an explanatory and prognostic function. The integrating potential of theory of law was associated with the adopting Marxist theory as logically primary.[16]

The only known realization of such a naturalistic program is Stanisław Ehrlich's theory of legal phenomena. By creating an empirical theory of legal phenomena, Ehrlich enriches the logically primary Marxism with his own concept of "social metabolism."[17] This notion denominates transforming information into decisions that, in their form of transformed and integrated information, impact natural-social environment and thus generate new streams of information. The process undergoes the necessary degradation within capitalism in which individual social groups lose their subjectivity, and the society as a whole becomes an object of manipulation by the alienated elites. The process of social development is based on a transition towards a higher form of social being (in socialism) where the degeneration of social metabolism is once and for all overcome.[18] In such comprehended process of social development, the author intertwines his own concept of

15 Z. Ziembiński, *Metodologiczne zagadnienia prawoznawstwa*, Warsaw 1974, pp. 78 and 239, cf. also J. Wróblewski, "Teoria prawa – wielopłaszczyznowa, empiryczna czy socjologiczna," *Studia Metodologiczne*, 1974, Vol. 12, p. 79.

16 K. Opałek, J. Wróblewski, *Prawo, metodologia, filozofia, teoria prawa*, Warsaw 1991, pp. 67–70.

17 S. Ehrlich, *Oblicza pluralizmów*, Warsaw 1985, p. 395; S. Ehrlich, *Dynamika norm*, Warsaw 1988, p. 304.

18 S. Ehrlich, *Władza i interesy. Studium politycznej struktury kapitalizmu*, Warsaw 1974, p. 451.

a norm as a group decision. Norms as decisions are created by the act of undertaking a decision (formulating a normative utterance) as well as the act of performing a decision (fulfilling the normative utterance). Here we see the phenomenon of normative causality where the act of formulating a normative utterance, the undertaking of a decision, is a causative factor that releases the act of fulfilling the utterance, of performing the decision. Combined, the two acts create the norm, that is, their interconnected occurrence is a necessary and satisfactory condition for the emergence of a norm as a group decision.[19] The author strongly objects against the reduction of a norm to normative utterance and, similarly to Petrażycki, charges dogmatics of law with unjustified reductionism. In this case it is not about giving to "phantasms" but about unjustified opposition of duty (normative utterance) and being (fulfilling the normative utterance). Adopting, in accordance with Marxism, that being and duty are united, the author claims that a norm in general and a legal norm in particular can be referenced only after a normative utterance gets heard, that is, has been fulfilled. Otherwise, a normative utterance is only a non-binding declaration of a viewpoint and cannot be considered a norm.[20] In consequence, a norm as a dynamic structure may not be considered statically as a criterion for assessing behaviors because such an approach reduces the norm to a normative utterance. This, in turn, implicates an unjustified separation of being and duty.[21] Let us point out that on the grounds of the presented concept, not fulfilling the normative utterance by the addressee is not an act of violating the norm because in such a situation the norm has not arisen at all. The author strongly highlights that each act of fulfilling the normative utterance creates a norm.[22] This means that there are as many norms as there are individual singular acts of fulfilling normative utterances.

In the case of the concept under scrutiny, seeing a norm as an empirical fact goes hand in hand with the thesis of the multitude and interconnections between the individual normative systems combine to make a singular global information-decision process. Ehrlich considers the fundamental classification to lie in the division of norms into formal and informal that are differentiated according to the criterion of the type of group for whose existence the type of norm is of constitutive importance. The thesis of the

19 S. Ehrlich, *Dynamika norm*, pp. 288–289.
20 Ibid., pp. 86–90; S. Ehrlich, *Norma, grupa, organizacja*, Warsaw 1998, pp. 32–33.
21 S. Ehrlich, *Dynamika...*, p. 96
22 S. Ehrlich, *Norma...*, pp. 37–38.

multitude and interconnections of the individual normative systems that, when combined, make up social metabolism, is yet another argument that justifies the necessity of multi-layer and interdisciplinary research of norms that would integrate the knowledge from different disciplines of jurisprudence and different branches of the humanities.

It is worth mentioning that in the presented concept, the global information-decisive process is an intended one. The goal is either the development of socialism and the fall of capitalism or worldwide peace, that is, the emergence of universal normative order that would guarantee continuity of specific life of humankind in the biological and social meaning.[23] In both cases, lawmaking is to be the fundamental factor introducing rationality in the impulsive course of information-decisive processes and this speed up the reaching of the ideal state of social metabolism.

4. Both the attempts of realizing the naturalist program of creating the empirical theory of law derive from different philosophical premises (philosophical positivism combined with a sort of psychologism on one side, Marxism on the other) both share some similarities. Both are radically critical of the dogmatics of law, which at worst falsifies the image of legal phenomena and at best offers a reductionist image of the said phenomena. Reductionism of dogmatics is to be based not only on treating norms as language utterances but also on the complete omitting the fact of there being a multitude of normative orders within the society. In both cases, understanding law as an empirical fact leads to unlimited multiplication of legal norms – there are as many legal norms as there are specific psychic experiences or fulfilled decisions. Transferring the norm from the sphere of duty to the sphere of being causes the non-emergence of a specific empirical fact (experience or behavior) and does not mean a violation of the norm because in such a case the norm simply does not exist. As a consequence, a norm ceases to be seen as a criterion of assessing of human behavior or – more broadly – as means of social control. In both cases, the naturalist postulate of axiological neutrality of the empirical theory of law is accompanied by axiologically active considerations of the social ideal. It seems the two concepts share one more feature: they are useless in practical legal discourse. This is proven by completely ignoring of the two concepts in specific disciplines of jurisprudence.

23 Ibid., pp. 209–210 and 215–216.

2 Is It a Crisis of Analytical Theory of Law?

Analytical research dominated Polish theory of law which can be explained with a few factors. These can be cultural factors (role of instituted law that influences the understanding of a legal norm as a language utterance). Also, Polish tradition of doing science, including the internally shaped models of viewpoint-neutral science (the influence of the Lviv-Warsaw school – for years the alternative to Marxist theory).[24] Finally, we may mention the issues of logic or the research procedure – the primacy of legal linguistic research as the tool necessary in identifying legal phenomena in their real aspect.[25] The consequence of works related to analytical theory of law dominating in the general science of law was the visible "removal" of empirical research of law from theory of law towards sociology of law. The emancipatory tendencies of each of these perspectives of researching law (in the case of analytical theory of law the impulse from the dogmatics of law was also vital) led in the Polish conditions to the specific appropriation of the term "theory of law" by the stream of analytical research.[26] In this situation, the

---

24 "In Poland, legal positivist [let us add that above all in the so-called refined version – added by the authors] played … the role of a doctrine that in the post-War era protected the education of lawyers against excessive ideologization. Positivism as a method offers the conviction of autonomy of law, its independence from political and economic phenomena. … Positivism, at least in the methodological sense, developed a model of a lawyer that was immediately applicable also within the concept of the state of law." M. Zirk-Sadowski, "Uczestniczenie prawników w kulturze," *Państwo i Prawo*, 2002, Vol. 9, pp. 6–7.

25 As Z. Ziembiński writes, "…it is impossible to consider that anything is a legal phenomenon … without referring what is being said to legal norms of a system in some or other wording. … Research of the real aspect assume in an open or concealed way the reference to decisions what utterances are legal norms of the discussed legal system." Z. Ziembiński, *Problemy podstawowe prawoznawstwa*, Warsaw 1980, pp. 78–79.

26 Z. Ziembiński writes that "in a system of legal sciences which does not possess a leading theory of law that encompasses in its research legal phenomena in their social aspect, there needs to be a place for sociology of law as a separate self-contained science." (*Problemy podstawowe...*, p. 68). It is symptomatic that, for example, Opałek as late as in his *Zagadnienia teorii prawa i teorii polityki* (1983) sets aside long stretches of considerations to empirical questions and directly references the notion of empirical theory of law. In his *Prawo. Metodologia, filozofia, teoria prawa* (1991), however, this notion disappears and the empirical questions are dominated by standard analytical-legal issues. In turn, J. Stelmach and B. Brożek (*Metody prawnicze,* Zakamycze 2004) among the so-called legal methods mention economic analysis of law as the only method which is close to empirical theory of law, describing it in the chapter "Analysis," apart from linguistic analysis (p. 135ff.).

question of the "end" or the "crisis of the theory of law" in consequence of the above-mentioned processes is primarily associated – or at least this is the point of view of the authors of this article – with analytical theory of law. It is in this very area that we may say "there was undoubtedly something like" Polish theory of law. Its excellent philosophical traditions, major scientific breakthroughs have shaped good practices of practicing general science of law for many years. Identified with the major names of the stream (Z. Ziembiński, J. Wróblewski, K. Opałek, W. Lang, J. Woleński), it justifies the claim to have the question in the title of this chapter refer to the achievements of this branch of science of law. Making this reservation which limits the scope of our diagnosis to the analytical stream of Polish theory of law, to some measure we are speaking against the above-mentioned idea of positivist universalism in our legal dimension, that is, against the idea of a "singular theory of law."

The question of the evaluation of the achievements of Polish analytical theory of law – with all the complexity of what can/should be called analyticity or the analytical method[27] and what needs to be omitted here as a necessity – can be simplified and reduced to two perspectives. First is a question on the so-called programs of constructing "theory of legal phenomena" in their legal (linguistic) aspect. Second is a question on the method or methodology of legal research or – in a narrower understanding – legal notion-tools that serve to order the preexistent "legal world" (doctrinal classification of law and legal language, dictated by the requirements of the scientific methodology, extrapolation of the "local" assumptions of the legal language into the realm of linguistics). The first perspective, although this has never been openly exposed, seemed to fill the enlightened idea of solving the problems of natural language by creating a universal language of science modeled after mathematics (Leibniz, Descartes) or physics (Carnap). In this respect, Polish theory of law situated itself closer to the continental stream of analytical philosophy and rarely (more frequently in the later period, influenced by H. L. A. Hart) drawing from the so-called common language school that found the programs of this type rather alien. The first of these perspectives never transcended the borders of enigmatically formulated postulate of "creating the theory of legal phenomena" in their "language aspect."[28]

27 Possible viewpoints are described in detail by J. Stelmach and B. Brożek, op. cit., p. 103ff.

28 Cf. e.g. Z. Ziembiński, *Problemy podstawowe prawoznawstwa*, p. 53. The idea behind Z. Ziembiński's theory of law, understood as scientific discipline, was "to create a theory of legal phenomena – a system of theorems that would register and explain all the notions within existence and transformations of law." Z. Ziembiński constructed

Lack of breakthroughs in the realization of the program was caused primarily by lack of need for this type of research endeavors on the side of specific disciplines of jurisprudence and legal practice.

It seems that the only, albeit a meaningful, exception is in the current multitude of proposals of new normative logics. The multitude of such projects[29] can on one side – taking into account the active character of "scientific life" in this area – serve as proof of the development of research on the formalization of legal language. On the other hand, the inconclusivity of the proposal, lack of mutual coherence, as well as creating more intricate procedures of applying the achievements in the problems of legal norms cause that the idea of simplicity, at the foundation of each formalization, is definitely lost. Each subsequent proposal of a new logic, while solving one of the problems, usually multiplies other problems that in turn open new ways for new projects. Although the academic environment in itself will not complain on this state of affairs and would consider the description of "crisis" a mistaken one, those who expect adequate results in legal practice would probably not share the satisfaction with the current scientific search for the solutions.

Undoubtedly, the need for the analysis of the individual notions of the language of practice and science of law was always evident; this was inspired by the difficulties and doubts arising on the side of the dogmatics of law. Here, however, we need to add that the solutions offered by theory of law were not always enthusiastically acclaimed by specific science communities. The role of theory of law was usually to systematize – to generalize, to conceptualize, mostly including the verification of the intuitively understood cognition – of the notions used by specific disciplines of jurisprudence. The emerging connection of general science of law with its own dogmatics can be seen as proof for the scientific character of analytical theory of law and even as the condition for its social existence.[30] Within this perspective of perceiving theory of law there can

---

methodological foundations that made it possible "to create a theory of legal phenomena." In our opinion, this was not an apragmatic "theory of legal phenomena" ("a set of theorems that would register and explain all the notions within existence and transformations of law") but rather a set of legal research assumptions that could serve to construct such a theory. For these reasons, the achievements of Ziembiński, as well as the whole Poznań school of theory of law, in our opinion ought to be identified with the latter of the above-mentioned perspectives.

29 The list and a short summary can be found in J. Stelmach and B. Brożek, op. cit., Chapter II.

30 "The term analytical philosophy … denotes a philosophy whose practicing is to be closest to practicing specific sciences, i.e. scientific philosophy." – T. Szubka, op. cit.,

be no "research program" – only activity which is to clarify and specify notions, concepts and other ideas formulated in the language of science and in common language, mostly with the use of logic and linguistic tools.

Analytical philosophy is a "typically academic activity that does not make claims for directly impacting social and political life … and is from definition worldview- and politics-neutral."[31] This activity was not meant to serve descriptive means because it was primarily realized by those who "actively practiced philosophy and tried to reform it. For this reason, the term 'analytical philosophy' had from the very onset a normative aspect: it referred to philosophy practiced in a proper way, i.e. obeying the methodological regime and providing the best cognitive results."[32] Following Frege, we could add that the only way to correct thinking was to lead through analysis of the language.[33] This kind of general characteristics in reference to law would only require a clause taking into account a rather complex mutual relation between the practical languages of science and practice, which ought to result in a much more reserved view of practical neutrality of analytical theory of law. In this understanding of legal "analytical philosophy," the reconstructivist analysis program appeared to be especially useful and the results of its application can, as we think, be considered the most representative component of the achievements of Polish analytical theory of law.[34]

In our understanding, the "end" or "crisis" of the general science of law requires the differentiation of the two above-mentioned understandings of

---

p. 26. Lack of own subject for analytical philosophy leads to the conclusion that also analytical theory of law is in fact a methodology of legal research and "subjects" or problems are provided by specific sciences. In this sense, theory of law cannot exist without the existence of specific disciplines of jurisprudence.

31 Ibid., p. 27.

32 Ibid.

33 Gottlob Frege's methodological theorem is, according to M. Dummett, "a fundamental axiom of analytical philosophy" – M. Dummett, *Origins of Analitical Philosophy*, London 1993, p. 128.

34 The identification with this exact role of theory of law is definitely visible in the titles of works of only one author – Z. Ziembiński. The examples are: *O nieporozumieniach dotyczących tzw. "norm zezwalających"*; *O czym mówią prawnicy, gdy mówią o ocenach*, *O zawiłościach związanych z pojmowaniem kompetencji, W sprawie elementarnego wykładu o wykładni*; *Próba uporządkowania podstawowego słownictwa prawniczego*, *O pojmowaniu celu, zadania, roli i funkcji prawa*, etc. The position of the author can be seen in: Z. Ziembiński, "Deskrypcjonistyczna i rekonstrukcjonistyczna analiza języka w prawoznawstwie," *Studia Prawnicze*, 1985, Vol. 3–4. In Polish theory of law, the reconstructionist program had supporters in, for example, J. Woleński and W. Patryas.

analytical theory of law. It seems that the former, aimed at creating "programs" of some universal legal research method that would mirror logic or linguistics, cannot be considered as embodiment of crisis in analytical theory of law. First, there are no breakthroughs that can later be considered in the categories of end or crisis. The idea of the founding fathers of methodological naturalism, of creating a universal language of science, a tool for researching facts that would be free of intuition and randomness – failed, and in the legal microscale was not even attempted. Second, the above-mentioned richness of normative logics is not an adequate point of reference to the poised question because we are not looking at research with the use of logical methods but at the earlier searches for tools that would be appropriate in such analysis. Where legal problems can be at all connected with logical research, the connection is usually based on law and jurisprudence as providers of inspiration and are sources of problematic questions which can even sometimes be impossible to solve on the grounds of classical logic and necessitate the search of some alternative logics.[35] Hence, summoning of the numerous concepts of non-classical logics cannot be seen as realizing some research program in analytical theory of law. It does not seem that there is something more to logic than the conceptualization of legal/theory-of-law intuitions related to the existing or potential legal situations and the elements (norms, acts) that constitute these elements. Contemporary logical dilemmas, even if they are inspired by legal issues, ought to be located in the potential discussion on the "crisis of logic" rather than in the discourse of the theory of law.

It seems that the question of the crisis of legal analytical research in the second of the streams is valid. This stream is an attempt to clarify of the existing individual notions of the language of science and legal practice in the level of general theory of law. The search for a universal – useful in all branches of law and legal disciplines – concept of interpretation of law, a model of a system of law, language construction of a legal norm or legal competence can be seen as typical, successfully realized scientific endeavors which can be currently confronted with questions of their crisis, or at least lowered attractiveness of this type of problems.

Diagnosing of a crisis with lower number of literature references, in this case a weaker utilization of the achievements of "Polish classics" in the literature of the younger generation of theoreticians of law is not yet an argument that would justify the announcement of a crisis, let alone the fall of the theory of law. Apart from scientific "fashion" which is an underestimated factor, although of a temporary

35 See: J. Stelmach, B. Brożek, op. cit., p. 83.

character by definition, what causes the noticeable "regress" of traditional analytical research is a visible pressure from argumentative-communication theories (theories of discourse constructed on the pragmatic aspect of the language) noticeable return of traditional philosophical problems (ontology and axiology of iusnaturalistic concepts) and the nowadays increasingly disregarded influence of postmodern thinking. In other words, in the science of law we are currently largely facing the flow of what the analytical faction of philosophers called speculative philosophy, a reaction to which, as we know, was the 20th-century rapid development of analytical research, also in jurisprudence.

3 First Response to Crisis: "New Philosophy of Law"

The phenomenon of wider opening to speculative philosophy can be easily noticed in the area of institutionally isolated Polish general reflection on law. The reason for the shift in accent can be most likely sought in a number of factors, with the argument of the passing "fashion" most likely to draw our attention. Undoubtedly, the almost universally perceived crisis of scientism is a factor here, especially in the humanistic and social reflection. The influence of scientism was a vital but – what is more important – an external factor for jurisprudence. It invaded the area previously inhabited by other ways of thinking, not being completely capable of undermining the viewpoint established by dogmatics of law within science of law. Scientist theory, the successor of philosophy of law and at the same time its evolutionary, highest, and last link, took it upon itself to serve to build a bridge between the dogmatics of law, insufficiently conscious of the methodological and philosophical problems, and other disciplines. The other disciplines, according to the scientist axioms, were to be intertranslatable and to found the mosaic of reliable knowledge. Dogmatics, in the light of the requirements of the modernistic intellectual climate, situated themselves rhetorically into scientist narration, however, as theory attempted to raise, they had issues related to the compatibility of their scientific practice with the scientist assumptions. In consequence, dogmatic character, deduced from the assumptions of legal positivism in the model, did not match the induced dogmaticity, that is, with what the groups that identified and were identified as dogmaticists considered the essence of their professional functioning.[36] Theory

36 J. Wróblewski also agreed, separating "purely positivistic" tasks of dogmatics with their essential function of constructing, developing, and applying the so-called notional networks in researching law from what they are actually involved in. He indicates that within specific disciplines in jurisprudence also practical aspects of the functioning

seemed to be aware of this, but it did not abandon its mission, seemingly feeding on the conviction of cognitive value of its assumptions. At the same time, philosophical status of the scientist approach, especially in the recent decades, underwent a massive change.

The main stream of changes is connected with the popularization of the thesis stating that science is not Cartesian description of reality but rather a fact of culture which means that "both its method and object ought to be perceived ... as cultural creations attaining the status of 'fixed reality' and 'reliable method' in the process of their forgetting their cultural construction."[37] This leads to a thesis which is profoundly dangerous to scientism and which was aptly worded by an Italian critical philosopher, F. Rossi-Landi: "there is no non-ideological area of reality which could call itself a realistic area: this cannot be the area designated and protected by the epistemological approach established by science founded on perceptory evaluations – what is more, this is one of the typical philosophical ideologies that still circulate the contemporary culture ... There is no science that would provide us with the ultimate guarantees, there is only the positivist myth of such science; what is more, it makes no sense to reference science in the singular"[38] According to many authors, such doubt is immanently inscribed into the modernist ways of thinking which from their definition are critical and constructed, following Kant, on the conditions of the cognition possibilities. The necessity to prove the truth of the assumptions led to their falsification. The local variety of doubt, of the highest importance to jurisprudence, turned out to be undermining of the idealist assumptions of language, inscribed into positivist logic. One of the consequences of philosophic determinations "outside" of the disciplines was "the collapse of the phenomenological concept of the language" which assumed at least the possibility of strict correspondence between language and thinking. An alternative was provided by the hermeneutic and structuralist concepts. Both are based on the assumption of the inadequacy of thinking and language, although the first one states that thinking is by definition richer and inexpressible in language, while the latter – just the opposite – sees the prerequisite and the shaping force of thinking in language. Both

---

of law are described, together with its social and psychic consequences, evaluations of binding law with the extra-systemic criteria, and de lege and de sententia ferenda remarks are made. J. Wróblewski, in: W. Lang, J. Wróblewski, S. Zawadzki, *Teoria państwa i prawa*, Warsaw 1979, p. 12.

37 A. Szahaj, "Postmodernizm a scjentyzm," in: A. Szahaj, *Zniewalająca moc kultury*, Toruń 2004, p. 20.

38 F. Rossi-Landi, "Semiotyka a ideologia," in: A. Nowicki (ed.) *Współczesna...*, p. 161.

also search for alternative categories to traditionally understood language, primarily reaching towards conversation and discourse as well as get involved in the "reference crisis."[39] This crisis, "announced" by the general philosophy carries a destructive potential to dogmatics of law, and in consequence also to theory of law. "Solving definitions and notional problems is a condition for judging further problems within legal interpretation … Within the positivist paradigm of science of law, the system of law is treated as an ontological category – law exists as a system. In consequence, the interpretation of law as a cognitive and descriptive activity ought to be based on the description of the actual meaning of a norm which is considered binding."[40] For legal dogmatics, closer to practice than to theory, and older than scientism, the potential refuge from these problems can be found in the autonomation in regard to the general reflection, combined with the so-called internal point of view.[41] An escape into autonomous "technique" is a typical reaction of the institutional scientific sub-worlds to hazardous changes in the intellectual entourage. Within scientific disciplines, sets of specialist information replace global interpretations. This facilitates maintaining the authority of a discipline "within" and in reference to its immediate environment at a reasonable level, as well as petrifies the "popular positivist consciousness," although at the same time it excludes integration.[42] As A. Peczenik wrote, for years "the faculties of law have been overflowing with the so-called technical lawyers that simply dabble in dogmatics of law on a lower level of abstraction, devoid of deeper reflection … They are right. Reflection made by the 1950s philosophers representing the main stream would mean the inevitable end of dogmatics."[43]

Theoretical reflection over this type of phenomena found itself in a peculiar situation. On the one hand, relations of cooperation developed with the dogmaticists require the adjustment to the dogmatic way of speaking, which

39 A. Kozak, "Dylematy prawniczej dyskrecjonalności. Między ideologią polityki a teorią prawa," *Proceedings of the Zjazd Katedr Teorii i Filozofii Prawa*, Warsaw, September 2008, p. 4.

40 Z. Pulka, "Interpretacja prawnicza jako rodzaj interpretacji filozoficznej," in: M. Błachut (ed.), *Z zagadnień teorii i filozofii prawa, Ponowoczesność*, Wrocław 2007, pp. 126–127.

41 "It is a way of thinking thanks to which powers attained in accordance with the law are for us equally real to horses or dogs." – A. Kozak, *Pojmowanie prawa w teorii wykładni*, Wrocław 1997, p. 59.

42 J. Habermas, "Na czym polega dziś kryzys?," in: J. Habermas, *Teoria praktyka*, Warsaw 1983, p. 471.

43 A. Peczenik, *Koherencyjna teoria argumentacji prawniczej*, text available at http://szczecin.ivr2003.net

in consequence results in the necessity to ignore the fluctuating general philosophical environment, very inconvenient to dogmatics. On the other hand, the tradition of general reflection on law which, prior to the triumph of scientism, was openly philosophical and was not able to cut their ties with philosophy, inspires to change our optics and tackle different problems. This, in practice, equals to the removal of oneself from the dogmatics situated in the mainstream of jurisprudence. In these conditions, a specific partition of the discipline is possible – into two sub-worlds which, referring to the popular concept of Teubner and Luhmann, can be called autopoietic and allopoietic, where the specific differentiating factor of poiesis is law. The first sub-world, in the name of remaining in the jurisprudence mainstream, is forced on occasion to ignore philosophy, which is expressed through spectacular silence on general issues such as the status of own theorems, concept of the language at the foundation of the individual concepts, ideological and axiological assumptions. The reflection of the first stream limits itself to formulating theories of at most "mid-range." Some time ago, S. Kaźmierczyk put it aptly when he said that such matters as the theory of a norm or concepts of interpretation were transferred from "theory of law" to "introduction to sciences of law"; L. Morawski described the phenomenon with the use of the metaphor of a bookkeeping theory. Such theory feeds on and legitimizes through requirements from dogmatics, sometimes assuming the shape of a "dogmatics of hard cases" – a resource reached for by the more reflexive dogmaticists if their discipline-specific set of instruments is not sufficient to handle a specific problem. The other stream, valuing "general reflection" over the need of unity with the jurisprudence mainstream moves away from jurisprudence towards general philosophy. It attempts to describe legal problems in the language of philosophy, discarding "theoreticity." It becomes gradually less analytical because contemporary philosophy is also becoming less analytical. The representatives of the second stream find common language with philosophers much easier than dogmaticists and practicioners of law. In their writing, they more often reference general philosophy literature or works from the general humanities than jurisprudence books. The second stream seems currently stronger than the first. This does not, naturally, mean that these changes are of fixed and irreversible character. Nevertheless, such diagnosis is rather attractive and provokes the introduction of diachronic simplifications – the general reflection of law outlived the period of scientism colonization and returns to the world of philosophy.

Other scenarios of the future general reflection on law are also possible. The strength of discipline ties in the heart of our area, resulting from analytical tradition may prove to be so strong that it could plot new canons enabling some identification base, program, and borders for reflection. It seems, however, that the currently dominating critical attitude and "hermeneutics of suspicion" in general philosophy are capable of dissolving the relatively homogenous discursive structure of the dogmatized jurisprudence and legal practice. As a consequence, ideological differences may prove stronger than the discipline habits. In other words, politicalness may exhibit a stronger influence than scientific institutionalization. Some symptoms can be observed in the United States where the postmodernist environments of the CLS gather philosophers of law, dogmaticists (if we can at all speak of American dogmaticism), and influential practitioners of law around a specific ideology, thus influencing jurisdiction.[44] In consequence, on the ruins of scientist jurisprudence we may see the emerging conservative, religious, gender-queer, ecological, post-colonial and other microparadigms. There is also a third option, in some aspects differing from the two plotted above. It may turn out, especially in reference to conservatism, within the society in general as well as among judges and professionals in law that J. Habermas' homeostasis of fragmentary stories, avoiding confrontation and involvement into general theoretical debates, is a permanent thing. In other words, legal debates without consensus may become the norm.[45] The divisions between "auto" and "allopoietic" reflection on law may deepen, and within the latter, discourse may become fragmentary around the issues which are important to general philosophy, especially social and political philosophy and epistemology, because these branches are most attractive to philosophers of law. These processes started fermenting in Polish congresses of the chairs of theory and philosophy of law which have resembled the tower of Babel in the last few years. Apart from classical debates on the scientific value of clarificatory or derivatory concept of interpretation there appear, with no surprise, discussions where the line of division runs along the dilemma of liberalism versus communitarism, affirmation versus critique, modernism versus postmodernism, while the traditional discussions of the theoreticians seem to be swallowed by the debates on what L. Morawski used to call the main problems of the contemporary philosophy of law. This drift towards postanalytical concepts is made easier by the recent political developments. Not attempting to evaluate them, we may rather uncontroversially say that radical systemic changes, not grounded in a formal change of the Constitution undermine the existing rules of legal discourses, allow for doubt

44 P. Schanck, "Understanding Postmodern Thought and Its Implications For Statutory Interpretation," *California Law Review* (65) 1992, p. 2505

45 A. Bator, "Debaty prawnicze. rozmowa bez konsensu," in: *Z zagadnień teorii i filozofii prawa. ponowoczesność*, M. Błachut (ed.), Wrocław 2007, p. 47ff.

in the seemingly deeply rooted canons of interpretation of law. Both parties of the legal-political dispute instrumentalize law in order to achieve their political goals, undermining the "certainties" developed some time ago by analytical theories and pertaining to, for example, methods of interpreting of normative texts. Both parties justify their points of view by the state of higher necessity or, referring to Schmitt's theories, legal state of emergency. For some, this necessity is conditioned by the shape of the state and the need for introducing reforms in which the attachment to traditions and "being true to the method" could do harm. For others, the need to loosen the ties of methodological constraints in the area of interpretation of law is legitimized by the need to protect the principles of the state of law. One way or the other, anarchist interpretation practice causes a growing dissonance between the analytical theories of old and what is occurring nowadays. The representatives of general reflection of law, especially those closer to the external point of view or realism, are willing to abandon analytical theories as extremely naïve or at least incapable of influencing practice – as the rules of a game that nobody wants to play. In these circumstances, theories grounded more heavily on political philosophies, theories for which unity of theory and practice, of description and fight is the foundation gain in meaning. This may be, however, considered, a passing phenomenon.

4 Second Response to Crisis: "New Style" of Analytical Theory of Law

The above-mentioned tendencies can be diagnosed in two ways. They can be considered signs of temporary crisis of the theory of law, for a meaningful proof of merely lowered interest in the hitherto prevailing research programs and ways of practicing analytical science of law. It is therefore possible that when the dust settles on the frequently lively discussed "concepts" and "philosophies," which are critical of scientific positivism, even in legal circles, analytical theory of law can have a lot of cleaning up to do. The scientism of the analytical research method was and sometimes is justified with the need of a therapy. The only question is whether and when a specific state of science will be diagnosed as needing analytical therapy. So far, this is not the most valid issue. Anticipating a simple restoration of analytical theory of law would nowadays be a mere speculation. Passively waiting for some better times would mean that we see sources of crisis in unfavorable social context of practicing science ("postmodern times," passing fads and scientific manners) and not in science itself. A higher value could be ascribed to a postulate for the analytical theory of law, known for its critical function, to make a move towards possible self-criticism. It therefore seems more important to ask whether theory of law is capable of reacting to the current crisis. In our opinion, there are capabilities hidden within it, and we may even say that certain such attempts in jurisprudence, including Polish, have already been taken, even if they have been careful ones. This exactly would be the "second response to crisis" that earlier in this text was called the "new style" of practicing analytical theory of law.

As the scientific methodology suggests, reactions to crisis within science, or its preexisting paradigm, could be of two types: patience and strong conviction that problems of science as well as ways of solving them are universal and ahistoric. Social need for certain questions, as the supporters of such attitude claim, can alter in time, but the responses are ready-made because they stem from the already adopted axioms – definitions, a selected set of definitions.[46] It is exactly within such an approach that analytical philosophy receives a normative character – the heuristic value of facts and customs is ignored and the goal of science is to make corrections to facts and customs as a consequence of applying a course of procedures based on adopted axioms. Reality is incapable of rejecting any theory and this can only be confirmation of its explicatory values; there are, naturally still facts that do not fall into the realm of a given theory but in this case the theory takes no interest in them.[47] Such theory cannot be falsified – it only may turn out, with time, that the facts explained by it are fewer and fewer and the theory itself is becoming more of a stylistic figure than a useful set of definitions. Usually, after some time such a theory meets a new set of axioms – more adequate to a given area or for some reason more convincing and attractive to scientific environment – and this causes the hitherto prevailing theories to pass into history. The fact that analytical theories "know no" history, this de facto means their scientific end. This can be called, quoting T. Kuhn, "a change of paradigm" or, if we are prone to emphasis, even a scientific revolution. Within such dogmatized style of practicing science, authors and supporters of the prevailing theories usually ignore and disregard the assumptions of the new research approach and

---

46 Such approach is sometimes labeled as foundationalism. See, for example, K. Wójtowicz, "O filozofii matematyki Imre Lakatosa," *Roczniki Filozoficzne*, Vol. LV, 2007, No. 1. Lakatos describes them as "formalism" or a "deductivist" style, see *Proofs and Refutations, The Logic of Mathematical Discovery*, Cambridge 1976, Cambridge University Press, passim.

47 It is "the theory that creates its subject, not the other way round" – J. Woleński, "Spór o status metodologiczny nauki o polityce," in: *Metodologiczne i teoretyczne problemy nauk politycznych*, Warsaw 1975, p. 40.

then show tendencies to desperate acts of defense – sometimes this is the defense of the only way of practicing science they know.

An alternative attitude to crisis may be one that I. Lakatos called, in reference to mathematics which is, as we know, the model for practicing analytical science, an informal or heuristic style.[48] As he claimed, in what we usually consider "a theory," we can distinguish two components: ideas common to the given theory that form its hard core and "auxiliary hypotheses" that serve the role of a safety belt. The feature of formalism was to focus on the defense of the hard core of a theory and in consequence to avoid the application and adaptation of the theorems because this could lead to the theory being modified or even falsified. This kind of dogmaticism was therefore connected with the tendency to ignore empirical and practical arguments and in a situation of a crisis – open inadequacy of theory towards the arguments – led to the emergence of another form "that assured true adherence and ultimate fundamentals, thus restoring the image of authoritative, reliable, and irrefutable mathematics."[49] Auxiliary hypotheses can excellently protect theories from falsification but only under the condition that their capability of revealing and ordering of new facts is shown, as well as their openness to previously unknown arguments and situations. It is therefore not as K. Popper imagined, that a theoretician proposes a theory and the reality simply voices its veto. Rather, the presented theory receives a response from reality, from social practice: that it is inadequate, incoherent, and maybe merely unclear, so – you can prove, by constructing auxiliary hypotheses, that the theory you are presenting gives some answers to the expected practice, only requiring adaptive measures, where we construct the "safety belt" for the theory. Alternatively, if you cannot prove it, modify the theory, adjusting the axioms that form its hard core to new challenges.[50]

It seems that in Polish theory of law of the recent years we can find examples that the above-mentioned language of methodological analysis can be applied to, and thus prove how, in the condition of the claims and questions from legal practice and specific disciplines in jurisprudence, we can adapt or modify the theorems that used to be formulated in a style close to formalism. Below, I will make references to two examples of this type of conduct that come from the achievements of the Polish analytical theory of law: the so-called derivative concept of interpretation of law and concept of competence and competence norm.

---

48 I. Lakatos, op. cit.

49 Ibid., p. 22.

50 These are shaped by three rules that combine to make Lakatos' method of proof and refute, pp. 87–88.

Either of these two highly influential concepts would, naturally, require a much more detailed description from the viewpoint of this article than the size of this text would warrant.

If we consider the theses proposed in 1984 by K. Płeszka and T. Gizbert-Studnicki[51] as the basics for the characteristics of derivative interpretation of law, we arrive at a conclusion that this concept adopts a whole series of unintuitive assumptions in legal practice – the concept of non-referential semantics, understanding the norm as an unambiguously characterized utterance, interpretation of law as translation from the language of the text of law into the language of norms – of openly counterfactual, formalizing character. The authors of the referenced article concluded, quite unsurprisingly, that "the derivative understanding may prove to be a handy tool in describing the dogmatic-legal interpretation" and this would occur in the company of some idealized comprehension of dogmatics of law itself.[52] Thus, the derivative concept of interpretation of law in its then form was separated from interpretational legal practice – operative interpretation – considering it inadequate in the area.[53] This characteristics, as far as we can tell, has never been openly challenged by the authors of the derivative concept but, as we can expect, has become a factor, or one of the factors, causing increased efforts in the next years to prove the practical usability of the concept, to defend its "hard core" in confrontation with the expectations of legal practice.

We can interpret M. Zieliński's 2002 *Wykładnia prawa. Zasady. Reguły. Wskazówki* as an important attempt to secure the derivative concept of law with the safety belt of "auxiliary hypotheses." The author reveals his intention in the following way: "on the one hand it is all about conserving the characteristic elements of this concept and on the other – about highlighting its aspects that could be momentous in interpretation practice."[54] We are far from claiming that the derivative concept replied to its own crisis in this exact way. Here there could be no mention of a crisis because the primary target group for the theoretical

---

51 This is a reference to the text "Dwa ujęcia wykładni prawa. Próba konfrontacji," *Zeszyty Naukowe UJ, Prace z Nauk Politycznych*, Vol. 20, Kraków 1984.

52 Ibid., p. 24.

53 Ibid., p. 25; see also B. Brożek, "Derywacyjna koncepcja wykładni z perspektywy logicznej," *Ruch Prawniczy, Ekonomiczny i Socjologiczny* 2006, annual LXVIII, Vol. 1, p. 86.

54 M. Zieliński, *Wykładnia prawa. Zasady. Reguły. Wskazówki*, Wydawnictwo LexisNexis, Warsaw 2002, p. 213.

model, dogmatics of law, highly praised the cognitive values of the concept.[55] The adaptation or modification was rather a response to the limitations resulting the formalism of the primary expression of the norm, so it was an activity that potentially anticipated the oncoming crisis. It was to show that analytical theory of law is capable of transgressing the limits of ordering its own language – that it can adequately adapt also to the expectations of legal practice, even for the price of abandoning a few of its own primary assumptions (such as that the legal norm as the result of interpretation does not need to be considered as a so-called unambiguously characterized utterance). The evolution of the derivative concept of interpretation of law is a good example for what needs to be done in order to maintain "the capability of discovering and ordering of new facts" as well as "openness to previously unknown arguments and situations."[56]

The example of the discussion on competences and competence norms seems to be equally educative. In Polish theory of law, there was an incredibly influential belief, mainly presented in the works of Z. Ziembiński – that the only components of the system of law are norms that have a predictive character – a norm as an order/prohibition of specific behavior. Reducing the varied methods of expressing normative character, as can be seen in legal texts, legal practice, and dogmatics of law, to a single, universal model of a language utterance can be considered proof for the formalism of this type of "concept of legal norm." A rather specific standard for the shaping of behavior, defined by the competence rule, needed to be reduced, as a consequence of the adopted assumptions on the comprehension of a norm, to the role of a component of the structure of the order/prohibition norm. Such an approach, although enlightening in its simplicity and clarity, which are highly praised values in reconstructionist analytical philosophy, did not meet universal acclaim in specific disciplines of jurisprudence.[57]

---

55 See R. Mastalski, *Interpretacja prawa podatkowego. Źródła prawa podatkowego i jego wykładnia*, Wrocław 1989, pp. 95–98; W. Jakimowicz, *Wykładnia w prawie administracyjnym*, Zakamycze 2006, pp. 19 and 377.

56 There needs to remain an open question of to what degree the changes (supplementations, applications) introduced into the derivative concept are to be "strengthened by a safety belt" of its hard core or to what degree they would serve to create a new form (falsification, rebuilding of the primary one).

57 The most radical one, full of negations, was proposed by A. Szpunar ("Udzielenie pełnomocnictwa," *Przegląd Sądowy* 1993, Vol. 9). An overview of administrative lawyers' opinions can be found in: M. Zieliński, "Dwa nurty pojmowania 'kompetencji,'" in: *Gospodarka, Administracja, Samorząd*, H. Olszewski and B. Popowska (eds.), Poznań 1996, p. 584ff.

Critics usually raised the argument that this kind of linguistic reduction fails to take into account the objective specificity of legal research, for example, the specific status of the subject of the competence, freedom of undertaking of the acts of competence performance. The considerations about law dominated by the ideas of holistic and uniform structure that encompassed the norms reduced to a single and simple language model, caused the neglect of the expectations that were voiced by the representatives of specific sciences of law towards theory of law. This remark can be reduced to the charge of formalism and, subsequently, disregard the arguments formulated by legal practice, with which most of the specific sciences identify themselves when they attempt a critical confrontation with the achievements of the theory of law.

These arguments were the foundation for the formulation of the so-called pragmalinguistic modification of the primary understanding of competence and competence norm.[58] The "strategy of defense" of the primary version of the discussed concept was – to quote Lakatos – the "focus on the defense of the hard core of the theory" typical for formalism,[59] the above-mentioned modification turned to making it more adequate to the expectations of practice.[60] Does the above-mentioned proposal merely secure the primary version of the concept of competitive norm with a "safety belt" in the situation of a crisis of its explicating capabilities towards a specific kind of questions? Or maybe it is a change of its original assumptions, axioms? This question cannot be answered here, although we are inclined towards the latter option. Something else is important here, namely – as was the case with the concept of derivative interpretation – doubts and perturbations associated with the application of the theory that was constructed initially as a closed, internally coherent order of theorems cause us to abandon the comfortable "notional geometry" of the analytical theory by "constantly improving the speculations by speculation and critique, with the use

---

58 See, for example, M. Matczak, *Kompetencja organu administracji publicznej*, Zakamycze 2004, passim.

59 A typical argument in such a defense is the argument of "not understanding the theory." "A claim that theoreticians of law put more attention to the analysis of the structure of the competence norm than the analysis of the notion of competence is a claim based on misunderstanding." (Z. Ziembiński, *O zawiłościach...*, p. 16).

60 M. Matczak writes: "The chance to overcome the weaknesses of predictive competence concepts lies in the application of pragmalinguistic approach to research of law and legal language. Such approach enables in particular to modify the view of Z. Ziembiński as well as provides new, more adequate – e.g. from the viewpoint of the research needs of public law – understanding of the notions related to competence." (op. cit., p. 202).

of logic of proof and refutation."[61] In order to reach this point, theory of law must stay in close connection with dogmatics of law.[62]

So, on the one hand the discipline we practice needs to remain a critical theory of scientific practice realized in the dogmatics of law and legal practice, and on the other hand the dogmatics of law and legal practice ought to keep their power of "vetoing" theoretical ideas. As long as the dogmatics of law continues to provide objects, problems, to such critical analysis, and theory of law is inclined to give sensible answers to the arguments, including agreeing to possibly override its starting assumptions, there should be no mention of crisis, let alone the end of theory of law.

61 I. Lakatos, op. cit., p. 19.

62 "Theory of law needed dogmatics as the object for critique. At the same time, dogmatics of law needed theory as inspiration." – A. Peczenik, "Stan obecny teorii i filozofii prawa w krajach Zachodnich," in: *Studia z Filozofii prawa* J. Stelmach, (ed.), Kraków 2003, p. 9. In another passage, A. Peczenik claimed that "[Scandinavian theory of law] devoid of contact with the grand tradition of dogmatics of law became marginalized." op. cit., p. 11.

Michał Paździora

Postanalytical Challenges to Legal Education in Poland*

Nathan Glazer, the author of a broadly debated article "The Schools on Minor Profession,"[1] qualifies law and medicine among the sciences that are characterized by strong professionalization. The decisive features that he takes into account are the type of work performed and the character of the profession. Glazer suggests that the work of a lawyer, similar to that of a medic, is of purely technical character. Their education is preceded by a tedious and long-lasting effort of gathering systemic knowledge and skills because of the requirement of long-term training are not accessible to laymen. Second, professionalization is closely connected with the stability of politics. The so-called weak profession schools, as Glazer claims, are susceptible to inevitable influences of fashion and politics. Pedagogy is in his opinion a classical example of a weak profession: its research results depend on the constantly changing views on the place of humans in the world, the desired patterns of personality and social roles, as well as the shape, size, and diversity of the society. Contrary, schools of strong professions have at their disposal something in the form of "deep structures" that do not yield to political pressure and changing fads. What can change is only the surface that serves rather esthetic functions and has no bearing on the matter of the discipline, just like in medicine where new eating habits or models of human body reinforced by fitness coaches do not bear any impact on the foundations of the discipline, which are founded on the knowledge of the unchanged construction of human organism or the functions of its individual organs. Taking into account Glazer's arguments, education in law, similarly to education in medicine, is based on scientific cognition of general rules and their applications to specific problems. Moreover, in the profession of a lawyer, just like that of a doctor, we need to apply professional norms that focus on practical problems related to the profession. To sum up, the level of professionalization of a specific profession

* The paper is part of the grant funded by the Polish National Science Centre Adam Czarnota "Constitutionalism. Rule of law, the political and public sphere" UMO-2015/17/B/HS-5/00768.

1 N. Glazer, "The schools of the minor professions," *Minerva*, 1974, Vol. 12, Issue 3, pp. 346–364.

is decided by the systematic and scientific knowledge foundation and technical skills in applying them, mastered by the adepts. What is important, it is believed that systematic foundations of knowledge are of scientific and standardized character, which causes the practicing of the profession highly specialized and, thus, limited for the non-specialists that apply to them.[2]

At the same time, a similar discussion took place in Poland, then a member of the Eastern Bloc, a state of real socialism of one-party structure with political Marxism as the dominating ideology. Although the accents were distributed in a different way, because of the ideological differences, the main axis of the debate remained untouched: what features distinguish legal disciplines and what character is assigned to the knowledge of law. In Poland, the discussion on education in law and professionalization of legal disciplines was solved in the consequence of the 1970s debate on the scientific status of jurisprudence. According to Paweł Jabłoński, the debate on the model of legal sciences played out in the background of the rejection of the role of philosophy in the cognition of law and opposing its function in relation to scientific theory.[3] Naturally, for the positivist-oriented representatives of legal sciences this comparison favored the scientifically developed theory of law and based on the conviction that jurisprudence ought to meet the methodological criteria defined for scientific theories. With the same move, there appeared the abandoning of some areas that were traditionally the domain of the philosophy of law. In turn, the philosophy of law started to be treated as a set of loose reflections, often considered inconclusive and outdated.[4] What was to decide the scientific character of legal science was not the area or object of research but the properties of the analytical research method. It was related to the methodological patterns that the nomological natural sciences propose. The goal of the "valuable" theory of law is to construct a scientific theory understood as a systemized set of scientific rules; characterized by notional and formal coherence. This theory could thus be characterized by prognostic and explanatory functions.[5] Although reaching for the analytical method can be explained by strong logical tradition in pre-war

2 D. A. Schon, *The Reflective Practitioner. How Professionals Think in Action*, United States of America 1984, pp. 21–23.

3 P. Jabłoński, "Polskie spory o rolę filozofii w teorii prawa," *E-Wydawnictwo. Prawnicza i Ekonomiczna Biblioteka Cyfrowa*: Wydział Prawa, Administracji i Ekonomii Uniwersytetu Wrocławskiego, Wrocław 2014, p. 51.

4 Ibid., pp. 51–53.

5 A. Bator, Z. Pulka, A. Sulikowski, "Czy koniec teorii prawa," *Czy koniec teorii prawa? z zagadnień teorii i filozofii prawa*, P. Jabłoński, (ed.), Wydawnictwo Uniwersytetu Wrocławskiego, Wrocław 2011, pp. 15–16.

Poland, mainly associated with the program of the Lviv-Warsaw School, its features that harmonized with philosophical minimalism of the positivist program were also important. Analytical philosophy has a purely academic character, strongly accentuates its political and social neutrality, and limits its activity on the grounds of jurisprudence to mainly constructing tools of the notional analysis of law. The goal of theory is therefore to propose objective methods of cognition, including methodological directives so that the result of conduct according to these rules is independent of individual preferences of the cognizing subject.[6] The area of interest of science practiced in this way is defined by notions of legal phenomena analysis and their interconnections, relations between legal norms, and the structure of the system of law. Analytical roots of science of law appear on two levels: in "focus on constructing a coherent and complete notional network for the reflection on law" and "development of specific style of characteristics of complex legal situations, based on the deconstruction of situations into elemental factors or aspects so that, later, their mutual connections and impacts can be taken into account."[7]

Similarly to Glazer's arguments, we find in this declaration the establishment of a "deep structure," independent of political and social context. The important factor in creating directives for the interpretation of legal texts is the assumption of the rationality of the lawmaker. The construction of the rational lawmaker is based on the assumption that the lawmaker is equipped with knowledge which is not contradictory and which is a system – knowledge then encompasses also the future consequences of theorems – and the assumption that preferences of evaluations that the lawmaker follows are binary asymmetrical and transitive relations. This concept is supplemented by the assumption of optimization, which states that the lawmaker will always select from the possible actions those that will lead to the most preferable state of things. The goal of proper methodologically oriented jurisprudence is the construction of such concept of legal interpretation, whose results will be achieved independently of the preferences of the cognizing subject, that is, the lawyer. Thus, the goal of science is achieved when it is the construction of systemic theorems of prognostic and explanatory character. The openly declared ideological and political neutrality of the cognition of law was to find confirmation in the objectivity and universality of the scientific method. In various declarations, especially in the Communist times, there were attempts to protect legal education from the influences of Marxism. The goals of legal education, however, were based on the assumption of the passivity of the cognizing

6 S. Czepita, S. Wronkowska, M. Zieliński, "Założenia szkoły poznańsko-szczecińskiej w teorii prawa," *Państwo i Prawo*, 2013, Vol. 68, Issue 2, pp. 3–16.

7 Ibid., p. 14.

subject which was required to closely follow the presented analytical research methods; this, in consequence, negated any sort of possibility to interact with the cognizing subject.

Yet another proof for professionalization lies in the systematic and scientific fundamentals of knowledge, capable of reaching to the "deep structure" of this branch of science and the technical possibilities of applying its fundamentals. In the first part, I will present the silently accepted assumptions of the analytical philosophy of law in Poland, as well as the entailed vision of legal education. In the second part, I will focus on the educational challenges of the project of post-analytical philosophy. The third part will be an outline of the desired changes.

1 Vision of Legal Education in Analytical Philosophy

In the introduction to *Leksykon filozofii analitycznej*, the analytical approach is defined not through the scope of research or subjects but through the style of doing philosophy. At the onset, what integrated analytical philosophers was the acceptance of three theses: (1) the goal of philosophy is to overcome philosophy through the analysis of language; (2) the only valid goal of philosophy is the analysis of language, common or scientific; (3) the only method at the disposal of philosophy is the method of language analysis. Today, naturally, we will not find an analytical philosopher who would consider at least one of the three theses legitimate. What makes analytical philosophy unique is its style, characterized by consistent, meticulous care for details in the expressed contents. Development in philosophy, if it exists at all, is based on eliminating problems that arise out of the blurriness and unclarity of notions, by strictly establishing the contents of the discussed phenomena. It is difficult to agree with the thesis saying that analytical philosophy is merely "a matter of style." As proven by Bertrand Williams, there is nothing that can be called a philosophical style what would be clearly and precisely defined by the directives of analytical philosophy.[8] Many post-analytical philosophers like Richard Rorty write in an "analytical style" but, at the same time, do not question the achievements or methods of analytical philosophy. Moreover, in an interview, Rorty once said that analytical philosophy should not be criticized because of its style and that it ought to remain close to its precise research methods.[9] According to Leszek Nowak, there is a specific paradox of

8 Bernard Williams, "What Might Philosophy Become?," *Philosophy as a Humanistic Discipline*, A. W. Moore (ed.), Princeton University Press, Princeton 2008, p. 204.

9 R. Rorty, *The Rorty Reader*, Christopher J. Voparil, Richard J. Bernstein (eds.), Oxford, UK, Wiley-Blackwell, 2010, p. 497.

analytical philosophy in the fact that the care for intersubjective communicability of philosophical contents, nourished by its supporters, has led to

> total anti-philosophical aggression [because the supporters would] perform too arbitrary divisions of traditional philosophies into respectful and worthy of reconstruction on one side and those at best worthy of academic critique on the other. There were times when this critique took the form of simple rejection that brought no results, especially no results that would be useful for the critic's own concepts.[10]

The opposition of post-analytical philosophy to analytical tradition results not from the rejection of the latter's style. As Rorty said, it is a good style, but it is just a drop in the sea of the transcendental project of analytical philosophy.[11]

The key importance of language in the comprehension of reality is highlighted in both the analytical and the post-analytical stream. In order to understand this key concept, let us quote Descartes' metaphor of the development of knowledge:

> Thus it is observable that the buildings which a single architect has planned and executed, are generally more elegant and commodious than those which several have attempted to improve, by making old walls serve for purposes for which they were not originally built. Thus also, those ancient cities which, from being at first only villages, have become, in course of time, large towns, are usually but ill laid out compared with the regularity of constructed towns which a professional architect has freely planned on an open plain; so that although the several buildings of the former may often equal or surpass in beauty those of the latter, yet when one observes their indiscriminate juxtaposition, there a large one and here a small, and the consequent crookedness and irregularity of the streets, one is disposed to allege that chance rather than any human will guided by reason must have led to such an arrangement.[12]

The description of a city – which Descartes sees as a symbol of constructing knowledge – may be understood as an urbanist metaphor of language. An unquenchable need to introduce order in the architecture of the city forces the architect to demolish it and start the construction anew. The construction of the city starts with planning the new spatial-functional layout. Without a planner, the architecture of a city is chaotic, communication is unclear, and finding the right way is difficult in the web of intersecting streets from different times of

---

10 L. Nowak, "Problemat ('mętnego') Hegla, czyli o tym, czego nie pojmuje krytyka w stylu popperowskim," *Rozum jest wolny, wolność – rozumna*, R. Marszałka, E. Nowak-Juchacz (eds.), Warsaw 2002, pp. 206–207.

11 R. Rorty, *The Rorty Reader*, op. cit., p. 497.

12 R. Descartes and I. Maclean, *A discourse on the method of correctly conducting one's reason and seeking truth in the sciences*, Oxford University Press, Oxford, New York 2006, Oxford World's Classics, p. 12.

development. In one of the anecdotes, Leibniz says that – as a child – he came up with a "universal system of signs" that could express all our thoughts. As he declared, this language would be extremely hard to construct but very easy to learn because of its huge usability.[13] Analytical philosophers, just like modern builders of cities, constantly search for a universal form of language unhampered by conventions. According to Toulmin, such language would not only express

> our thoughts in such a precise manner as arithmetic expresses thoughts or as geometrical analysis expresses lines … [but] it would also embody and codify ways of argumentation so that people with different intellectual views could reason together not worrying about notional havoc or making mistakes.[14]

The victory of analytical positivism in Polish jurisprudence resulted in the establishment of a very coherent education program that was based on the scientific cognition of law. It is hard not to see a self-fulfilling prophecy here. Legal education constructed on the model of analytical positivism achieves its "objectivity of cognition," "objectivized rules of cognition," or "reflection of objective properties" by projecting the practice of an image of a scientist; that is, proposing the scientist's models to explain their practices in the consciousness of the educated so that the explaining constructs become the determining rule.[15] It is difficult to find direct implications for legal education within the debate on the scientific character of jurisprudence in Polish literature. The very legal education, in fact, becomes a non-issue. As M. Stambulski remarks, the analytical vision of legal education can be called a "theory of the Nuremberg Funnel."[16] In theories of education, the "Nuremberg Funnel" is a mistaken assumption that the process of learning is based on setting a proper tool (a "funnel") to the head of a student and "pouring" knowledge.[17] We will find that, similarly to Descartes' metaphor, the rules of modern epistemology based on the search for certainty and the need

13 S. Toulmin, *Kosmopolis. Ukryty projekt nowoczesności*, translated by T. Zarębski, Wrocław 2005, p. 122.

14 Ibid., p. 123.

15 M. Paździora, M. Stambulski, "Co może dać nauce prawa polityczność?: przyczynek do przyszłych badań," *Archiwum Filozofii Prawa i Filozofii Społecznej*, 2014, Vol. 1, pp. 55–66.

16 The name is derived from the place of publishing and the title of a 17th-century manual of poetry by G. H. Harsdörffer, *Lejek poetycki. Jak opanować w sześć godzin sztukę tworzenia niemieckiej poezji bez odwoływania się do łaciny*. Cf. M. Spitzer, *Jak uczy się mózg*, Warsaw 2008, p. 15.

17 M. Paździora, M. Stambulski, "Co może dać nauce prawa polityczność?: przyczynek do przyszłych badań," op. cit., p. 64.

to establish a universal method of cognition. Understanding the deep structure of jurisprudence is like understanding the rules of laying out a city plan. On a side note, why should all the cities not be identical, based on the same architectural plan? Leibniz's dream of the universal language would then come true. The burden of constructing the language lies on the academic teachers of law, and the only thing left to students of law is the purchase of a map and adherence to the rules of reading this map, which does not entail the involvement in actual city building. According to A. Schon, this kind of education, realized by rules of technical rationality, constructs a harmful positivist epistemology of practice. In this model of practice, the foundation is the domination of scientific cognition on which practice completely depends. The scientific element defines the procedures of diagnosing and solving the emerging problems. Everyday conduct, however, requires only the skills of applying fundamental knowledge. This creates an educationally harmful hierarchy, in which general rules appear on the highest pedestal while specific solutions to problem situations at the very bottom.[18]

2 Educational Challenge in Post-Analytical Philosophy

What was the essence of language for Descartes and Leibniz, in Wittgenstein's analogy appears to be a metaphysical illusion that philosophy constantly falls for: "Our language can be seen as an ancient city: a maze of little streets and squares, of old and new houses, and of houses with additions from various periods; and this surrounded by a multitude of new boroughs with straight regular streets and uniform houses."[19]

According to J. Hanessen, "the search for the meaning of language would be similar to the search for the meaning of a city."[20] According to Wittgenstein, there is no single function of language, so there is no single constitutive rule that would constitute "the essence of a language game." Like the search for the city center

18 D. A. Schon, *The Reflective Practitioner*, op. cit., p. 24.

19 L. Wittgenstein, G. E. M. Anscombe, *Philosophical investigations/Philosophische Untersuchungen*, Blackwell, Cambridge, Mass 1989, 3rd ed., repr. Paragraph 18.

20 A remark made towards a text of J. Hannesen, "While Reading Wittgenstein PI §§1-19 (1): A Cautionary Tale," K. Johanessen, *Interpreting Wittgenstein: Four Essays*, The Wittgenstein Archives at the University of Bergen, Bergen 2008, p. 67; qtd. aftr T. Zarembski, "Gry językowe, jedność dyskursu i gra podawania i poszukiwania racji," *Ludwig Wittgenstein – konteksty i konfrontacje*, P. Dehnel, L. Rasiński (eds.), Wrocław 2011, p. 90.

when we cannot trace back its origins, in the search of the meaning of language we need to dislocate some language games from others only to point out a single constitutive rule that determines all the remaining language games. In this context, T. Zarembski highlights that "what we call 'language' may encompass varied areas, of which none assumes an especially designated place."[21]

What also raises objections among post-analytical philosophers is the naturalistically misshapen image of language that forms the fundament of analytical philosophy. Charles Taylor indicates that the misshapen image is the result of false belief that "each understanding of someone else's language is based on applying a theory."[22] In the popular thought experiment of William V. O. Quine, the process of comprehending is presented according to the guidelines of modern epistemology: an independent observer learns the language of the encountered tribe by combining the utterances with conditions of their correctness. Because the language of the tribe is inaccessible to the linguist through any other language, the only way of comprehending this language is to observe its natural users and the external circumstances that accompany the acts of communication.[23] According to Taylor, the necessity of understanding how a language articulates the Wittgensteinian "form of life" makes the uninvolved observer an absurd. Moreover, "to treat a reality from the point of view of a neutral observer means to treat this reality as something which makes it impossible or meaningless to participate in it and interact with."[24] In other words, understanding or interpretation is not based on the necessity to apply theory but is always a matter of specific practice. Of course, practice is not only practical actions but also what William James calls the whole of human life with everything inside it: emotions, intellectual passions, and moral needs. The dream of a universal language is based on an assumption that the symbols of this language will be capable of expressing our thoughts independently of context that finds expression in social practices and institutions. Metalanguage or, as Rorty would have it, "the final language" needs not only transcend the boundaries of subject language but also prove their conditions of truth. As Taylor demonstrates, the ambitious aspiration appears to be only a dream which one follows in search of practical matters – emotions, aspirations, goals, or social relations – and becomes impossible. Our

21 Ibid., p. 89.

22 Ch. Taylor, "Teorie znaczenia," transl. W. Jach, A. Orzechowski, *Język, dyskurs, społeczeństwo. Zwrot lingwistyczny w filozofii społecznej*, L. Rasiński (ed.), Warsaw 2009, p. 177.

23 W. V. O. Quine, *Na tropach prawdy*, transl. Barbara Stanosz, Warsaw 1997, pp. 67–69.

24 Ch. Taylor, *Teorie* ..., op. cit., p. 177.

practices are partially constituted by language and, in order to understand them, we need to know the underlying language.[25]

The challenge in education lies in reversing this task: the education problem is not about constructing a universal language but how to practically learn a language that already exists. The central issue of analytical education program arises here. Education in the style of post-analytical philosophy appears much more modest. The task of the philosopher is to constantly order the rules of grammar so that we can find our way in a specific language game. Similarly to the plan of a city, we are forced to abandon hope of becoming the sole planner; while, in the case of describing the grammar of law, we are forced to condone the lack of an external point from which all grammar could be described. Education is the plotting of a map with the reservation that no map is the holistic representation of the city. This map only shows some of the city's aspects, some characteristic points to reach the goal. For example, the subway map is not a faithful depiction of the communication network of the city. It presents in a simplified way the selected aspects of the transportation system. It is, however, useful to tourists who want to move around by using the subway, although it makes no mention of the street network. The task of philosophy is to plot subsequent, more or less detailed maps.[26]

The top-down system of rules may encompass only what has already been comprehended. Similarly to a medical treaty, which creates the paradigms of recognized illnesses, analytical philosophy of law creates only pattern decisions based on what has already been scientifically processed and didactically comprehended. In the face of quickly changing reality, the technical capability of applying the rules is insufficient. What Wittgenstein reveals is the flexibility and temporary character of grammar rules. Just like we cannot learn a language by not using it, so we cannot master the rules governing legal practice when we are not part of the community. Returning to the metaphor of the "Nuremberg Funnel": if passivity is required on our part, we merely learn how to be passive.

3 From a Legal Academic to an Academic Lawyer

Law as a whole is composed of norms that bind in a given state, order according to adopted rules, and coexist with the examples of their interpretation and specific applications; doctrinal guidelines and informal rules associated with the broadly understood legal culture. In the post-analytical perspective, law is a

25 Ibid., p. 171.
26 Ibid., pp. 155–156.

whole constructed of elements that impact one another and which cannot be completely analyzed or controlled. In other words, law is the practice of acting in accordance with a given form of life. The difference between analytical and post-analytical approach to researching law may be visualized again with a consideration of Wittgenstein's philosophy: "*The treaty* assumed the reduction of all the games to one and concluded that inability to reduce or improper execution thereof leads to nonsense. *Investigation* … forbid all reductions because they misshape the language and inevitably lead us into philosophical traps."[27]

The transition from the *treaty* to the *investigation* is based on the ultimate abandoning of the scientific method in philosophy. J. Tully calls the desire to seize law as a whole a philosophical misunderstanding, which is the result of the drive towards generality[28] and captivation by the scientific method that calls for a contemptuous approach to specific cases.[29] In L. Rasiński's interpretation, to abandon the search for metalanguage in research of language is founded on the privileging of grammar over logic. Language is not constructed around a single rule that could be described and explained by theory.[30] The status between the language and the world has no logical representation. When researching language, we need to focus on the social character of creating meanings; that is, on grammar "that is something previous, at least logically, in reference to experience, because it determines what we may sensibly say about our experience."[31] The research of law ought to take the form of considering grammar as the form of life that constitutes law.

The challenges presented by post-analytical philosophy to legal education in Poland are based on engaging problems that are characteristic of practical philosophy. This is especially evident in four areas. First, the appreciation of what is said above what is written. The tasks of philosophy of law may be limited to the creation of rules, if the interpretation of legal texts is disconnected from social context. The rebirth of legal rhetoric is solid proof that meanings should not be considered as extra-temporal and -contextual relations but as

---

27 J. Woleński, "Ludwig Wittgenstein o naturze refleksji filozoficznej," *Filozofia współczesna*, Vol. II, Z. Kuderowicz (ed.), Wiedza Powszechna, Warsaw 1990, p. 16.

28 J. Tully, *Strange Multiplicity…*, op. cit., p. 104.

29 Cf. L. Wittgenstein, *Niebieski i brązowy zeszyt. Szkice do Dociekań filozoficznych*, transl. A. Lipszyc, Ł. Sommer, Spacja, Warsaw 1999, as well as the remarks in L. Rasiński, *Śladami Marksa i Wittgensteina. Krytyka społeczna bez teorii krytycznej*, PWN, Warsaw 2012, pp. 182–186.

30 L. Rasiński, *Śladami Marksa i Wittgensteina…*, op. cit., p. 183.

31 Ibid., p. 150.

references to specific social practices. Second, returning to specific things. The goals of analytical philosophy of law are largely based on the creation of general and abstract theories. Therefore, casuistry was often applied in order to evidence the observed regularities, and the examples that did not match the proposed explaining models were omitted. Post-analytical philosophy of law draws our attention to the fact that model solutions do not rely on the deep structure of jurisprudence but belong to individual types of problem situations. Third, treating local things in a serious way. Foregrounded casuistry reminds us that philosophical activity mainly relies on collecting reminders. Historical, social, and cultural conditioning should become the new subject of philosophy. Fourth, the highlighting of the temporal aspect of the adopted concepts. Rationality of the adopted solutions is not only based on formal calculations but also depends on the time where it can be efficient.

The distinction between a "legal academic" and an "academic lawyer" in the title of this section comes from Minkkinen[32] and serves to show the vector of change. It coincides with two types of thinking within the legal education. The legal academic is an example of a lawyer who is completely committed to the function of practicing law. Their task is to serve the professional legal practice. We have seen this approach when analytical positivism was realized in Poland. According to this vision, legal education focuses on ensuring the stability of legal practice through controlling it on the basis of the positivist epistemology of practice. Although we cannot speak of a conscious educational practice, this approach continues even though the political-social reality changed dramatically; Poland is an EU member state and develops a market economy. The more frequently emerging projects of change within the legal education, initiated by the appropriate ministry and planned within the educational institutions, only create an illusion of change. The proposed changes to make the legal education more practical define the education's goals as providing it with the most refined tools of cognition and efficient means of argumentation. Law still shows itself as something external to the control of academic education. The universality of the cognitive method of law was only replaced by the universality of the tools for applying law.

Paradoxically, if academic education is not separated from professional legal practice, it then loses its control over this practice. Unlike with the legal academic, the role of the academic lawyer is not reduced to merely serve in professional

32 P. Minkkinen, "The Legal Academic of Max Weber's Tragic Modernity," [available at papers.ssrn.com], accessed December 3, 2017.

preparation. According to this model, legal education is connected with humanities and social sciences by a common vocation: to serve in understanding the world better and create possibilities for the development of future professionals. Minkkinen finds support in the argumentation of Martti Koskenniemi[33] who, similarly to Tully, indicates in his project of constitutionalism that we cannot pinpoint the central rule that could help us in ruling international disputes also in the international law:

> It is not a commitment which seeks to realize given principles or ready-made social arrangements. It aims to construct the whole as a structure of open political conflict and constant institutional revision. The whole will be seen as a system which enables, as far as possible, particularized solutions, aimed at realizing authentic commitment. But it gives no intrinsic weight to solutions, once adopted, and it is ready to make constant adjustments once this seems called for. It positively excludes imperialism and totalitarianism. Beyond that, however, it makes no pretention to offer principles of the good life which would be valid in a global.[34]

The possibility of adopting a point of view which is radically critical towards legal practice may serve to understand it better. The turn towards Wittgenstein's grammar investigations proposed by post-analytical philosophy does not mean the questioning of legal practice and rejection of its professional form. According to Minkkinen, this allows academic lawyers not to feel bound by loyalty towards practice. By rejecting the role of a tool that prepares them for professional life, academic lawyers may position the analyzed problem in the proper place of legal education as an interdisciplinary academic environment. This is similar to Wittgenstein's method of grammar investigation that does not stop at the point of researching logical relations – how words combine – but drives towards grammatical relation where our ways of using words match specific situations. The rejection of some usages as improper in specific situations does not mean that they lose practicality as tools.

---

33 M. Koskenniemi, *From apology to utopia: the structure of international legal argument*, Cambridge University Press, New York 2005, http://www.myilibrary.com?id=42200.

34 Ibid., p. 255.

Adam Sulikowski

Law After the Death of God. Jurisprudence and Some Assertions of the Contemporary Philosophy

Religious metaphors are handy in presenting the condition of law because the connections between legal and religious thinking are evident. Leszek Nowak convincingly writes on the subject that

> there seems to be one area of thinking, apart from theology, where the additional word "dogmatics" is used and even there it comes with some – rather justified – pride. It is the dogmatics of law, i.e. jurisprudence of different areas of law, civil, penal, administrative, constitutional, just to name the elementary few. It is therefore worth making a comparison with theology.[1]

Without going into details, I will state that the comparison reveals more similarities than differences: apart from the above-mentioned attitude towards dogmatic considerations, there is a thetical concept of binding of norms, rules of text exegesis, and the specific image of the rational lawmaker. Ernst Kantorowicz, a specialist in theology and theory of law, argues that the latter has two "bodies," one alive and specific, the other eternal and ideal.[2]

Friedrich Nietzsche in *The Joyful Wisdom* included the story of a madman who runs among citizens in broad daylight with a lantern in hand:

> A madman jumped into the [crowd] and drilled them with his eyes. "Where is God?" he asked, "I want to say it! We have killed him – you and me! We are all murderers of God! … Do we not yet hear the laments of the undertakers of death who buried God? Do we not yet smell the decomposition of God? – gods also decompose. God is dead! God remains dead! And we have killed him!"[3]

In my understanding, this metaphoric diagnosis also aptly expresses the condition of contemporary jurisprudence. Even though lawyers – the citizens on the

---

1 L. Nowak, "Metodologiczne kryterium demarkacji i problem statusu teologii," *Nauka* 3, 2004, p. 126.

2 H. Kantorowicz Ernst, *The King's Two Bodies: A Study in Mediaeval Political Theology*, Princeton, NJ, Princeton University Press, 1998, passim.

3 F. Nietzsche, *Die fröhliche Wissenschaft*, qtd. after M. Żelazny, "Nietzsche: śmierć Boga," *Literacje* 1 (16), 2010, pp. 55–56.

square – go about their business as if nothing has happened and do not notice any changes, the man with the lantern – a wise man aware of the contemporary achievements of philosophy but weird in the eyes of the pragmatically aligned professionals – seems to see and know more. The madman knows that in the light of changes invisible to the crowd, normal everyday activity of lawyers loses its primary meaning because law that they represent has become an empty myth. The crowd seems reluctant to take the responsibility for the things announced by the madman. They do not seem to feel that they are a part of the collective murderous "we" along with the madman and his lantern. This man is perceived as a dangerous weirdo capable of committing murder that he would later blame on peaceful citizens. Thus, general philosophy seems to be guilty of the death of the legal God and, although both jurisprudence and philosophy stem from their times and conditions, philosophy did plead guilty while for many lawyers "confessio est regina probationem." In order to clarify these claims, we must formulate the answer to a few questions typical of the legal investigation activity. First, who, or rather what, was the lawyers' God? Second, what does his death signify and how did it happen? Third, what are we going to do about it?

It is rather easy to answer the first question. The God of lawyers is the modern positive law. Naturally, the legal God – like in *Dialectic of Enlightenment* – assumed the place of the God of the *ancien régime*, adopting many of his structures. However, this process does not form the core of my investigation, so the thesis in which it has occurred will be used as an assumption, and I will directly move to the discussion of the modern understanding. Jurisprudence understood as a set of official discourses on law initiated its emancipation process in modernity from positivizing the subject of its own investigation. The catchphrase of positive philosophy is the postulate of nomocracy; that is, of creating a clear, stable, and lawfully binding set of rules by "a man that has reached maturity." These rules would keep "the jugglers that serve sweet and bitter drinks from the same flask" at bay, as Jeremy Bentham used to write about the pre-modern lawyers.[4] The positivization of law was somehow secondary in reference to the needs of legal practice and the new "priestly" professional group of dogmatic lawyers that began to replace the moralists as situated between law and legal practice.[5] In accordance with the positivist credo – in a cult of the mathematized natural science – the frontline of the scientific battle in the research of law is

4 Qtd. after K. Sójka-Zielińska. "Wykładnia w programach kodyfikacyjnych epoki Oświecenia," *Teoria i praktyka wykładni prawa*, P. Winczorek (ed.), Warsaw 2010, p. 73.

5 L. Morawski. *Główne problemy współczesnej filozofii prawa. Prawo w toku przemian*, Warsaw 2010, p. 15.

occupied by professionals, who were supposed to establish its objective in the form of proper understanding of legal texts. As Zbigniew Pulka writes, "as part of the positivist paradigm of jurisprudence, the system of law is treated as an ontological category (law exists as a system). [In consequence,] interpretation of law as a cognitive and descriptive action should base on the description of the actual meaning of the norm that we consider binding."[6] Thus, as J. Leszczyński successfully proves, positivism defined "the project of dogmatics as a science that performs strict exegesis of a legal text according to the spirit of scientism."[7] What is interesting is that law accessible as a set of texts that did not undergo specialist processing is a rather chaotic and asystemic material. The clue lies in the fact that in order for law – as weird as it sounds – to precede research, a set of rules must have appeared that enabled the perception of law as such an object. As Leszczyński states in a different passage, where he refers to the sociological rules of institutionalization, "solving the problem of the positivization [of law] is primarily achieved through institutionalizing the dogmatics of law. It is chiefly the institutionalized dogmatics of law that constructs knowledge according to the adopted standards and thus legitimizes it."[8] Positive law, from its definition as preceding and objective towards the dogmatics, gains these two features due to the existence of dogmatics and especially the disciplining and training of scientists that restricts the registry of the possible interpretation behaviors. Similar conclusions appear in A. Peczenik's comparative study of legal dogmatics; the logic of connections simply means that lawyers-engineers apply law in the course of their everyday activity; it is for them and the realization of their needs that the dogmatics of legal knowledge is created at universities which enable the identification of positive law.[9]

For God to be who he is, there needed to arise religion that made him what he is. At the same time, religion draws legitimization from the existence of God that it created. Naturally, there are texts that can be derived from the lawmaker and legitimized by his authority. Similarly, in religions there exist holy writings that can be assigned divine origins. The writings, however, have their drawback of

6 Z. Zbigniew. "Interpretacja prawnicza jako rodzaj interpretacji filozoficznej," *Z zagadnień teorii i filozofii prawa. Ponowoczesność*, M. Błachut (ed.), Wrocław, Kolonia Limited, pp. 126–127.

7 J. Leszczyński, *Pozytywizacja prawa w dyskursie dogmatycznym*, Kraków, Universitas, 2010, p. 97.

8 J. Leszczyńki, op. cit, p. 160.

9 A. Peczenik. *Scientia Iuris. Legal Doctrine as Knowledge of Law and as a Source of Law*, Dordrecht, Springer, 2005, p. 2ff.

not being perfect, while God is perfect. The writings are also not textually complete; they do not serve a direct answer to every question, while a priest needs to complete them. In order for God to assume a specific shape and speak, there needed to preexist the priestly dogmatics. For law to assume a divine systemic shape and be able to speak, the dogmatics of law needed to emerge. Dogmatics, according to the assumptions of positivism and in the spirit of scientism, identified itself as science.[10] Moreover, this science and its achievements were to form a part of the process of constructing complete knowledge of the world. According to the thesis inherited from the philosophical ancient regime, scientific knowledge is coherent and internally translatable because its whole constitutes the image of logos; that is, of word. Logos existed at the beginning. Therefore, dogmatics needed to be combined with other areas of certain knowledge. These connections were to be served by specific legal discourse called the theory of law or general reflection of law. The theory of law was primarily supposed to be a metadogmatics; that is, an assurance that the work of legal scientists fulfills the criteria of scientific character and constructs a coherent and complete system of Knowledge and Truth. Metadogmatics was also supposed to be the "dogmatics of complicated cases"; a coherent set of theorems that a dogmaticist may call upon when realizing their pragmatics-aligned tasks. In the post-religious multi-layer system of knowledge, the place for theory was the space between dogmatics and positive philosophy. Naturally, the tension between cognitive naturalism and the so-called antinaturalism, almost always present in law, influenced the heterogeneity of theory-of-law discourses. Nonetheless, the theory-of-law mainstream focused on constructing ordered legitimizing relations between the dogmatics and other acclaimed scientific discourses, with the most important being connections with language sciences or with positive philosophy of language. The legal God depended on a single para-religious dogma, also in the existential meaning, which is sometimes called the assumption of referentiality.

But how and why did the legal God die? First, we need to define how far we want to search for the reasons of death. Michel Foucault aptly plotted the problem during his famous 1972 seminar on the reading of the files of a triple murder committed in 1835 in Normandy by Pierre Rivière. The effect of the seminar was the book *Moi, Pierre Rivière, ayant égorgé ma mère, ma sœur et mon frère...*[11] When discussing the course of the investigation and lawsuit on the

10 R. Alexy, *Theory of Legal Argumentation*, Oxford, Clarendon Press, 1989, p. 262.

11 M. Foucault (ed.), *Moi, Pierre Rivière, ayant égorgé ma mère, ma sœur et mon frère...*, Paris, Gallimard, 1973.

case of the Normandy murder, Foucault exhibited how other discourses – psychological and sociological –permeate into the simple language of criminal law that used to operate in the categories of guilty/not guilty only in reference to the direct culprit. Such discourses postulate the distribution of guilt to cover broader circles; the victims become accessories to murder, their immediate environment that "saw and yet did not react" as well; the local community, the general social structures, the system of education, poverty, the economic system, and so on. When considering the issue of the death of the legal God, we also must consider the scope of investigation. Similarly, to the case of Pierre Rivière, the direct culprit is relatively easy to point out: it is the philosophy of language that dealt the fatal blow by destroying the myth of referentiality. As A. Peczenik writes: "Reflection made by the representatives of mainstream philosophy around 1950 meant the inevitable end of dogmatics."[12] A. Kozak makes a similar conclusion when indicating that the main cause of the fatal changes was

> the breakdown of the phenomenological concept of language that assumed the possibility of at least a close congruity between language and thinking. An alternative was provided by hermeneutic and structuralist concepts. Both base on the assumption of the inadequacy of language and thinking .... Moreover, both search for alternative categories to traditionally understood language, reaching first and foremost towards conversation and discourse, as well as engaging in the "crisis of referentiality."[13]

The assumption of referentiality is the foundation of legitimizing of dogmatic activity. It founds the official relation of responsibility between the effects of the lawmaker and the effects of dogmatics. This relation, although rarely brought up by the dogmaticists, makes their efforts binding. Proving the existence of this relation was the task of theory and therefore the changes within the mainstream philosophical understanding of language and comprehension caused a phenomenon which was especially harmful to the general reflection on law. As the interdiscourse that situated itself between dogmatics and the general philosophy of language, the theory of law found itself split between two supporting elements drifting in opposite directions.

The changes within the philosophy of language were especially deadly to the "religious complex" of jurisprudence, but there were other blows that also came

12 A. Aleksander, "Koherencyjna teoria argumentacji prawniczej," 2003, http://szczecin.ivr2003.net.

13 A. Kozak, "Dylematy prawniczej dyskrecjonalności. Między ideologią polityki a teorią prawa," *Proceedings of the Zjazd Katedr Teorii i Filozofii Prawa*, Warsaw, September 2008, p. 4, manuscript.

from the direction of philosophy and caused heavy injury. For example, the anti-Cartesian or antihumanistic changes in the philosophy of the subject heavily impacted the dogmatic visions of free and rational subject of the law whose importance in legal science cannot be overestimated. As B. Kaszowska-Wandor writes, since Heidegger, mainstream philosophy has focused on the deep and destructive (to the older concepts) critique of the idea of the free subject, hence a strong radicalization of the critical approaches ensues:

> On the one hand, there is indicated the fictitiousness of the subject as a merely temporary structure that serves specific extrasubjective means. On the other, there is negated the notion of freedom as the fundamental indicator of subjectivity. The radicalization is primarily based on indicating increasingly powerful determinism as the feature of the existence of mankind. This determinism, in the antihumanistic thought, is stretched to new and broader areas of human existence.[14]

The structure of this text allows to approach these phenomena more broadly, so I will quote a different text of my authorship[15] only remarking that philosophical ascertainments of the few recent decades almost demolish axiology and the dogmas of civil law, although it is evident in other branches of law as well. The sharp punches to the body of the legal God were furthermore dealt by the philosophical critique of the ideological purity of science. Its description would take thick volumes, so I will again use a suggestive quote, this time from an Italian Marxist-semiologist Rossi-Landi, who writes that

> there is no methodological sphere of reality that would claim to be a realistic sphere: this will not be the sphere defined and protected by the epistemological approach established through science based on sensual judgment; moreover, this is one of the most typical philosophical ideologies that still circulate in contemporary culture …. There is no science that would provide us with eternal guarantees, there is only a positivist myth of such science. Furthermore, to speak of science in the singular actually makes no sense.[16]

This approach which I support, is naturally rather radical and is in no way representative of the whole heterogenity of contemporary considerations on the contents of science in science, but the very fact that such a vision exists in official

---

14 B. Kaszowska-Wandor, "Przepisywanie humanizmu. Od renesansowej humanitas do współczesnej antropotechnologii," *Humanizm. Historie pojęcia*, A. Borowski (ed.), Warsaw, Neriton, 2009, p. 464.

15 A. Sulikowski, *Posthumanizm a prawoznawstwo*, Opole, Wydawnictwo Uniwersytetu Opolskiego, 2013, passim.

16 F. Rossi-Landi, "Semiotyka a ideologia," *Współczesna filozofia włoska*, A Nowicki (ed.), Warsaw, PWN, 1977, p. 161.

discourses endangers the foundations of the legitimization of legal dogmatics and the post-ideological visions of the scientific character.

Naturally, following Foucault's mechanism of broadening the circle of culprits, we may consider philosophy as the only direct guilty and claim, which is actually an often case, that the accessories are the still more abstract factors, such as the general disintegration of contemporary *episteme*, transformations of capitalism, transition from the industrial to the post-industrial society and the resultant disintegration of the ethical model of passive loyalty towards rules that long governed factory, university, and courtroom work. The replacement of the cult of the rule and procedure with the cult of creativity definitely weakened the discipline of law. Other things to blame can be the crisis of the peace of Westphalia in international relations, which is a fundamental concept in modern science of law, that the independent state is the primary source of law. We may even blame the progressing ethnic, cultural, and axiological heterogenization of modern societies that causes increasing tendency to problematize the legal institutional imperatives that usually are outside the consciousness of the immersed individuals and groups; we may see the culprits in differently described cultural, ideological, technological, and other changes.[17] Following the example of Nietzsche, we may seek for the beginning in the mistaken assumptions of the theology that created the dead legal God, in the imperfection of the human activity, or in the legal "will of power."

Naturally, the death of God does not easily find its way into the minds of both the practitioners and dogmaticists of law. They go about their daily business as they used to, just like the citizens on the market of Nietzsche's story. As A. Peczenik writes that, despite the changes,

> the dogmatics of law – which borders on a miracle – did quite well for itself … continued the traditions of notional jurisprudence, although in a much less resolute manner. However, it had to pay a high price. The faculties of law overflow with so-called technical lawyers that simply stick to the dogmatics of law on a lower level of abstraction which, however, lacks deeper reflection.[18]

The dogmaticity of law gradually becomes less reflexive if theological metaphors appear, it becomes less episcopal and more common. It creates theoretical

---

17 See more in A. Sulikowski, *Współczesny paradygmat sądownictwa konstytucyjnego wobec kryzysu* nowoczesności, Wrocław: Wydawnictwo UWr, 2008, passim; *Konstytucjonalizm a nowoczesność. Dyskurs konstytucyjny wobec tryumfu i kryzysu moderny*: Wrocław: Wydawnictwo UWr, 2012, passim.

18 A. Peczenik, op. cit.

concepts for its own needs which are not only incompatible with the concepts formulated on the basis of other dogmatics but may also be internally conflicting. Andrzej Bator aptly summarizes this phenomenon in his text "Debaty prawnicze. Rozmowy bez konsensu."[19] Bator's diagnosis is in many places convergent with the general remarks on the contemporary condition of knowledge formulated by Jürgen Habermas, who argues that short-term and coexisting (albeit conflicting and competitive) syntheses of specialist information formulated in the language of scientism, and with silent promise of coherence with other syntheses, are replacing global interpretations.[20] In this way, we still may maintain the common positivist consciousness and the post-theological promise of the mono-narrative of pan-knowledge that results from the dogma of the word as being the first. This is what the death of God is like.

What are the consequences of the death of God? Naturally, the answer depends to a large degree on the emotional reaction to the depicted process. For many, including myself, the death of the legal God is not a tragic event because they feel they are also to blame, at least when invoking the criminal construct of dolus eventualis. It was the critical theory of law, drawing on classical philosophy, that hindered legal theology's reaction to the blows. This is the consequence of the specific function of critical theorizing which is a form of anti-theology – following the distinctions proposed some time ago by Leszek Kolakowski – a "clownish" philosophy that does not believe in the assurance of contemporary priests in the situation "as is" keeps formulating the remarks of "it is not as you think"; "it is the effort of constantly questioning of obviousness, i.e. constantly disavowing of existing revelations."[21] For the "jester" thought, the death of the legal God is a sort of victory because it opens a discussion on the political and ideological character of dogmatics and legal practice which – under the pretense of a divine myth of law – previously was invisible and untouchable. Critical thought, however, needs to be constantly reactive, because God may be dead but the priests and the faithful continue living and they repress the death of God to continue their cult. Religious thought does not tolerate a

---

19 A. Bator, "Debaty prawnicze. Rozmowy bez konsensu" M. Błachut (ed.), 2007, op. cit., p. 41ff.

20 J. Habermas, "Na czym polega dziś kryzys? Problemy uprawomocnienia w późnym kapitalizmie," *Teoria praktyka*, translated by M. Łukasiewicz. Warsaw, PIW, 1983, p. 471.

21 L. Kołakowski, "Kapłan i błazen. Rozważania o teologicznym dziedzictwie współczesnego myślenia," [in:] L. Kołakowski, *Nasza wesoła apokalipsa. Wybór najważniejszych esejów*, Kraków, Znak, 2010, p. 62.

vacuum. "A rain of gods falls from the sky during the burial of a single god that became outdated. The godless worship their saints and the blasphemers build chapels."[22] Evidently, the death of the legal God strengthens Bentham's "jugglers." These jugglers are primarily the courts, especially those of high instance that lose the self-restraining barriers if formal control ceases to exist; the myth of the existence of God (or of positive law) in his posthumous impotence ensures the potential legitimization of almost any decision. Much has been written on the subject of the increasing role of courts and court activism. The process is therefore noticeable and commented upon. In the short and simplified version that does not take account for a plethora of subtleties and differences across the individual theoretical visions, it is based on courts that engage in solving social, economic, and political problems by calling upon arguments from an increasingly blurry and less resistant law; in other words, the voice of the dead God justifies judicial power. According to some, judicracy is a state of affairs that is not excessively dangerous; it is even desirable because the rule of the judges is more "rational," "liberal," and efficiently prevents totalitarian practices. The most known and reflective supporter of such statement is Jürgen Habermas. In his opinion, judicracy can be the surrogate of the proper process of communicative verification of legal norms and of separating the norms that can be inadmissible to all those that are legitimized by legal myths of divinity but do not deserve to be maintained. This process, for obvious reasons, could not find place in the conditions of a dogmatic approach to law; the power of judges in the societies located on the post-conventional stage of moral development can be the least institutionally complicated basis for the verification processes.[23] It seems, however, that Habermas fell in the same trap that the less "seeing" philosophers of law like Ronald Dworkin,[24] Aulis Aarnio,[25] or Robert Alexy[26] fell into when they

22 L. Kołakowski, op. cit., p. 81.

23 The societies located on the post-conventional stage of moral development are those that are capable of critical consideration of their institutional background and for which tradition cannot be an argument that efficiently legitimizes the visions of good and evil. J. Habermas, *Faktyczność i obowiązywanie. Teoria dyskursu wobec zagadnień prawa i demokratycznego państwa prawnego*, translated by A. Romaniuk, R. Marszałek, Warsaw, Scholar, 2008, pp. 87, 133–134, 272.

24 R. Dworkin, *Biorąc prawa poważnie*, transl. T. Kowalski, Warsaw, PWN, 1998, pp. 62–63.

25 A. Aarnio, *The Rational as Reasonable: A Treatise on Legal Justification*, Dordrecht, Springer, 1987, pp. 7–10.

26 R. Alexy op. cit, p. 8ff.

relied on the ethical attitudes of judges, their sense of extralegal standards, capability of the apolitical setting of rational consensus, and the feeling of justice. Habermas also believes in the liberal myth, which states that the removal of the political is possible through the adoption of certain ethical standards. Naturally, for Dworkin, Aarnio, and (partly) Alexy, proper ethical attitude is based on the trust in the existing rules and cultural practices, while for Habermas on the readiness to question them – even in order to construct a rational agreement. However, the belief in the potential to restrain the political and the ideological is common to them all. Habermas' vision may be treated, on the one hand, as a diagnosis of the situation and, on the other hand, as the way to exit the crisis. It may be convincing in its first aspect but its normative understanding appears as excessively utopian. From the external point of view, the "legal field" – if we want to use the words of the critical sociologist Pierre Bourdieu – is the field of ongoing fight and rivalry, also in the political understanding, while the legality of agencies is no stronger from their multi-aspect involvements. The maintenance of the belief in the judges' capability of stimulating communication processes may be treated as a sign of hypocrisy in the meaning that P. Bourdieu assigned to the term.[27] The danger of this hypocrisy was aptly described by Chantal Mouffe, when she wrote that it leads to the unrecognized "violence concealed behind the references to rationality which is often the case with liberal thought which masks the inevitable borders and exclusions under the pretense of neutrality."[28] According to Mouffe, the unrecognized irremovable political and its concealing under "deliberate" lawmaking is dangerous not only for the moral or axiological reasons but also because it leads straight to populism that gathers the actual political and emotional power by formulating the arguments of destroying the pseudo-neutral "system" and, thus, weakening the fundamentals of law.[29] The increase of the power of "anti-systemic" political powers in different states can be the sign of such weakening of fundamentals. This may be why we are approaching a new wave of totalitarianisms which may be considered in the legal science perspective, to quote A. Kozak as "spasmodic attempts to regain the certainty and validity of reference in the rules of the game established in the Enlightenment era." From the recent history of the totalitarian systems, the

---

27 P. Bourdieu, "Les juristes, gardiens de l'hypocrisie collective" *Normes juridiques et régulation socialem*, F. Chazel, J. Commaille (eds.), Paris, LGDJ, 1991, pp. 95–99.

28 C. Mouffe. "Demokracja, władza i 'to co polityczne,'" *Paradoks demokracji*, Wrocław, Wydawnictwo DSW, 2005, p. 42.

29 After A. Kozak, I comprehend this term as readiness of the institutional social environment to accept the claims of law to have the binding effect.

"sovereign," which is completely real in the empirical understanding, created law that made actual resistance, and the loyalty of education-court-clerical cadres assured its "divine embodiment," which was supported with efficient methods of eliminating or reducing the doubtful and those who thought otherwise. The creators of totalitarian systems more or less consciously materialized the thesis that the "non-ideological" and the "apolitical" may only be achieved through complete subordination of the system to the only valid ideology. We may say, somewhat perversely, that they followed Spinoza and Hegel towards their claim that freedom is the knowledge of necessity, and reached the acceptance of the suggestion once voiced by Auguste Comte in his rhetorical question: "If we do not allow free thinking in chemistry or biology, why should we allow it in morality or politics?"[30] It is doubtful, however, if we can return to the reliability of law via the preexisting theoretical ideas. The dead cannot be revived. Totalitarianism may bring fictitious signs of life but definitely not for long. The philosophical radical right for over 200 years has seen the solution to the problem in the restitution of the pre-modern ways of thinking about law. However, these are even more dead than legal positivism; their numbness appears in the capability of an idea to be treated seriously in the social practices. An inevitable consequence of the "sinful" renunciation of the return to pre-modernism is Spengler's threat of the invasion of ideologically integrated peoples of the East, for whom the traditionally comprehended God and tradition are one and the same. The threat may actually exist and the "universal morphological mechanism of civilization"[31] will come true again but we do not yet know if the proposed medicine is better than the disease itself.

An interesting attempt to reanimate the surrogate of the divine reliability of law in the scientist version appears in the recently popular naturalist searches. They fall under the paradigm of positivism in the philosophical meaning, although they irrevocably reject the dead legal positivism. Quoting W. Załuski, the representative of the Kraków naturalists, "law has … biological roots not only in the trivial sense of being the product of biological beings, meaning us. On a deeper level, it supervenes our natural dispositions or is an expression thereof."[32] One of the goals of the naturalist searches is the reconstruction of the "concept of human nature supported by the theory of evolution," which could serve to

30 Comte after A. Kozak, 2007, p. 68.

31 O. Spengler. *Zmierzch Zachodu. Zarys morfologii historii uniwersalnej*, translated by J. Marzęcki, Warsaw, KR, 2001, p. 48.

32 W. Załuski, *Ewolucyjna filozofia prawa*, Kraków, Wolters Kluwer Polska, 2009, p. 108.

verify the contents and form of law.[33] To practice the reflection on law with the use of evolutionist attitudes and theses ensures a "high level of scientific character" according to the traditionally scientist stories. What is more, it ensures what used to be the object of positivist desires of legal sciences: the hard object of research, the ontology of law that can be convincing and definitely seems more resistant to critique than the old ontological theories, just like those based on traditional Cartesianism, Kantism, or neo-Kantism.[34] Naturalist concepts may be attractive to theoreticians, but in the foreseeable future will not be capable of legitimizing legal practices so they may prove unattractive from the point of view of the orphaned believers in the legal God. On a side note, they are also prone to attacks from the destructive "philosophy of suspicions." An attempt to create a philosophy that would be impervious to such attacks could be A. Kozak's juriscentrism, which is called even by its author a post-postmodern concept of law. For the purpose of his considerations, the author calls the philosophical critique of the positivist divinity of law a postmodernist concept and is to respond to this critique with his book.[35] There is, sadly, no place in this text to discuss this definitely interesting theory. Let me only state that juriscentrism, aware of the meaning of philosophical transformations and the legitimacy of the resultant critique of jurisprudence, postulates the submission to legal institutional imperatives, the dampening of the impact of other institutions, and treating the nebulous and chaotic set of legal texts, increasingly heterogenous "doctrine of law," and the increasingly political interpretation as the "divine system;" that is, keeping faith despite the destruction of its intellectual justifications. Maciej Pichlak calls this attitude "patience towards law":

> juriscentrism is therefore a faith that has overcome the trial of doubts and skepticism suggesting an answer to the last question. A juriscentrically aligned lawyer is not differentiated by the fact that, while remaining blind and deaf to the possible objections towards law, towards the weaknesses of its own object of faith, and the resultant doubts, still sees something more in the legal order, some specific value that makes it, nonetheless, worthy of some faith.[36]

Artur Kozak himself based the justification of his concept not on the reliability of law but rather on fear:

---

33 W. Załuski, 2009. op. cit.

34 M. Zirk-Sadowski, *Wprowadzenie do filozofii prawa*, Kraków, Zakamycze, 2000, p. 24ff.

35 A. Kozak, op. cit., passim.

36 M. Pichlak, "Artura Kozaka cierpliwość wobec prawa," *Filozofia Publiczna i Edukacja Demokratyczna*, 2014, Vol. III, Issue 1, p. 242.

> The destructive force of anti-foundationalism and skepticism left only rubble behind. What can we build upon it? We cannot bring back to life the universal ideas of Evil or Reason. We need to reference what is basic and proper to any living being: to the self-preservation instinct. Everyone wants to keep unchanged form and this is the point of origin for the post-postmodern concept of law: everything is a convention. But if we, as a society, want to keep the current form, some of the laws must be necessary and not subject to dispute. This is not a matter of Truth and Error, Good and Evil, or Power and Freedom. This is a matter of Life and Death.[37]

We may accuse Kozak's idea of the same naivety we find in the visions of Habermas, Dworkin, and Aarnio, which assumes that the carrying force of the postulated ethical program will be stronger than the cognitive dissonances, all the involvements of the elders of legal knowledge, and their susceptibility to realize individual political goals. Besides, it seems that the legal institutional imperatives are not all that certain and systemic as it may seem. Their homeostasis is rather accidental and instable. If we agree with A. Bator,[38] it is a gradual weakening through the expansive potential of increasingly numerous dogmatic-heretic visions of law, among which each is ready to become a metacategory, a reference point for the evaluation of genuineness, sensibility, or usability; but at the same time these do not constitute a system.

In this situation, it is little wonder that the philosophy's radical left-wing postulates of "liberal antitheology" or the deconstruction of the institutionalized remains of the legal God in the subjective spirit of Foucault's "souci de soi" through constant delegitimization and undermining of the neutrality of priestly practices and concepts, while at the same time maintaining a modern historiosophic optimism and conviction that removing the divine aspect from law is the sign of progress. As Jacques Derrida wrote in his "Force of Law,"[39] deconstruction is justice.

Situating myself decidedly on the left side of the philosophy of law, I would like to express a self-reflective doubt at the end of this text, again with the use of post-theological metaphors. My doubt stems from the question on what will happen if the truth about the death of the legal God reaches the ears of the citizens and the faith crumbles. Critique is dependent on the advantage of the supporter of a specific dogma. As Kołakowski says, "The advantage of the supporters

---

37 A. Kozak, 2007, op. cit., p. 75.

38 A. Bator, "Debaty prawnicze. Rozmowy bez konsensu." [in:] M. Błachut (ed.) *Z zagadnień teorii i filozofii prawa*. Ponowoczesność, Kolonia Limited, Wrocław 2007, p. 47.

39 J. Derrida, "Force of Law: The 'Mystical Foundation of Authority,'" D. Cornell, M. Rosenfield, and D. G. Carlson (eds.), *Deconstruction and the Possibility of Justice*, Routledge, New York 1992.

of mythology over the critics seems an inevitable and natural tool."[40] However, when the critics of old, today in the mainstream, become the new priests – will this not change the vector of jest? "The attitude of the jester is a constant struggle of reflection on the possible rationale behind conflicting ideas, therefore it is dialectical in nature and an overcoming of what is because it is."[41] Hence, will the jester, true to the ethos of the jest, not shout one day: "Lo and behold, God is alive!"?

40 L. Kołakowski, op. cit., p. 80.

41 Ibid., p. 79.

POLISH CONTEMPORARY PHILOSOPHY AND PHILOSOPHICAL HUMANITIES

Edited by Jan Hartman

Vol. 1 Roman Murawski: Logos and Máthēma. Studies in the Philosophy of Mathematics and History of Logic. 2011.

Vol. 2 Cezary Józef Olbromski: The Notion of *lebendige Gegenwart* as Compliance with the Temporality of the "Now". The Late Husserl's Phenomenology of Time. 2011.

Vol. 3 Jan Woleński: Essays on Logic and its Applications in Philosophy. 2011.

Vol. 4 Władysław Stróżewski: Existence, Sense and Values. Essays in Metaphysics and Phenomenology. Edited by Sebastian Kołodziejczyk. 2013.

Vol. 5 Jan Hartman: Knowledge, Being and the Human. Some of the Major Issues in Philosophy. Translated by Ben Koschalka. 2013.

Vol. 6 Roman Ingarden: Controversy over the Existence of the World. Volume I. Translated and annotated by Arthur Szylewicz. 2013.

Vol. 7 Jan Hartman: Philosophical Heuristics. Translated by Ben Koschalka. 2015.

Vol. 8 Roman Ingarden: Controversy over the Existence of the World. Volume II. Translated and annotated by Arthur Szylewicz. 2016.

Vol. 9 Tomasz Kubalica: Unmöglichkeit der Erkenntnistheorie. Leonard Nelsons Kritik an der Erkenntnistheorie unter besonderer Berücksichtigung des Neukantianismus. 2017.

Vol. 10 Renata Ziemińska: The History of Skepticism. In Search of Consistency. 2017.

Vol. 11 Jan Woleński: Logic and Its Philosophy. 2018.

Vol. 12 Wielslaw Gumula: On Property and Ownership Relations. 2018.

Vol. 13 Andrzej Zaporowski: Action, Belief, and Community. 2018.

Vol. 14 Andrzej Bator / Zbigniew Pulka (eds.): A Post-Analytical Approach to Philosophy and Theory of Law. 2019.

www.peterlang.com